THE TALL SHIPS

GARTHPOOL (EX JUTEOPOLIS). LAST BRITISH SHIP

Frontispiece *(By courtesy of "Syren and Shipping")*

IN THE DAYS OF
THE TALL SHIPS

By

R. A. FLETCHER

Author of
" Steam-ships, the Story of their Development,"
"Warships and their Story,"
"Travelling Palaces,"
etc.

BRENTANO'S LTD.

NEW YORK   LONDON   PARIS

First Published 1928

CONTENTS

ILLUSTRATIONS

INTRODUCTION

THE story of the Sailing Ship in the nineteenth century is the connecting link between the great era of exploration and the intense materialism of the commerce of the present day. It unites the spacious days of the bearers of letters of marque, of privateers, of pirates, of the Spanish Main, of the mysterious Far East, of the wonderful Pacific Islands, of the fabled wealth of South America and the Indies, East and West, with the consolidation of the British Empire as we know it. It saw the gold discoveries of Australia, South Africa and California, the Crimean War, and the Indian Mutiny, and in all these the Tall Ships played their part. The ships which bore the fortune seekers of those days to real or fancied El Dorados, to wealth or to disappointment, were the fore-runners of the floating palaces which to-day carry passengers to the same countries, or from almost any port in the world to any other port, with a certainty which is calculated to within an hour or two. We are prone to forget—the Nation as a whole has already forgotten—what is owed to the memory of the Tall Ships and their intrepid commanders; the debt is as great to them as to the commanders of the finest modern liners.

The nineteenth century saw the stateliest and most beautiful creation for which the mind of man has been responsible in the whole of his history. When Ruskin wrote his marvellously expressive eulogy of the beauty of the sailing ship, and described the now despised windjammer as man's most beautiful work, he did the ship no more than bare justice. It is given to few men to voice as he did the beauty of the sailer, yet there is no more captivating sight under the broad dome of heaven than a large sailing ship under her full spread of canvas. No one who has seen a four-master, whether barque or ship, under every sail she could carry, gliding through the trades with the wind on her quarter, and her canvas gleaming like snow in the brilliant tropical sunlight, can ever forget the sight. Every man who has responded to the call of the sea knows the beauty of the sailing ship, whether he be an old-time shellback, or a modern seafarer who has only been in steamers. Nor is Walt Whitman's appreciation of the " sea-ship " any less merited. The English writer showed an insight into the æsthetic beauty of the sailer as a spectacle ; the " good gray poet " showed an insight into the mystic personality of the ship. The two writers together may help us to understand the spirit of the sailing ship as she was. Any sailorman of the old school will tell you that every sailing ship they knew had a will and a personality of her own. " No wonder the *Cutty Sark* was so fast, she had the spirit of a witch in her," an old sailorman told me once, and he believed it.

Scientists may tell us that the ships and the sea are only dead matter, but you and I who love the sea and the ships know better. Has not the sea called for centuries to Englishmen, and has the call ever been in vain ? There is in the blood of the real men of Britain a love of the sea, inherited from our Viking ancestors and from the no less adventurous men who lived along the east and south and west coasts. If there were not this inherited reply to the call of the sea, would so many have ventured forth upon the unknown oceans in little vessels that would hardly be

regarded as seaworthy nowadays ? Whenever the call
has been heard the British have answered. Probably that
call was at its loudest and greatest in the nineteenth
century, when Britain owned more sea-going ships than the
rest of the world put together, and the sailing ships were
at the height of their fame and had attained a degree of
development beyond which further progress seemed impossible. And the captains and crews of the best of the ships
were worthy of the vessels they sailed. From seventy-five
to fifty years ago it was possible to get British crews
for British ships. Then the foreigners —Dagos or Dutchmen, as all foreign sailors are classified by the English
sailor—came in sufficient numbers to undercut them in
wages, ill-paid though they were, until at last it was not
uncommon for a British ship to sail from a British port with
a crew consisting mostly of foreigners, some of whom did
not know enough English to understand the orders given
them. All honour to the British who still sailed in British
ships, and made something like sailormen of the motley
Continentals they had to deal with.

Almost all my life I have been a lover of ships, and some
of my earliest recollections are of them. As a boy I was
taken to see many of the famous clippers which made
shipping history in the China tea races and the Australian
wool trade. Later it was my privilege to round Cape Horn
in a little composite sailing ship of less than a thousand
tons. I have always maintained an interest in sailing
ships, visiting them at every opportunity, taking photographs of their hulls, rigging and decks, noting their
peculiarities, and forming acquaintance and friendship with
their masters and mates, some of whom to-day I number
among my closest friends. For years it has been my desire
to write something of the sailing ship of the last hundred

years, not as a complete history, for that is impossible, but as a small tribute to the memory of the Tall Ships themselves and that of the men who sailed them.

I do not pretend that this book is a complete realisation of that desire. For reasons of space I have been unable to mention many ships which were the talk of their day; while including some I have had to omit references to and stories of many of their masters—their adventures afloat and ashore, their skill in seamanship, their disasters due to icebergs, gales, fire, collision, stranding, disablement, and other perils of the sea, and how they overcame them or were themselves overcome. Nevertheless, I think I have included sufficient to show what manner of men they were; also, without indulging in too many technicalities, I have endeavoured to indicate the chief features of the different types of vessels they commanded. If there is no mention of every incident in the career of every well-known sailing ship and its master, it must be attributed, not to lack of willingness on my part, but to the necessity of leaving out a great deal in order to find room for the remainder. In the last hundred and twenty five years there have been thousands of sailing ships, and every successful voyage was more or less a romantic adventure; but unfortunately some voyages ended in tragedy. I have mentioned many fast passages, and some very slow ones, ocean races, instances of international rivalry, famous ships and their captains, and equally famous owners. It must not be forgotten that the ships which were most in favour and were looked upon as the most successful were those which made their passages with commendable regularity and had little or nothing in the way of exciting incident or adventure. Those ships and captains that avoided mis-fortunes were the most appreciated by their owners, officers, crews, and passengers, to say nothing of the shippers and consignees of their cargoes.

In the early days of the last century all sailing vessels were constructed of wood. Then the principal ships were the East Indiamen, the finest examples of the ship-builders' skill the world could show. Splendid ships they were, too, designed with an eye to beauty of form, to weatherliness, and in those days of high freights to earn fortunes for their owners and commanders. They were armed, and had to be able to protect themselves against French cruisers or out-and-out pirates of no nationality, and seldom came off second best in the encounters.

The bulk of British overseas trade, however, in those days, was carried in smaller vessels, generally good in their way but not equal in tonnage or equipment to the East Indiamen. They were the free trade ships and barques, so called because they were free to carry cargo to and from any port from which they were not excluded, as they were from India by John Company's monopoly. This monopoly was attacked more than once by other owners who desired to share in the Company's prosperity. Though the Company's good fortune did not last, its rivals produced a number of ships the equal of many it possessed, and these were followed by others which surpassed them. These in turn gave place to the Blackwall Packets and China Clippers. There also came the American bid for the supremacy of the world's mercantile marine, which, after the Americans seemed to be having matters all their own way, was met by the patriotic determination of Mr. Richard Green, of Poplar, whose name should be venerated as long as ships enter and leave the Thames, through whose efforts and stimulating energy English shipping again took first place, and in spite of attempts by

Americans, French and Germans to seize the honour, has retained it ever since.

There was little, if anything, to choose for either speed or beauty between the best of the British and American clippers after the British revival, but in the later races home from China with the season's teas the best of the British ships often gave points and a beating to their American rivals. The tea clippers were peculiar in one respect : they were built to be raced, to be driven as hard as the dare-devil skippers in command could drive them, to carry sail when it seemed impossible that spars and cordage could stand the strain. One of the fastest of these ships was the *Cutty Sark*, which some regard as the fastest ; she is the sole survivor of that glorious fleet. Thanks to the public spirit of a retired master mariner and his wife the *Cutty Sark* was repurchased from the Portuguese who had bought her, and is now spending her old age at her anchorage in Falmouth Harbour. The tea races were killed by the steamers which used the Suez Canal—a shorter route than that of the sailers by the Cape of Good Hope, and the clippers mostly went into the Australian trade.

The wooden vessels were followed by the composites : that is, those with iron frames and wood planking. One of the finest of them was the historic *Torrens*. These were succeeded by the iron ships, many of only a few hundred tons gross, and it is no exaggeration to say that the handy little ships and barques of the early part of the second half of the last century could be numbered by the thousand. The shipyards round the coasts, big and little, which had turned out hundreds of wooden ships from coasters to deep water vessels, now devoted themselves to iron vessels, and rang day and night to the clanging of the hammers. Now most of the smaller building ports are silent.

When steamers appeared about a hundred years ago they were opposed and ridiculed, but far-seeing men recognised their superiority over wind-driven ships. They were not then the great powerful creations to which in these times we are accustomed ; the engines of the steam ships, as they were called, were often mere auxiliaries to their sails, but the bare fact that they could act independently of their canvas showed an undoubted superiority over the sailer, and foreshadowed only too clearly the ultimate doom of the latter. Still, sailing ships continued to be built, and when steel replaced iron as the material of construction, their types and size improved until the " Red Duster " was displayed proudly in all the chief ports of the world by beautiful three-masted and four-masted ships and barques. No further improvements in sailing ships seemed possible, and none of the latest were able to excel the best of the clippers in anything but carrying capacity.

Some owners of sailing ships kept faithful to them as long as any money could be made out of them, and longer; but they knew that the day of the sailing ship was nearly done, that she could not compete successfully against the cheaper and more reliable steamer, and so they sold them to foreigners.

A few of them are still to be met with, mostly under other names, doing their best to maintain the glorious traditions inherited from the days when the sailing ship helped to make the history of the world. Many others have been broken up for the sake of the metal of which they were constructed, and their story has almost passed into oblivion. Others, again, are doing duty, after being stripped of everything above their lower masts, as coal hulks and floating storehouses, their very names forgotten. Surely by their records they deserved a better fate.

There are not many of the world's more important ports

where one or more of these former aristocrats of the ocean may not be found ending their days in this humble if useful rôle. They are to be seen in the Calcutta river, and at other Indian and Far East ports, at all the chief Australian ports—the famous *Samuel Plimsoll,* for instance, which spent the years of her old age at Perth, Western Australia, as a hulk, was not long ago, when too decrepit to be of further use, towed out to the open sea and sent to her last rest beneath the surface of the ocean she had crossed so often. A few more may be come upon near the mouths of African rivers, and yet others are to be found in many of the South American ports. Most of them have had their names changed, and have been so altered that they reveal little or nothing to indicate their former identity.

A few others, after having had their upper masts and all spars removed, have been equipped with motor engines and are employed in trade on the great rivers which discharge into the Plate. Many ships have been lost : many are known to have been wrecked, or sunk in collision, or sent to the bottom during the war ; and others, which left port in all their pride and beauty, have been posted "missing."

Year in and year out, when sailing ships rounded Cape Horn at certain seasons, almost daily, the "greybeards," as the immense waves in those seas are called, or the rocks, or the icebergs, exacted their toll, and ship after ship was added to the list of those missing with all hands. In the last twenty-five years few have been replaced, and in the last fifteen years none have been built to take the places of those sold foreign, or broken up, or converted into hulks.

Long before the end of the nineteenth century the sailing ship in British hands was not an economical proposition ; owner after owner, some with and some without regret, joined the ranks of the steam ship owners.

For fully half a century the sailing ship put up a splendid fight against her mechanically propelled rival, and scores of voyages were made in which the sailers beat their rivals hollow, wind permitting. Some of the old sailer captains used to take a pride in passing, if they could, every steam ship going in the same direction as their own ship, when the wind was favourable and strong, and some used to offer sarcastically to report the steam ships " all well."

The sailing ships, however, though they might beat the steam ships occasionally, could not compete against them in the two important factors of greater regularity and comparative indifference to weather conditions. The adoption of iron, and afterwards of steel, as the material of which both sailers and steam ships were constructed, helped to hasten the doom of the sailer, for the simple reason that steam ships were built of far greater size of these materials than would have been safe or economically advantageous with sailing ships.

In the last fifteen years of the nineteenth century very few large sailing ships were built in the United Kingdom ; in the present century there have been hardly any, and since the war none. So rapidly has the British owned sailing ship disappeared that the total of the deep water sailers in active service now registered throughout the British Empire amounts to one, and she, the *Garthpool*, formerly the *Juteopolis*, is making what is expected to be her last voyage.

Among the lines of the past may be mentioned the Blackwall packets, Green's ships, Milne's " Invers," Wigram's stately craft, Thompson's flyers, John Willis's pets, Devitt's floating homes, Hood's ships, Duncan Dunbar's ships, the Loch Line, the White Star, Trinder Anderson's vessels, the New Zealand Shipping Company, and their rivals Shaw Savill, the " Counties," the " Sierras,"

2

the " Stars," the " Monarchs," the " Glens," the " Halls,"
the " Falls," and many more. They all made shipping
history, fostered and furthered British trade and commerce, and carried Britons oversea to extend the Empire.
National gratitude should accord them some recognition
of their achievements, and of the heroism, resourcefulness,
bravery, and too often the self-sacrifice of those who
commanded and manned them.

It is sad to realise that never again shall we see the
fleets of homeward bound vessels speeding up the Channel
with a strong wind on their quarter, every sail set and
pulling its hardest, their canvas shining in the sunshine
from courses to skysails and towering above the weather-
beaten hulls. The ships themselves, with bows and sterns
alternately dipping and rising, and the clean graceful
clipper stems throwing the cloven waves on either side in
a smother of foam, presented a picture unmatched and
unmatchable. If the tide could not carry them into the
Thames estuary, or if the wind took an unfavourable
direction, they anchored one after another in the Downs,
till there have been as many as a hundred at a time.
Those that were lucky enough got tugs and so reached
London earlier than their rivals.

Perhaps Liverpool, because of its geographical position,
even better than London, could witness the coming and
going of its fleets of sailers, of which there might be a
hundred and fifty in a day ; it is on record that in one year
the deep sea sailing ships which entered and left the Mersey
numbered over seventy-five thousand. When, a few years
ago, a sailing ship captain disdained a tug, because he had
a strong favourable wind, and brought his ship under nearly
full sail into the Mersey, half the waterfront denizens of
Liverpool turned out to see the extraordinary sight.

Picture a group of these ships at sea, almost becalmed in the doldrums, or pushing on with the favourable trade winds, rocking gently to the motion of the ever-restless waters, and as it were bowing to each other with the stately grace of aristocratic ladies of the old school; indeed, they were aristocrats of the old school of ships. There was never an ungraceful sailing ship when once she was on the blue water under canvas, though to seafarers she might present every defect of which a ship could be capable. Ugly, squat, uncomfortable, and ill-kept as some of them appeared in dock, it could not be denied that when they were on the open sea and had their sails spread, and moved in accord with the rhythmic motion of the waves, they presented a certain beauty to the spectator which entirely belied the bad impression they might create in dock. But to sail in such ships was quite another matter.

Who that has seen a sailing vessel, be she coasting schooner or grand four-master, set forth on a voyage, has not felt the glow of the spirit of romance and adventure which were part and parcel of every sailing vessel, and has not wondered how she would fare ? With a well-built, well-found, well-commanded, and well-officered and well-manned ship, all should be well, and generally was well ; unfortunately these conditions did not apply to all ships for some were jerry-built, or uncared for and shockingly and criminally neglected and overloaded intentionally, and apparently it paid their owners better to load them heavily and over-insure them and lose them, than it did to have them make the voyage. What happened to their crews did not matter. Not all owners were of this stamp. The majority were honourable men, but there were enough black sheep to justify the noble work of the late Samuel Plimsoll, the seaman's friend, whose best monument is the marks to be found on each side of every sea-going vessel, sail or steam. But it would be interesting to know how many were lost on their first voyages after the Plimsoll marks were raised a few years ago, so that their owners could try and make more profit. The effect on the ships was that their total deadweight was increased and their freeboard and buoyancy were lessened. The poor old ships could not stand it.

Never again shall we see the fleets of sailers leaving port, painted afresh and with their brasswork shining, and casting off their tugs and setting their canvas, and perhaps catch the chorus of the sailors' chanty. Beautiful as brides the ships looked. They were old Ocean's brides. The spray he playfully cast about their bows was his kiss of welcome, the foam along their sides the pillow for their comfort that they might rest the more contentedly upon his bosom. But the Ocean has ever been a fickle wooer, and too often his kiss of welcome has been his kiss of betrayal. The world is the poorer for the disappearance of the sailing ship. Those who are old enough to remember the days of the wooden ships and the undivided topsails, who have noted the changes that culminated in the fine ships of the closing years of the last century, have something to be proud of in knowing that they lived in the days that produced the finest sailing ships and the finest seamen of their type the world has ever known, and some-thing to regret that those ships and men have gone for ever. The number of those who were trained in sail, whether officers or men, is becoming smaller. Yet training in sail was in vogue until the war clouds threatened Europe in 1912, after which, with the aid of the war, it died out entirely. Some lovers of the sailing ship have openly hoped that the windjammers would be given another lease of life if fitted with internal combustion engines, but the experiments made in that direction and the results on the whole have not all been unqualified successes, and do not justify the hope.

When the old-time sailormen used to transfer to steamers it was said by those they left behind that they had " chucked the sea and gone into steam." Modern sailors have not " chucked the sea," though they have " gone into steam." They have heard the call of the sea and obeyed it ; they cannot help it. The sea is the same, but the conditions of sea life are different, and the changes are for the better. The sea is as loving and as repellent, as faithful and as treacherous, as wilful and as contrite as ever ; sometimes raging like fiends let loose, and then sobbing and moaning, like an exhausted and fretful child over its broken toys, over the shattered victims of its fury, and in the strange voices which travel over the sea singing its requiem over those whose lives it has taken. I, like thousands of others, have heard those voices as I have trodden the deck of a sailing ship at night ; I have talked with the men in the forecastle and on the poop, of things which only those who have been at sea in a sailing ship can know ; I have seen the effects of the constant companionship of their floating home, of their continual trust in the unstable sea and wind, and know how near some of them have got to the truths of Nature, and knowing this, I can understand how strange beliefs—which landsmen call superstition— have taken possession of their minds. The men of the deep-water sailing ships were influenced to a marvellous extent by their surroundings, perhaps even more than they realised themselves. It is as a token of love and respect and esteem for those old shellbacks and their ships that I have written this book, inadequate though it be for the purpose.

IN THE DAYS OF THE TALL SHIPS

Those were the days of the old time clippers,
The tall ships ready for the setting forth to sail.
 Every spar and rope would quiver
 As they went down London River,
To welcome once again the kiss of spindrift, wave and gale.

Those were the days of the tough old shellbacks :
Men who ran their eastings down or battled round the Horn.
 When once they'd set the courses
 And had seen the wild white horses,
They were glad to be afloat but cursed the day that they were born.

Those were the days of the deep water sailors :
Men who never cared a jot how hard the wind might blow.
 On sheets or halliards hauling,
 And the mate or " old man " bawling,
And the good old chanty going of the luck of poor Ranzo.

Those were the days when they spread along the footropes,
And the frozen mainsail nearly tore their nails out by the roots.
 But although 'twas frozen hard
 They stowed it on the yard,
And in chanty sang they'd pay old " Paddy Doyle for his boots."

Those were the days of the dawdling in the doldrums :
Sails all slapping idly and sheets and braces slack ;
 Ships only making leeway,
 And scarce a yard of seaway,
And drifting o'er the Equator and sometimes drifting back.

Those were the days of the superstitious sailors :
Strange beliefs and omens drawn from birds and wind and sea :
 Lost ships beside them steering,
 Lost men at the weather earring—
Souls of drowned sailormen in seagulls flying free.

These are the days when the long-lost ships returning
Drift in misty half-lights to the moorings that they knew ;
 Strange phantoms from the ocean,
 Gliding on with stately motion,
Manned by souls of sailormen, ghostly ships and crew.

These are the days of ships long since gone under :
Drifting back to home and port upon the flowing tide ;
 Ghost ships scarred and broken,
 Every shattered spar a token
Of their struggle with the rocks or sea the day or night they died.

R. A. FLETCHER in the Nautical Magazine

CHAPTER I

TYPES OF SHIPS

W HAT were the Tall Ships like ? What sort of ships were they which went from the British Isles to all the available ports of the world during the last hundred and thirty years ? Many of the famous Tall Ships were small craft : little full-rigged ships, barques and brigs and brigantines and even sloops. A hundred years ago few, except the East Indiamen, were above five hundred tons. Yet they made their voyages to the Cape, and the East, and Australia, and even beat their way round Cape Horn to the West Coast of South America. Many of them carried passengers, too. One little barque of under two hundred tons is said to have gone from London to Melbourne in the 'thirties. As she had passengers, it shows what risks people were prepared to run in those days, and seemingly they thought little or nothing of it, and were only glad when the five months' voyage and its discomforts were over.

If the unusual spectacle of yards crossing masts should be seen in a United Kingdom port now-a-days, it may be taken as certain that they belong to a foreign-owned vessel. The chances are, too, that she was built in a British yard. Go and look at her, for it may be the last time you will have the opportunity. If her new port of registry is in a country bordering on the Mediterranean, it is very probable that she will be ill-kept and dirty. But you will still be able to notice the beautiful form and proportions of the hull, the tall, graceful masts, the swinging yards, and the slender rigging.

The finest sailing ships now afloat belong to the Americans, the Germans and the French. Most of the American-owned, square-rigged ships are the property of one or other of the salmon canning companies on the Pacific Coast. Indeed. this trade was the last refuge of the few remaining sailers, and last year and this have seen many of them converted into hulks, their places being taken by steamers. Scattered about the ports of the world are many British-built sailing ships, still afloat but stripped of everything above their lower masts, and ingloriously ending their days as hulks. They are as much to be pitied as the fabled racehorse which dropped dead of old age between the shafts of a greengrocer's cart.

Most of the old British ships that were sold to the Norwegians, Swedes, Finns, Germans, or Russians had good care taken of them, but others were sadly neglected. When the *Carradale*, a beautiful four-masted Clyde-built steel barque, was in the Port of London four or five years ago, I visited her. Her then first mate, a typical Finn, took me over her and explained with pride how careful her owners were with her upkeep. She was beautifully clean, her brasswork polished brightly, her decks scrubbed, and her cabins a model of neatness ; even the crew's quarters were clean and tidy. Aloft, too, there was not a frayed rope, and the mate told me her sails were in as good condition as the rest of the ship.

A contrast, this, to the *Cutty Sark* when her Portuguese owners brought her back to London.

But before dealing with these large modern vessels, it is necessary, in order that references in other parts of this

FINNISH BARQUE CARRADALE

Photo by R. A. Fletcher

Facing page 24

book to the rig of ships may be understood, and to appreciate their development, to say something of the types of deep-water vessels which sailed the Seven Seas during the last century. These ranged from cutters and sloops and coasters to five-masted, full-rigged ships, and six-masted and seven-masted schooners.

For the first quarter of the last century a great deal of the coasting trade of the British Islands was carried in cutters and sloops. At times longer voyages were undertaken, and they are known to have crossed the Atlantic. Both these are single-masted vessels, with the mast placed about a third of the length from the bows. They carried an immense mainsail, and sometimes a topsail above it, and two or three head sails, known as staysails or jibs, and, according to old prints, some had a square topsail or a square foresail, extended on yards.

The real modern cutter rig has no square-sails. Those with the square-sails were often termed sloops. Square-sails on one-masted vessels were discarded three-quarters of a century ago. The present meaning of the word sloop is a one-masted vessel which differs from the cutter in this detail : the cutter has a rope or stay extending from near the head of the lower mast to the stem of the vessel, whereas the sloop has the stay taken to the outer end of the bowsprit. Plenty of examples of these rigs are to be found in the pleasure and fishing craft at many seaside resorts, though even here they are being superseded by mechanically propelled vessels.

Many of these cutters in the old days carried passengers. The advertisements of the period describe the accommodation as " commodious and comfortable," and set forth in glowing terms such luxuries as they had. One advertisement announced that the fare included bedding for the passengers, another extolled the superior lighting of the interior by means of candles, and yet another announced that passengers would be provided with food instead of having to bring their own. These vessels maintained a fairly regular service both ways, between London and the east coast ports as far north as Aberdeen.

There was, too, the added excitement of a possible fight with a French vessel, in which event the captain would call for volunteers from among his male passengers to assist his crew, while the women and children, if any, would be kept below. Fortunately fights, except in the early years of the century, were of rare occurrence. The voyage from Granton or Newcastle to London took about a week, and sometimes a day or two less in very favourable weather. A westerly gale, however, has blown more than one of these coasters over to the Dutch coast, and it is recorded that one of them put into a Norwegian port for shelter and provisions, having been blown right across the North Sea. She reached London about six weeks late. She must have been a good sea boat, and superbly handled, for the North Sea can be a very rough place when the stormy winds do blow. Another of these vessels was blown so far out of her course that she sought shelter and provisions at an Icelandic port.

The passenger, goods and mail service between Liverpool and the Isle of Man used to be carried in cutters which, in very favourable conditions, made the journey in a day. Under unfavourable conditions they might take anything up to a week. One of these cutters was blown out of her course and sighted the Welsh coast, a change of wind brought her back to within sight of the island, and yet another change took her south-eastward again ; altogether she sighted the Welsh coast and the island three times.

At last she was able to make the Mersey, and thankful her passengers must have been to get ashore after six days and nights of it. Now the Isle of Man Company's steamers cross in four hours or a little less, and have been known to do the double journey twice in twenty-four hours at the height of the passenger season. There is a splendid painting of one of these cutters at the Peveril Hotel, Douglas.

Voyages to the Baltic and the nearer Continental ports, and even to the Mediterranean, were sometimes made in vessels of this class. The discomforts must have been great, and the dangers greater, on such voyages, but the fact that they were successfully undertaken is a glowing testimony to the daring seamanship of their captains, officers and crews.

Let us turn now to vessels having two masts. We find among them many variations in rig. A vessel with her principal mast forward, and a small mast near the stern, is known as a yawl or ketch. There are still some of them to be found among our coasters, and very sturdy little craft they are. The sailing barges, with their big mainsails extended on a diagonal sprit, and the small mizen at the stern, are not yawls or ketches, though often called so, but as barges are not deep-water ships in the sense in which I am dealing with them in this book, I say no more about them.

A two-masted vessel, with the after mast as high as, or higher than, the foremast, was a schooner, a brig, or a brigantine. The origin of the term schooner, as meaning a two-masted vessel, instead of a long glass out of which Dutchmen used to drink their beer, is unknown. There is a story that an enterprising American built the first two-masted vessel with fore-and-aft sails only ; he and his friends at the launch were at a loss what to call a craft of this type. She went down the slips so swiftly and took the water so gracefully that an excited onlooker exclaimed, with true American ability to invent slang, " See how she schoons." So a schooner she was called. Some American writers accept this yarn as gospel. Believe it if you like. Be that as it may, British vessels with two masts were in existence long before this alleged incident, but it is not known when they first began to be called schooners. The term schooner is applied to most British vessels having two or three masts, on which are set fore-and-aft sails only, and sometimes wrongly includes yawls and ketches. The Americans have built many schooners with three and four masts, a few with five, and fewer still with six masts, and one with seven. This was the *Thomas W. Lawson*. She was a fine steel vessel. Some difficulty was experienced in naming her masts and sails. Starting from the front, the first four were easy enough, being fore, main, mizen, and jigger. The fifth was called the spanker and the sixth the driver. Invention came to a temporary standstill until someone called the seventh the pusher. I wonder what some old square-rigger shellback would have thought, and said, if he could have been transferred to the *Thomas W. Lawson* and been ordered to set the pusher topsail.

Most American schooners are three or four-masted. These large fore-and-aft schooners are peculiarly suitable to American coastal navigation, particularly along the Atlantic seaboard ; they are anything from 500 to over 3,000 tons net register. The great advantages of this rig are that a large sail area is spread, and that only small crews are needed, for there is next to none of the going aloft inseparable from vessels carrying yards and square-sails, and a great deal of the pully-hauly work is done by donkey engines. Some of the more modernly equipped schooners carry internal combustion engines on deck, instead of steam donkey engines, and a motor may also be used to drive a dynamo for lighting the vessel by electricity.

A peculiarity of some of the American schooners is that the foremast carries a yard to which a large square-sail is attached ; this sail is not stowed on the yard as an ordinary square foresail would be, but from the deck either half of it can be hauled out from the mast to the yard arm, and in again when not required, or both halves can be set at once if necessary. When it is stowed it is brailed to the mast, and all the ropes are operated from the deck. It can be set or furled far more quickly than if it were attached to the yard in the ordinary way. It is another instance of the American fondness for labour saving appliances.

" What is the difference between a topsail schooner and a brigantine ? " is a question that is often asked and easily answered. A topsail schooner carries a transverse yard slung at the crosstrees of the foremast. Here another mast is fixed—fidded is the nautical term—and this upper or topmast carries another yard from which the topsail hangs ; sometimes there is a third yard above that, called the topgallant yard, to support the topgallant sail. If you wish to speak of these in the nautical way you will pronounce topsail as tops'l and topgallant as to'galn.

A brigantine has all these sails on her foremast, and in addition she has a third mast fidded to the topmast, and this spar carries, besides the topgallant yard, the royal yard which spreads the sail known as the royal. The second, or after, mast is fore-and-aft rigged only. On the stays extending from the mainmast to the foremast she may set as many as three or four triangular or irregular

shaped sails, which are named according to the stays supporting them. The mainmast of a brigantine carried on
the after side an immense spanker and above this a gaff-
topsail. It should be added that the fore-yard of a brigantine invariably spread a large square-sail known as the
foresail, whereas a topsail schooner rarely had any such
canvas, her foresail being a fore-and-aft sail supported
by a gaff on the after side of the foremast.

The last two-masted vessel to which reference need be
made is the brig. They were usually from 150 to 200 tons.
Brigs are virtually obsolete now ; one or two may be met
with in the Baltic, and a few in the Mediterranean, but as
they die out or are withdrawn from service their places
are taken by steamers or motor craft. The brig was often
a very graceful craft, and for her tonnage her spread of
canvas was fairly large. It is interesting to note that the
brig was the last type of sailing vessel in the British navy ;
the Admiralty kept two or three as training ships, long
after they had no other sailing ships into which to put the
sail-trained boys. In brigs, both masts were square-rigged
almost alike ; the foremast and mainmast each consisted
of three spars, and each mast carried four yards. The
mainmast was almost always loftier than the foremast.
The rigging and sails of the mainmast differed but slightly
from those of the foremast, except that the spanker or
driver of the mainmast was an invariable feature, while the
trysail of the foremast was not ; the braces of the yards on
the mainmast were carried forward, mostly to the foremast ; there were also some slight differences in the
arrangement of the fore-and-aft stays of the two masts.
In regard to the trysail, many brigs and some brigantines
had a spar, called the trysail mast, fixed down the after side
of the fore lower mast, and on this a small fore-and-aft

sail might be set in dirty weather. A brig thus equipped was called a " snow," though no one seems to know why. A hermaphrodite brig was an older name for the brigantine.

All deep-sea sailing vessels, whatever their rig, were fitted with a bowsprit, which served the double purpose of giving additional support to the foremast by means of the forestay and other stays, and carried a jibboom which projected beyond the end of the bowsprit with the object of allowing further jibs to be set on the stays between the jibboom and the upper part of the foremast. On account of their length—and some American ships had them of a length that seems little short of ridiculous and was certainly risky—a small spar was fixed under the end of the bowsprit to stiffen the stays that were brought down from the jibboom to the stem. This small spar was called a dolphin striker, and sailors have been known to tell landsmen that its chief use was to spear the dolphins as they played about the bows in the tropics so that the crews might have fresh fish for breakfast. In the very few vessels that carried a flying jibboom, as a second jibboom fitted to the first one was named, a second dolphin striker is said to have been carried sometimes. The drawback to too long a jibboom was that it was liable to snap as the ship dug her nose into a wave, and this would mean that the foretopgallant mast, having lost the support of the stays, might snap also, and when once this sort of thing started, there was no telling where it would end. The big modern steel sailers were almost invariably given stump bowsprits, the jibboom being dispensed with altogether. They did not need the additional sail carrying space provided by the jibboom, their greater dimensions enabling the jibboom to be done away with, the bowsprit sufficing to carry all the stays required.

Many brigs, brigantines, and schooners were very fast sailers for their size, and bore a large spread of canvas. They were mostly good seaboats and easily handled, and these qualities caused them to be used in the slave trade from Africa to America, and in the opium smuggling into China.

It is interesting to note that though brigs have died out and very few brigantines are left, there are still some representatives afloat of the little British ocean-going schooners. Year in and year out a small fleet of these vessels thrash their way back and forth across the North Atlantic, chiefly carrying fish from Newfoundland, St. Pierre and Miquelon to Gibraltar or Spanish or French Ports, and taking home products in return. There used to be, before the war, a fleet of small schooners belonging to a south coast firm, and averaging from 90 to 120 tons gross, which performed their transatlantic voyages, winter and summer, with a regularity which spoke volumes for the seamanship of those who commanded them and was a glowing testimony to the strength of their construction, their suitability for their work, and the excellence of their equipment. Two of them were well known as the *Little Secret* and *Little Mystery*. The romance of the sea can never die out while such vessels and such crews as manned them are afloat.

Once I saw one of these ocean-going schooners showing what she could do in a howling North Atlantic gale, with the sea running mountains high, as the phrase goes. The sailing ship I was on was under very reduced canvas. As the schooner crossed our bows less than half a mile distant we could see her leaning over till her lee gunwale was under water. Her three little scraps of sail, looking not much bigger than handkerchiefs, tore her along at a great pace amid a smother of foam, and clouds of heavy spray and sometimes green water swept her from end to end. We could see two oilskin-clad figures at the wheel ; they must have been firmly lashed or they would have been washed away. She seemed a living, a mad thing as she rushed down the slope of one wave and up the next, bounding ahead in a fashion that even the famous *Dreadnought*, the " wild boat of the Atlantic," when under Captain Samuels could not have surpassed.

Three-masted vessels were classed as luggers, schooners, barquentines, barques, and ships. Luggers were fore-and-aft vessels only, and were used chiefly for English Channel work. Deal was one of their principal ports. The schooners were either fore-and-aft, or carried square-sails on the foremast. A barquentine had her foremast fidded and rigged like that of a brig, her main and mizen masts having topmasts only and carrying fore-and-aft sails. A barque had her fore and main masts square-rigged, and her mizen mast fore-and-aft rigged. A ship, strictly speaking, was a three-masted vessel, with not fewer than four square-sails on each mast. Some of the older wooden ships and barques carried trysail masts.

In the early part of the last century, when suitable wood was fairly common, and this country had not been denuded of her oak forests to meet the needs of the Royal Navy and the mercantile marine, wood was the only material used. In those days freights were high enough to justify the importation of selected wood from the Continent and even from India, and not a few of the famous East Indiamen were actually built in India itself. As copper does not corrode in salt water, all the bolts had to be of that metal. Vessels of good sound timber, properly copper-fastened, might be expected to last a lifetime. Many of them have

lasted more than an ordinary lifetime. Some of the old
wooden hulks which may be seen in out-of-the-way
corners at one or another of our ports, were famous ships
in their day, the pride of their dead and forgotten owners,
the joy of their masters and crews, and the talk of con-
temporary sailormen in all the Seven Seas. Perhaps the
most famous remaining example of the old wooden sailing
ship is the *Success*. Some particulars of her remarkable
career are given in another chapter.

An interesting controversy was revived in 1925 over the
question which is the oldest vessel afloat. Steel vessels
do not last anything so long as those of iron, and iron ones
are said to be longer lived than those of timber ; yet the
oldest vessels afloat are built of wood.

The oldest which survived into the present century was
the Italian ship *Anita*, broken up a few years ago at Genoa.
Presumably she had outlasted her usefulness. She is
credibly stated to have been built when Queen Elizabeth
was on the throne of this country ; if that be so, she had
knocked about the world for three centuries. It is no
wonder she lasted so long, for her hull is said to have been
of oak a foot thick. This no doubt explains her reputation
of being the slowest ship that ever existed. Probably she
was so heavily constructed to enable her to withstand the
attacks of the Barbary pirates or other enemies. It is a
pity she could not have been kept as a relic of the times
when she first took the water, for she is said to have been
a representative of the type that Columbus used when he
sailed on his memorable voyage which ended in the discovery of America.

A few old sailing vessels may still be found in the Mediterranean, but it is to the Baltic that one must go now to
find maritime Methuselahs. Those going strong up to a

KETCH GOOD INTENT

Photo by W. A. Sharman

Facing page 34

very recent date, and they may possibly be in existence still, include the *Constance*, a small coaster built in 1723. A Swedish vessel, now called the *Emanuel*, took the water in 1749; in her early days she was a pirate, but now is engaged in the peaceful trade of carrying timber; the same family has owned her for close upon a century. Up to a few years before the war a little Danish schooner was still going strong after 140 years active service; she is said to have been owned and commanded by members of the same family throughout her career.

The oldest British patriarch of the sea is the little ketch *Good Intent*, which was built at Plymouth as far back as 1790, and is of less than 22 tons register. When she was sold at Cardiff in 1919 she was in such good condition that £200 was given for her. The ketch *Seal*, built at Southampton in 1810, is believed to be still afloat. When she was thirteen years old a storm carried her into a field near Poole, Dorset, from which she was dragged back to the shore and set afloat again. It is not very long, as time goes in the life of these old craft, since she sailed from Bideford for Durban, where she arrived in due course. Up to a year or two ago there was at Harwich, and may be still there, a small vessel, mastless but still able to float with the tide, of a type which showed that she belonged to the days of a long distant past. I was unable to ascertain her real name or history, and I did not accept any of the stories which imaginative and thirsty longshoremen told me of her alleged adventures. She was only moderately full in the bows, her most interesting feature being her stern which was high and square, and bore a lot of carving.

The *Great Republic* and the *Shenandoah* were the largest wooden sailing ships ever built, and both were launched in

America. A description of the vessels is given in another chapter.

There is a limit to the size at which wooden sailing ships can be built. The bigger the ship, the more massive must be the timbers put into her to stand the strains to which every vessel is subjected. Thus the time would come when so much timber would have to be used in her construction that she would not earn enough to pay for her building and upkeep. Every ship, whatever the material of her construction, must be strong enough to stand the strains known as hogging and sagging, to say nothing of the screwing strains to which the hull is subjected by the motion of the sea. When a hull is supported by a wave at bow and stern, and is comparatively unsupported amidships, she has a tendency to sag in the middle ; when she is well supported on a wave amidships, and her bow and stern are not so well supported, the strain is equally great, and she has a tendency to droop at the ends, thereby raising or " hogging" her amidships. If means are not taken to strengthen a hull to enable her to withstand these strains, she will eventually break her back.

As iron and subsequently steel came into general use for shipbuilding, many vessels were constructed of those materials of greater size than had been customary with wood, and four-masted vessels became common. When the four-masters—or four-posters, as they were dubbed later—had the fourth mast rigged fore-and-aft, and the other three masts square-rigged, they were called four-masted barques ; Americans liked to call them shipentines. When all four masts were square-rigged they were known as four-masted ships. A few five-masters have been built, notably by the Germans and French. The five-masted barque *France* attracted a great deal of attention when she visited London a few years ago. She was built for cargo carrying rather than for speed, but her enormous spread of canvas enabled her to be driven at a fair pace. She was wrecked off New Caledonia about four years ago. Probably the most noteworthy five-masted barque is the German built and owned *Potosi*.

The vessels of the early part of the nineteenth century were for the most part bluff-bowed and square-sterned. It was the custom to place the foremast nearer the bows than was the practice later. When vessels were given finer bows, more like a wedge, it was found that the weight of the foremast so far forward caused them to ship a great deal of water, so to increase the buoyancy at the bows the foremast was placed further back, and the mainmast was shifted further back also. These changes, together with the increase in the size of ships, caused certain alterations to be made in the sails. As ships were built of greater dimensions, sails were increased in size and more of them were set. When the fine-lined vessels, and the still finer lined clippers were introduced, longer bowsprits were fitted, which in turn supported longer jibbooms. This, together with the placing of the foremast further from the bows, enabled much larger headsails to be set. Both the foretopmast staysail and the jib had already assumed proportions in many vessels which made them very awkward customers to handle, and they well deserved the name of " man killer " which was given them because of the number of men they had hurled into the sea in dirty weather to drown. The greater number of stays introduced between the foremast and the jibboom allowed a greater number of sails to be set.

Another and most important change was the division of the square topsail into two, called the upper and lower.

The weight of an old-fashioned topsail was very considerable, and to reef one in a gale, or to stow it, was an exceedingly difficult task. Some of the old captains looked upon the innovation with anything but favour, for old sailing ship men were a very conservative class and extremely suspicious of anything new. They agreed with the owners in this detail, if not in any other. The division of the topsail necessitated another yard, and each yard meant another pair of braces to handle. Once having seen, however, and possibly being half converted by some master who was already an admirer of the divided topsails, the divided sail in operation, they could not help being convinced of the utility of the new-fangled idea. For one thing it enabled the upper part of the sail to be taken in and stowed without interfering with the lower half ; the latter could be reefed, for reef points were inserted in both upper and lower topsails.

Then, as vessels of still greater size were built, the top-gallant sails were divided also, with corresponding advantages. In course of time when the sailing ship reached its maximum size some four-masted barques and ships carried divided topgallant sails as well as divided topsails. The *Lancing*, which was one of the finest specimens of her type and one of the fastest, and was recently afloat, is an example. Four-masted barques were more popular than four-masted ships, and several of the latter after a voyage or two had the square-sails taken off the fourth or jigger mast and fore-and-aft sails set on it. For one thing they required fewer men. In a few very large vessels a further division of a sail was introduced affecting the spanker, two gaffs being fitted, one a considerable distance above the other, so that the upper portion of the sail could be taken in, or only the lower part set ; a fore-and-aft topsail was set above the upper gaff. One of the finest examples of a four-masted barque thus fitted is the German *Peking*, which belongs to Herr Laeisz of Hamburg.

Some of the very large sailers, both British and foreign, of the most modern type had their cabin accommodation in a deckhouse amidships, the deckhouse extending completely from one side of the ship to the other. A great advantage of this was that it prevented the ship being swept by big seas from end to end, and also stopped a great deal of water from coming over amidships. The roof of the deckhouse formed a commodious deck. Bridges or gangways connected the middle deck thus formed with the fo'castle head and the poop. Vessels thus constructed were sometimes steered from amidships, and when this was done a second wheel was fitted under or on the poop which could be used in case of emergency.

In the *Peking*, which is a remarkably well equipped barque, the after steering wheel was placed on the main deck under the poop, and the whole space was enclosed so that the steersmen would remain dry and neither they nor the wheel could be washed away, let the weather be what it would. Small thick plate glass windows were placed in the front of this steering cabin, which could be shut if required ; looking through the windows the men could keep an eye on the sails and steer accordingly, and the captain or officer on watch could give them his instructions by means of a speaking tube from the chart house on the middle deck. Her captain told me that the after wheel had never had to be used, as the amidships steering arrangement had never failed.

Probably the most famous vessel owned by this firm was the celebrated five-masted full-rigged ship *Preussen*. She was wrecked two or three years before the war off

Dover, and the remains of this once magnificent ship are still to be seen. It may interest some to know that the square-sails of the *Peking* were the same size as those of the *Preussen*, and that the *Peking* actually carried some sails which were made for the other ship.

As an illustration of the way in which steel supplanted wood or iron in ship construction, it may be stated that the whole of the hull of the *Peking* was built of steel, even to the decks, though that above the deckhouse amidships was sheathed with wood. All the *Peking's* masts were continuous steel tubes from keel to truck; her spars, even to the royal yards, were of steel, and all her standing rigging was of steel ropes. Hempen or flexible steel ropes or steel chains were used for the running rigging, according to the work they had to do.

Pictures of the sailing vessels of the first half of the nineteenth century show that the stays of the masts were brought down outside the gunwales, and after being extended on frames or baulks of timber to give them greater purchase in holding the masts firmly, were carried down the outside of the ship and there fastened. These baulks were known as the chains or channels, and many passengers enjoyed sitting on them on the weather side when passing through the tropics. With vessels of a larger size the shrouds and stays were fastened through the deck by means of bolts fixed to the frame of the vessel.

In what are romantically called the good old days of the sailing ship, the captains, especially of the racing clippers and of any ship which it was desired to push along, showed a wonderful ingenuity in setting additional sails. Many pictures of the clippers show what could be done in this way. There may be seen at the ends of the yards of the few old time sailers still afloat a ring; this was called

CHILIAN BARQUE ALEJANDRINA
Negative in possession of R. A. Fletcher

the ear-ring ; the man who could take his place at the weather ear-ring was reckoned a smart sailor. To increase the sail area, and thereby the speed, temporary spars called studding-sail—contracted to stunsail—booms were extended horizontally beyond each yard arm even to the royal yards, and these ear-rings were used in making fast the stunsail booms. The captain of a clipper might set on his fore and main masts eight additional sails on each, four on either side, and possibly two or three more on each side of the square-sails on his mizzen mast. These, however, did not exhaust his ingenuity. Another sail, perhaps a couple of yards wide, would be laced to the bottom of the spanker and called a bonnet, and additional spars might be fastened to the spanker boom and gaff to enable yet more canvas to be spread. Other additional sails were " save-alls," " water sails," and " Jamie Green."

Some ships carried above the royals another sail known as the skysail. The *James Baines*, a famous ship in her day, had another higher still, the moonsail, on her main-mast. A few American ships are reputed to have reached even nearer the clouds with a " skyscraper " above the moonsail, and yet another above that impiously called " God's curse." I think the name must have been given to it by some poor wretch who had been sent aloft to furl or set it, with a knowledge that a hefty bucko mate had his eye on him. The actual propelling power of these very exalted handkerchiefs or kites was not great. In a few modern ships nothing was set above the topgallants. " Bald-headed " was the sailor's word for such ships.

It must have been a splendid sight, and unfortunately one that will not be witnessed again, when one of the fine ships, with every inch of canvas that could be crowded on her, was tearing along with a heavy breeze on the quarter, with every sail stretched to its utmost and pulling its hardest, while the vessel threw a great wave of foam from her bows. It was worth living to be on a sailing ship when the "Old Man" cracked on, and was unwilling to shorten sail until there was imminent risk of something carrying away if he did not. Stunsail booms on the racing tea clippers often snapped under the strain, but no sooner was one broken than another was set in its place. Captain Woodget, of the *Cutty Sark*, is said to have crowded on sail on one of his races home from China with tea, to such an extent that he smashed nearly every stunsail boom he had.

NOTE.—During the war, 1914-18, many old sailing ships which had been withdrawn from service were re-equipped, and even a few which had been wrecked were given a new lease of life to meet the demand for tonnage. Among the latter was the iron ship *Andrina*, which stranded near Cape Horn, and after being ashore for twenty years was re-floated and re-rigged by Chileans and named *Alejandrina*. The accompanying photograph of her was taken after she came to England.

CHAPTER II

THE EAST INDIAMEN

THE pride of place in the closing years of the eighteenth century and the early years of the nineteenth century was held by the East Indiamen, the magnificent vessels built for the service of the East India Company. No fleet, before or since, has been so extravagantly maintained. Towards the end of the eighteenth century they attained a degree of perfection which it was claimed at the time could not be surpassed. One of the finest of them all is asserted to have been the famous *Pitt*, or *William Pitt*, which distinguished herself both as a trader and as a fighting vessel. No other British ships of their time even equalled them. Probably their chief rivals in the middle of the eighteenth century were a few French or Dutch ships. The Dutch were the first to be driven from the rivalry, but only after many a hard sea-fight, besides the wars between the Company's land forces in India and the Dutch settlements in the Indian Peninsula ; thereafter the Dutch confined their activities in the Far East to the Dutch East Indies. The French were more persevering, and held on till well into the early years of the last century. There was many a sharp fight between French ships, both warships and privateers, and the ships of the East India Company. Mention is made of some of these contests later in this chapter.

The East India Company is said to have owed its incep-
tion to an expedition of three ships, of which but one
completed the round voyage, near the end of the sixteenth
century. The reports of trade prospects the sole surviving
ship brought back were so favourable, however, that
another expedition was planned. This consisted of five
vessels, and it achieved considerable success as some
trading stations were established in India. The tonnage
of the vessels of this little fleet is of interest. The biggest
was the *Dragon*, 600 tons, the next was the *Hector*, 300 tons,
the *Susannah* and *Ascension* were of 200 tons each, and the
fifth was a little storeship, the *Guest*, 120 tons.

To us, in these days of mammoth steam ships, it is almost
like tempting Providence to undertake an ocean voyage
in such little sailing vessels, especially one like the *Guest* ;
but it seems to have been taken for granted that if a vessel
could get over one wave she could get over the next :
so the merchant adventurers of those days, to judge by
their charters, adopted the Cromwellian advice to put their
trust in God and, mindful of human enemies, kept their
powder dry in view of emergencies. These five vessels
were heavily armed and carried 480 men. The expedition
was profitable.

The Company's first charter was granted in 1600 ; in
this it was described as " The United Company of Merchant
Venturers of England Trading to the East Indies."
Subsequent charters extended its influence and strengthened its monopolies. A ship called the *Trades Increase*
was built in 1609 ; she is stated to have been of 1209 tons,
the largest constructed for trading purposes up to that
time. She was lost on her first voyage. This entailed a
financial loss which might have crippled an undertaking
less well protected than the East India Company. In

1611 the *Globe* brought in a profit estimated at 218 per cent, and in 1612 the capital invested in the voyages of the *Globe*, *Victor*, and *Thomas* is said to have returned a profit of 340 per cent. For year after year the completed voyages of the Company's ships showed immense profits. If a vessel were captured by enemies or pirates the loss was more than covered by the profits made by the other vessels.

The first charter conferred on the Company the sole right of trading with the East Indies, *i.e.*, with all countries lying beyond the Cape of Good Hope or the Straits of Magellan, for fifteen years. Trespassers were warned off, under penalty of losing their ships and cargoes. The temptation of the enormous profits to be made was too great to be resisted, in addition to which subjects of other nations did not recognise the right of the British Government to grant a monopoly at all. Therefore they went on trespassing and making profits, and some of their ships were caught and paid the penalty.

In the Company's early voyages the cost was borne by the subscribers, who seldom made less than 100 per cent on the round voyage, though against profits of this magnitude had to be set an occasional loss of ship and goods. After 1612 the voyages were made for the benefit of the Company as a whole. By 1679 the Company was employing eleven ships of 400 to 600 tons. That does not mean that it did not have more than eleven ships in those seventy-nine years, but that in that year it had eleven; doubtless some had been lost, but such records as are available of the shipping of those times are very few and incomplete and unreliable.

" Old prints of these waggons," Lieut. W. H. Coates writes in " The Good Old Days of Shipping," " shew them to have been fearful and wonderful crafts ; castles were raised at both bow and stern for battle purposes, and their sides simply bristled with guns ; while the marvel is, considering their towering sides, their enormous castellated projections, and their ill-cut bellying sails, not that they took so long to get to their destinations, but that they ever arrived at all."

Well into the eighteenth century the ships were clumsily constructed, but during that century the shipbuilders on the Thames side, who were practically the best shipbuilders in the country, introduced and applied and developed the most scientific and reliable methods known at that time, and before the century closed they were launching the finest ships the Company had. The builders of ships of whatever requirement remained faithful to one type. All vessels were constructed with bluff bows as round as an apple, and the stem was generally burdened or decorated with a tremendous amount of heavy wood work, such as may be seen on the models of the wooden walls of Old England in the United Services Museum in Whitehall or the Naval Museum at Greenwich. These bluff bows retarded progress greatly by their shape, as instead of dividing the water on either side they piled it in front and then had to push it out of the way ; they also rendered it exceedingly difficult for a vessel to beat to windward, and the lee way vessels made in trying to do so was enormous. Some, if it were attempted to sail them with the wind more than a couple of points before the beam, went as far sideways as they did forward.

Bows of this shape were favoured by shipbuilders and owners in this country long after the Americans had demonstrated the advantages of what came to be known as schooner or clipper bows. It was the fashion or custom to place the foremast far forward, and it was contended, quite correctly, that the full bows were necessary to give the hull the buoyancy forward required to support the weight of the foremast. The Americans showed that if the mast were placed not so far forward the bows could be made sharper, without impairing the buoyancy forward, and that by giving the vessel more rise or sheer, as it is called, towards the bows, the buoyancy would actually be increased, and that the sharper bows would enable the vessel to sail faster and closer to the wind.

Such charts as navigators had in the seventeenth and eighteenth centuries, and even later, were very incorrect and incomplete, in spite of the care which most ship masters, and especially those in the East India Company's ships, showed to keep their charts as accurate as possible ; the navigating instruments, too, were far from reliable. Taking all the circumstances into consideration one cannot help admiring and being amazed at the daring these navigators showed in undertaking these voyages, and their skill in arriving at their destinations. There were also the country's enemies to be reckoned with—and England was more often than not at war with some state during the seventeenth and eighteenth centuries—and the probabilities that the pirates would not leave them alone. No wonder the Company wanted its ships to be the best obtainable, and armed them heavily and gave them large and well-trained and severely disciplined crews.

The East Indiamen seem to have been as severe in the matter of discipline as the ships of the Royal Navy. Flogging was the rule for even trivial offences, and confinement in irons was another punishment much favoured by those who had it in their power to inflict it. Soldiers, sailors, and passengers all got a taste of the " cat " when it was thought they deserved it. Captain Larkins, though strict, was not inhuman ; a dozen lashes at the gangway was about his maximum. On the other hand, Captain Rawes, who commanded the *Warren Hastings* a few years later, gave two dozen as a minimum. He was not popular on board, which is not a matter of surprise, and when he went ashore at Canton, it is recorded that " at noon, to the joy of all the officers, Captain Rawes left the ship for Canton."

In his journal of his voyage in the *Marquis of Wellesley* in 1812, Addison reports that six men were improperly pressed out of the ship by H.M.S. *Clorinde*. Admiral Pellew ordered them to be returned, and this was done, but because they did not like their compulsory return to the Indiaman, the acting chief officer of that vessel, a man named Cleland, ordered them two dozen each, then and there. This greeting would not be likely to endear Mr. Cleland or the ship to the six men. Another custom which prevailed was that of sending detachments from ships to other ships to see punishment inflicted, as an intimation of what they might expect if they did not behave themselves.

Though the Company was a believer in strict discipline and in the stimulating effects of the cat-o'-nine tails, it was careful of the welfare of faithful servants of whatever rank. After eight years in the Company's ships seamen were given pensions if they wanted them, and pensions were also given to the wives and children of those killed or too seriously wounded in the Company's service to be employed any further.

For taking on board persons without the written permission of the Company's agents, the offender might be fined £20 for a black servant, and anything up to £500 for a European. Passengers bringing native servants from

India had to enter into bonds to bear the cost of their keep in this country and of their return to their own.

Only certain firms of repute built ships for the Company, and they charged something like £40 a ton and sometimes more ; but the ships were the best that money could procure. Other firms, which offered to build as large and as fast ships at much lower figures, were told that the Company's ships, or ships intended for the Company's service, must be not only suitable for the carriage of valuable cargoes, but must also be able to hold their own against armed enemy vessels, even against odds, and must be sufficiently powerful to act as warships in case of need. Only those firms, whose ability to meet the Company's requirements was beyond question, were permitted to build for the Company's service. These conditions prevailed well into the nineteenth century. How the change came about will be explained later.

The East India Company was a generous employer to the masters and mates of its ships, and the perquisites, or indulgences as they were officially called, enabled the former to earn large fortunes. If the masters did not receive much or anything in the way of actual salaries, the deficiency was made up to them several times over in other ways. At one time the command was bought and sold, and sums varying between £2,000 and £10,000 are known to have been given to secure the post. The purchaser could resell it if he liked, and his heirs had the same right. This custom naturally led to abuses ; some who bought their masterships were unfit to hold command ; the practice was stopped and the Company granted compensation when a master gave up his ship, as he often did when he had made enough to live upon in comfort on shore for the rest of his life. Following this reform, the Company

4

instituted an examination or test for its masters and mates. The master's earnings depended greatly on what the ship earned. When a ship was chartered by the Company, the latter estimated that she would carry considerably less cargo than her tonnage ; it was on the lower estimate that the full rate of freight was charged, which might be £18 a ton for the homeward voyage, and half rates on the balance of the tonnage. Thus a vessel of 1,200 tons might carry 1,100 tons at £18, and 100 tons at £9. Masters, after their supposed proprietary rights in their commands were abolished, were each allowed on the outward passage up to 56 tons of cargo space free, but rather less on the home voyage. They were also at liberty to sublet their own private cabins to passengers, which must have been a very profitable transaction, as it is on record that a general officer has paid as much as £234 for a passage to India, and that the fare even for a subaltern amounted to £95. Captains were also allowed what was known as primage, a percentage upon the total gross amount earned by the ship during the voyage out and home, and they further had practically the whole of the fares of the passengers, except the Company's troops, though the Company deducted what it cost to feed the passengers. The Company's ships generally carried from twenty to thirty passengers, so the captains did not do so badly.

Another very remunerative perquisite was the dunnage, or articles used to protect cargo being brought from India from injury while in the ship's hold. Unless stowed properly, cargo has a tendency to roll with the rocking of the vessel and would very quickly be damaged. In these times strong planks are generally employed for the purpose, and belong to the owners of the ships, but in the days of the East Indiamen the captains were allowed to supply the dunnage, and as they sold it when they got to England they made a nice little sum out of it, especially as the dunnage consisted of articles such as bamboos, rattans, nankeens, and anything else that was cheap and would serve the purpose and fetch a good price in this country. Nor did the captains always have to buy it. Some of it was given them by native merchants, possibly not always from the purest of motives, and was accepted in the spirit in which it was given. The abuse of the privilege of supplying dunnage led to the Company interfering. The Captains were notified that as too much dunnage was brought home, " occupying tonnage to the exclusion of goods, or cumbering the ship," anything not absolutely and *bona fide* necessary and used as dunnage would be charged against the commanders and officers.

The captain of an East Indiaman made somewhere about £6000 or more a year ; some who commanded the larger and more popular ships are said to have made as much as £10,000, and one particularly fortunate captain is said to have made a voyage of twenty-two months, from London to India, China and back, and to have raked in no less than £30,000. If he did not retire then, he ought to have done so, if only to give somebody else a chance. The mates and other officers were also allowed a certain amount of cargo space in which they could carry goods on their own account, and the allowances in the matter of refreshments were on a generous scale.

The Company paid attention to sartorial matters, and issued regulations affecting the uniforms the various ranks had to wear. The full dress uniform of a commander consisted of a blue coat with black velvet lapels, cuffs and collar, with a bright gold embroidery, " as little expensive as may be " ; waistcoat and breeches of deep buff ; the buttons were to be of yellow gilt metal with the Company's crest. They had to have cocked hats and carry side-arms, to be worn under the coat, and black stocks or neckcloths were the rule. The undress uniform included blue coat with lapels, black collar and cuffs, deep buff breeches and waistcoat, and buttons like those on the full dress suit. The uniforms of the other officers were rather similar, but less elaborate. When any of them had to attend the Court of Directors, full dress uniform had to be worn. Boots, black breeches and stockings appear to have been forbidden.

After the Company instituted its rules for its officers it adhered to them rigidly. No one could act as master of an East Indiaman unless he was twenty-five years of age or over, and he must have put in at least one voyage as chief or second mate in the regular service of the Company, or have commanded a ship in the Company's extra service. Chief mates had to be twenty-three years or more, and were required to have made a voyage as second or third mate in the service between England and China or India. A similar service was required of second mates, who must be not under twenty-two years of age, and third mates had to be twenty-one years of age, and to have made two voyages as midshipmen or in some other capacity in the Company's service ; fourth mates had to be not under twenty years of age, and must have made a voyage to or from India or China in one of the Company's ships, or in a vessel belonging to some other satisfactory service, of which he had to produce certificates.

The crews, as already stated, were large. The *Earl of Balcarras*, built in 1815, of 1417 tons, carried a commander, six mates, a surgeon and his assistant, six midshipmen, purser, gunner, carpenter, master-at-arms, armourer, butcher, baker, poulterer, caulker, cooper, two stewards, two cooks, eight boatswains; gunner's, carpenter's, caulker's, and cooper's mates; six quartermasters, one sailmaker, seven servants for the commander and leading officers, and seventy-eight seamen. Five supernumeraries, such as supercargoes, were allotted to each ship, one of whom had the privilege of appearing on the quarter deck.

The crews of other ships were in much the same proportion to their tonnage, vessels of from eight hundred to thirteen hundred tons carrying from 102 to 130 men. What is more, they were practically all British. Many a modern sailing ship of twice those tonnages has gone to sea with a crew of about a quarter that total, and mostly dagoes at that. The usual two-watch system was maintained for the crew, but the officers were divided into three watches. Naval discipline was the rule, and on Sundays divine service was held, attendance at which was compulsory, and any captain who did not hold it was liable to be fined two guineas by the directors " for every omission not satisfactorily accounted for in the log book."

Sir R. B. Dyke Acland, K.C., in an article in " The Dolphin," giving an account of the log of the *Warren Hastings*, says : " On Sundays on the way out ' The ladies and gentlemen attended divine service in the cuddy.' It is a curious fact that while this entry appears on the outward voyage on every one of the nineteen Sundays except four, on one of which divine service was performed apparently without the assistance of the ladies and gentlemen and on the others they were either coming into port or actually at anchor, it never appears on the homeward voyage at all, though on four Sundays out of twenty-five the words ' performed divine service ' are inserted in the log. Whether a long sojourn in the East

had demoralised the ladies and gentlemen, or whether
Captain Larkins had come to the conclusion that his
ministrations were of no use it is impossible to say."

The history of the East India Company shows that it
was justified in holding a high estimate of its own importance and that of its ships. It seemed to think it had come
to stay for ever, and steadfastly resisted any suggestion
of reform in its methods. Having under its charter a
monopoly of trade with India, it charged what it liked and
saw no reason why the monopoly should not last as long
as India did. In its most prosperous days practically every
voyage brought in a very handsome profit. The ships
were specially built for the Company's trade by private
firms, and chartered to the Company, which went to the
length of appointing their commanders long before they
were completed, and sent the commanders to supervise
the construction in order that they might become thoroughly familiar with the vessels. The Company paid the
builders at the rate of £40 per ton; its detractors said
that equally suitable vessels could be built and equipped
for £25 a ton. The Company replied to this by asking
whether any ship could be built for £25 a ton as capable
of contending against an enemy as the Company's more
expensive ships, or if such ships would be fit for the
service of the country, i.e., in the navy, during war. Besides the ships built for it in this country, the Company
had its own shipyard at Deptford and also owned a number
of very fine ships built at its own establishments, or by
private firms, in India, but these " country ships," as they
were called, were not at one time employed in the Company's trade between England and the East.

In the Company's lordly view a ship was only fit for its
high class trade for four voyages, or say eight years;

this ended their life so far as the Company's service was concerned. If thought to be in especially good condition a ship might be permitted to make two more voyages for the Company, though not many did so, and then they were usually sold to be broken up. Having been built for the Company's trade, in the peculiar way the Company liked, they were not suitable as they stood for any other trade ; the breaking up process resulted in some cases in the ships being practically rebuilt and re-equipped for employment in other trades. Nor were they suitable for the royal navy. Designers of naval vessels had profited by and copied to some extent the designs of French frigates, but the East Indiamen were still of the old full-bodied model in order that they might carry more cargo. The French, it may be remarked in passing, have always shown a genius for ship designing, and the British have shown an equal genius for copying them, and sometimes for improving on them. But British ship owners and builders have always been a conservative people, with a few notable exceptions, and much preferred to go on as their predecessors had done, and could always find reasons for saying that suggested innovations would not work. So the Indiamen were slow and heavy and stately ; they were never hurried in ordinary circumstances, partly because they could not be and partly because the Company did not want them to be.

It is probably not accurately known how many ships the Company had in the whole of its career. The number must have been very great. Its trade was enormous, and the out and home voyage was expected to last two years, and was sometimes longer. The number employed varied enormously from year to year. For instance, in the season of 1809-10 no fewer than forty-seven vessels, totalling 32,500 tons, were sent to Bombay, China, Bengal,

Madras, and Penang. In the years 1819-20 the Company sent to the same stations twenty-three vessels totalling 26,200 tons, besides twenty-one vessels which had been chartered, of 10,948 tons ; but in 1829-30 only twenty ships belonging to or permanently engaged by the Company were despatched, in addition to twelve chartered vessels.

One reason why the East Indiamen were so slow was that the practice prevailed, and was encouraged by the Company, of making all snug for the night. No matter how fine the weather might be, or how favourable the wind, the royals and in some cases the topgallant sails were taken in, and the ship dawdled along under easy canvas till daylight came and the sails would be set again. It may have added to the comfort of the more or less august passengers on board to be as gently rocked as possible in the cradle of the deep, but it helped to make the voyages unnecessarily long, and it did not reduce the real perils of the sea. If a vessel were dawdling in this fashion it was more likely to be carried off its course by some current, and more than one of the disasters which befell the East Indiamen may be traced to this cause.

One of the most remarkable wrecks of a Company's ship was that of the *Winterton*, commanded by Captain Dundas, which sailed from England early in 1792. She arrived at the Cape on July 20th and remained till August 1st. The captain intended to take what was known as the outward passage to India, but variable winds obliged him to bear for the Mozambique Channel. After a spell of light winds and calms, a south-west wind sprang up on the 19th, and the captain tried to make Madagascar, as his observations made him sure as to his locality some eighty miles from the nearest part of the coast. Shortly after three o'clock the next morning, the night being clear, and in a perfectly smooth sea and no breakers or surf within hearing, the ship struck. Daylight disclosed that she was on a reef about six miles from the shore. As the vessel was leaking too badly to be saved, the boats were provisioned and rafts constructed to enable the people to reach the shore if possible. The wind increased, and the surf rose. One raft ultimately got ashore with some of the survivors, who found that the poop of the vessel had drifted ashore with others. Those lost were the captain, mate, three lady passengers, and forty-eight seamen and soldiers. The natives robbed them of practically everything.

On September 12th, the third and fourth mates, and four seamen, and a male passenger named de Souza, who spoke Portuguese, left Tulliar in the ship's yawl in an attempt to get to Mozambique. Aided by currents, they reached the African coast in eight days, but being short of water decided to put into a small river they saw and found some natives who spoke Portuguese. It was a Portuguese possession, and the governor supplied them with provisions and a pilot and sent them to Sofala, where they arrived on the 29th. The governor of Sofala had a boat about the size of an Indiaman's longboat, and gave it to them as they wanted to try and reach Delagoa Bay. This boat was so leaky that they had hard work to keep it afloat, and were glad to return to Sofala a few days later. The governor now sent them overland to Senna ; the governor of that place, hearing they were on the way, sent palanquins for them which were very welcome as the travellers were in a deplorable state from fatigue, exposure, and lack of food. They arrived on December 6th, and notwithstanding all that could be done for them three of the party died soon afterwards. The survivors went to Killeman in a local vessel, and thence by a local sloop the third mate and de Souza reached Mozambique five months after they left Madagascar.

There being then no royal Portuguese ship in the harbour, which the governor might have sent to the rescue, Dale, the third mate, freighted a private vessel for Madagascar, at the same time sending a report home of the wreck by a French vessel sailing for Mauritius. The relief ship sailed from Mozambique on March 1st and on March 24th anchored in St. Augustine's Bay, whence he set out to rescue his companions at Tulliar ; he found that nearly half of those he had left there had died from privations, there being only 130 alive. Seven died on the way back to Mozambique. Dale and the purser of the *Winterton*, and Lieut. Brownrigg of the 75th regiment, freighted in the name of the East India Company a vessel to take them to Madras. They left Mozambique on June 10th and the island of Joanna on the 19th, and when within a few days' sail of Madras were captured by the privateer *Le Mutin*, from the Isle of France. This was their first intimation that Great Britain and France were again at war. Dale, Brownrigg, and twenty-two seamen were taken on board the privateer, whose captain put an officer and some of his own men on the prize and ordered her to Mauritius without delay. The privateersmen made their captives as comfortable as they could. On July 15th the privateer approached Tutecorin, where she met and fought a Dutch East India-man, the *Ceylon*, Captain Muntz, and the Dutchman captured the privateer and liberated the Englishmen. Next they got to Callancoetah, and finally reached Madras by boat on August 20th, 1793, exactly twelve months after the *Winterton* was wrecked. Dale and some of his compan-ions were given passages on the *Scorpion*, a sloop of war, for England. The only incident of note during the homeward voyage seems to have been that the *Scorpion* was chased by a French frigate. Otherwise the sloop made such a slow voyage that it was supposed she had either gone down or been captured by an enemy. Nothing was ever heard of those men who were left on the prize to be taken by the privateer's men to Mauritius.

The Company in 1794, in the absence of an English man-of-war from the Indian seas, had to undertake the policing of those waters, where French privateers were not slow to seize the opportunity to ply their trade, and pirates preyed upon anything they could capture. The pirates usually left the East India Company's ships alone, for they knew by experience that they were well armed and well manned and ready for a fight, and would show no quarter to any vessel owning allegiance to the " Jolly Roger," or flag flying the death's head and crossbones. The Port of Calcutta was more or less blockaded, and the French privateers had British shipping to some extent at their mercy.

The Company's ship *Pigot*, under Captain George Ballantyne, was lying in Rat Basin, near Bencoolen, about eight or nine miles from Sumatra. The French privateers, the *Vengeur*, 32 guns, and 350 men, and the *Resolue*, 28 guns and 160 men, attacked her alternately, as the narrowness of the channel prevented them attacking simultaneously. The *Vengeur* at times came within a hundred and fifty yards of the *Pigot*, and after an hour and three quarters it had enough of it. The *Resolue* took her place and in twenty minutes followed the other French vessel out of range of the Indiaman's guns. They anchored about two miles away while they made good their damages, and then they sailed away. The *Pigot* lost one man, but her masts, sails and rigging were badly knocked about. She had 32 guns and only 102 men.

An even more remarkable action, which Captain Brenton in his " Naval History of Great Britain," describes as " much too honourable to pass unnoticed," was that fought shortly afterwards by the Company's ships *William Pitt*, Captain Charles Mitchell ; *Houghton*, Captain Hudson; *Nonsuch*, Captain Canning ; and *Britannia*, Captain Cheap. Captain Mitchell was in command of the squadron. On January 22nd they saw two strange vessels, and chased them and compelled them to fight, and in forty minutes both gave up. They were the *Vengeur* and *Resolue* ; the former had 15 killed and 26 wounded. On January 24th the Indiamen were attacked by four French ships, the *Prudente*, 40 guns, *Sybille*, 44 guns, *Duguay Trouin*, armament not stated, and *Isle de France*, ten guns. The French, finding the fight was going against them, fled and made good escape. They next turned up at Rat Basin, Bencoolen, and captured the *Pigot*, which was undergoing repairs there. Captain Mitchell, on returning to England, was knighted for his brave conduct, and the Company presented him with £8,000.

About the end of January, 1797, six French frigates surprised a fleet of five Indiamen near the east of Java. These were the *Woodford*, Captain Lennox ; *Ocean*, Captain Patten ; *Taunton Castle*, Captain Studd ; *Canton*, Captain Lushington ; and *Boddam*, Captain Palmer. All had specie and valuable cargoes. Captain Lennox hoisted the flag of Rear-Admiral Rainier, and two of his ships hoisted the colours of ships of war, and advanced towards the French. The latter made off. The French squadron was commanded by Rear-Admiral de Sercey, who was greatly angered when he learned later that he had been successfully bluffed and that his squadron of six warships had fled from five Indiamen.

At various times certain of the Company's ships acted as guard ships at ports which it was thought might be threatened, or cruised in company with British warships, at the request of the government, to look out for and intercept enemy ships. In 1799 the *Earl Howe* and *Princess Charlotte* were sent by H.M.S. *Victorious* to cruise in the area between Pigeon Island and the Palmyra Rocks, and were retained on this duty until the end of the following year. The commanders and officers of the East Indiamen were granted commissions for this cruise to give them the status of naval officers.

Another expedition in conjunction with naval ships in which the Company's ships distinguished themselves, was that against Malacca in 1811. There were four ships of the line, fourteen frigates, and seven sloops of war, and the Company's cruisers *Malabar*, *Aurora*, *Mornington*, and *Nautilus*.

In connection with the preparations for the capture of the Cape of Good Hope from the Dutch, a country ship was sent to cruise off the Cape, and the packet *Swallow* reported that twenty-one Dutch Indiamen were on their way home. This squadron was sighted during the night by the Company's ship *General Goddard*, under Captain Money, who sailed his ship into the middle of them. They fired at him but he did not reply. Instead, he kept with them until daylight, when the *Sceptre* and other vessels came up and helped the *General Goddard* to secure seven of the Dutchmen. This victory had not a little to do with the capture of the Cape of Good Hope.

The officers and men of the East India Company's ships seem to have been animated by the rule " When you see a

French vessel, attack it." French ships in those days to British sailors were like the proverbial red rag to a bull, though it must be admitted that the French were no less ready for a fight as a rule.

Occasionally the British caught a tartar. Several lively fights took place in the year 1800. The East Indiaman *Kent* tackled, or was tackled by, the French ship *Confiance*, of twenty-six guns, which was commanded by the famous Surcouf. A hot fight raged at close quarters for two hours. The artillery of the Frenchmen was superior in weight, and perhaps slightly so in number of pieces. After the *Kent* had her commander and twenty-two men killed and thirty-four wounded, she was captured. The French losses were also heavy.

Captain Bulteel, of H.M.S. *Belliqueux*, having six or seven East Indiamen under his convoy, chased three French frigates and captured one, the *Concorde*. While he was securing his prize, Captain Meriton in the *Exeter*— who apparently never shirked a fight with the French if he could get into one—and Captain Hamilton in the *Bombay Castle*, came up with the French frigate *Medee* carrying thirty-six 12 pounders and 315 men, and captured her. Another French vessel, of forty guns, escaped by superior sailing. " This is another instance of the gallantry and public spirit of the captains and crews of the East India Company's ships, and a singular instance of a ship of war being taken by merchantmen," Captain Brenton records in his history. He adds that " The chase was long, and at midnight Captain Meriton, finding himself coming up fast with the enemy, while the *Bombay Castle* was far astern, placed lights in all his ports. Having two tiers of guns, and running alongside the frigate, he commanded her to surrender. The French captain immediately complied, supposing himself under the guns of a ship of the line. He was brought on board the *Exeter*, with his officers, and delivered his sword to Captain Meriton. The *Bombay Castle* coming up, the prisoners were divided between the ships. The French captain, looking very attentively at the little guns on the quarter deck, asked what ship it was he had struck to ; to which Meriton sarcastically answered : ' To a merchant ship.' The Frenchman begged to have his sword, and to be allowed to return with his men to his ship, and fight the battle over again. This modest request was civilly declined."

In June of that year the Company's ship *Ariston*, under Captain Campbell Marjoribanks, was attacked by a French sloop, supposed to be the *Confiance* ; if so, she must have been repaired rapidly after her fight with the *Kent*, but the enterprise was quite in keeping with Surcouf's reputation for daring. The *Ariston* was attacked shortly after she had anchored off Bencoolen. Captain Marjoribanks offered a determined resistance, and after his ship had cut her cable —to save the time of raising the anchor and getting it on board—she assumed the aggressive. The Frenchman hauled off, and the *Ariston* chased her and fired several broadsides at her. The sloop, however, was better able to beat to windward than the heavy *Ariston* and succeeded in getting away after a pursuit lasting some hours.

The same year the Company's ship *Hughes* was sent to cruise in the Bay of Bengal to protect commerce, as some French ships were known to be prowling about for victims. She met and fought a French ship, which, like many French ships, proved to be a faster sailer, for she managed to make her escape after the expedient had been resorted to of throwing some of her guns overboard to lighten her.

The Company's ship *Phoenix*, under Captain Moffatt,

fought a duel with the French privateer *General Martillac* in November, 1800. The Indiaman cleared for action, and as the vessels got within pistol shot the privateer manned his rigging and prepared to board. The *Phoenix* let him have half a broadside, whereupon the privateer struck. She had sixteen guns and 120 men.

In the same year the French frigate *Bellona* attacked the Company's ship *Admiral Gardner*, under Captain Saltwell, and found her too tough a nut to crack, for the Indiaman beat her off.

One of the most remarkable battles in the history of the Company's ships was fought in 1803. The Company's China fleet was homeward bound, for sailing in convoy was necessary for mutual protection, with several country ships and other vessels under its care, and without itself having any escort of British men-of-war. In this comparatively defenceless condition—except that the East India Company's ships were armed as usual, and the sailers carried guns, as was the custom of merchant ships in most parts of the world in those spacious times—when the whole squadron might be regarded by legitimate enemies like the French, or illegitimate enemies like the pirates, as a prize worth fighting for, a squadron of powerful French warships was sighted. These were the *Marengo*, of 84 guns, the *Semillante*, of 40 guns, the *Belle Poule*, of 40 guns, a corvette of 28 guns, and a brig of 18 guns ; the whole French squadron was commanded by Admiral Linois.

Brenton, in his history, in describing the affair, says that the French, when off the Straits of Malacca, fell in with the homeward bound fleet consisting of the following ships : *Camden*, Captain Dance; *Warley*, Captain H. Wilson ; *Alfred*, Captain J. Farquharson ; *Royal George*, Captain F. J. Timmins ; *Coutts*, Captain R. Florin ; *Wexford*,

Captain W. Stanley Clarke ; *Ganges*, Captain W. Moffatt ; *Exeter*, Captain H. Meriton ; *Abergavenny*, Captain J. Waresworth, junior ; *Henry Addington*, Captain J. Kirkpatrick ; *Bombay Castle*, Captain A. Hamilton ; *Cumberland*, Captain W. W. Farren ; *Hope*, Captain J. Pendergrass ; *Dorsetshire*, Captain R. H. Brown ; *Warren Hastings*, Captain T. Larkins ; *Ocean*, Captain J. C. Lockner. With these were eleven country ships. Brenton says the *Marengo* had 80 guns, and the *Suffisante* (not *Semillante*, as Lindsay has it), 44 guns.

The following particulars are taken from Brenton's account of the action : " Captain Dance, with great judgment, put his ships' heads towards the enemy ; four of his best sailers he sent down to reconnoitre, and having ascertained what they were, called in his look-out, and formed the line of battle in close order under an easy sail. As soon as the French ships could fetch into the wake of ours they put about, and at sunset were close in rear of the India fleet, which was in momentary expectation of an attack, but at the close of day the French admiral hauled his wind. Lieutenant Fowler, of the Royal Navy, who was a passenger with Captain Dance, volunteered to go in a fast sailing vessel to order the country ships to keep on the lee bow of the India fleet ; by this judicious arrangement Captain Dance kept himself between the country ships and the enemy. Lieutenant Fowler, having executed his order, returned, bringing with him some volunteers from the country ships to serve at the guns (a noble proof of the public spirit of our sailors.)

" The Indiamen lay-to in line of battle during the night, with the people at their quarters. At daylight the enemy were three miles to windward, also lying-to : the British ships hoisted their colours and offered battle, but the enemy not choosing to come down, at nine a.m. the India fleet steered its course under easy sail ; the enemy then filled and edged towards them. At one p.m. Captain Dance, perceiving that the French Admiral intended to attack and cut off his rear, made the signal for his fleet to attack and engage in succession. The *Royal George* led, and was followed by the *Ganges* and *Earl Camden*. The ships performed the manœuvre with admirable correctness, and stood towards the French under a press of sail. The latter formed a very close line, and opened their fire on the headmost ships, which was not returned until ours had approached as near as they could get, the French having a great advantage in superior sailing. The *Royal George* bore the brunt of the action ; the *Ganges* and *Camden* came up, and also began to engage ; but before any other ships could get up, the French admiral hauled his wind and stood away to the eastward under all the sail he could set. Captain Dance made the signal for a general chase, but, after a pursuit of two hours, finding the enemy gained on him, he very properly desisted.

" The action was very short : one man only was killed on the *Royal George*, and one wounded ; the other ships had none hurt, and received little damage in their hulls or rigging. To say that Linois was deceived by the warlike appearance of our Indiamen, and the blue swallow-tailed flags worn by the three largest ships, may save his courage at the expense of his judgment. ' An Indiaman,' says the Count de Dumas, ' has often been mistaken for a ship of the line.' But when did the Count de Dumas ever hear of seventeen British ships of the line lying-to, to await the attack of a French 80-gun ship and two frigates ? "

In commenting on this remarkable affair, Captain Brenton adds : " Our Indiamen are certainly very fine ships, and have, generally, such an appearance as to be sometimes mistaken for ships of the line ; but their complement of men is very inadequate to their size, for fighting, particularly when required to lie alongside a ship of the line. None of them, we believe, had more than 100 men, their heaviest metal 18-pounders. The *Marengo* had 700 at least, with a weight of metal on her lower deck, and a scantling, which rendered her an overmatch for all the ships of that fleet that could at one time have brought their guns to bear on her. The two frigates were also very powerful ships, so that the conduct of Captain Dance entitles him to all the praise which can be bestowed on a sea officer." Another account says it was Captain Timmins who suggested to Captain Dance that they should assume the aggressive.

The fleet of China ships and their cargoes were valued at six million pounds, and it is stated that the revenue on the tea they carried amounted to three million pounds. Commodore Dance was knighted for his distinguished conduct, and the captains, officers and crews of the ships also received rewards.

To show how valuable the convoys sometimes were it may be stated that Admiral Rainier when homeward bound from Madras in the *Trident* called at St. Helena and took the China fleet under his charge. The fleet consisted of thirty-nine ships, and was valued at fifteen millions sterling. The French, naturally, wanted to intercept it, but Admirals Cornwallis and Gardner kept the French Admiral Gantheaume shut up in Brest.

The Company's ship *Cumberland*, when under the command of Captain Farrer, in 1805, and sailing in the convoy of Sir Thomas Troubridge, fell in with the French battleship *Marengo* and a large frigate. The ship received from her enemies several broadsides, and returned them, at pistol shot range, so close were they, and then the vessels parted.

Having made the error of mistaking Indiamen for ships of the line, Linois, after capturing two or three Indiamen, made the mistake of thinking a warship was an Indiaman, when he tried conclusions with the *Blenheim*, and got away while he could. Not long afterwards he encountered a British squadron under Admiral Warren. His ships, the *Marengo*, on which he was wounded, and the *Belle Poule*, were captured, and he was brought a prisoner to England.

In 1806 the East Indiaman *Warren Hastings* and the French frigate *Piedmontese* had a duel lasting for four hours. The French ship hauled off more than once during the action to effect repairs, and returned to the fight, which ended in the *Warren Hastings* being captured.

The islands, Mauritius and Bourbon, were exceedingly valuable to France on account of the facilities they afforded the French to repair and refit their vessels, and the British government in India decided to capture them in 1809. The first French victim was the frigate *Caroline*, of forty-four guns and 400 men ; she had only a few weeks before captured off the Nicobar Islands the Indiamen *Streatham*, Captain Dale, and *Europe*, Captain Gelston, and three other Indiamen. They are stated to have been ill-manned with crews of English, Lascars, Chinamen and Portuguese, all of whom except the English abandoned their guns when the enemy started shooting. The captor took them to St. Paul's Bay, Bourbon, and not long afterwards the French captain had the mortification of being himself captured and seeing his prizes restored to British ownership. The cargoes of the Indiamen were reshipped

and the captains and crews reinstated, and the vessels
resumed their journey.

In July, 1810, the French commodore Du Perrée, whose
ships had been particularly active in the Bay of Bengal,
sighted the outward-bound East Indiamen *Ceylon*, Captain
Meriton, 26 guns, 110 seamen and 250 soldiers ; *Windham*,
Captain Stewart, 26 guns, 110 men and 250 soldiers, and
Astell, Captain Hay, 32 guns, 120 men and 275 soldiers.
Meriton, as senior officer, was in command. He had taken,
when in an Indiaman, a French frigate, and thinking he
might repeat the exploit, he waited for the attack. The
fight was a severe one ; the brunt of it was borne by the
Ceylon and *Astell.* Captain Meriton was wounded—he
ultimately recovered—and the chief officer of the *Ceylon*
surrendered the ship. The *Windham* was also taken, but
was recovered in another fight. The *Astell* escaped. Her
colours were shot away three times during the engagement.
The *Astell* is reported to have been attacked by a superior
French force again in 1812, and to have beaten off her
assailants and got away.

The Isle of France capitulated in 1910.

Peace was concluded and broken at intervals, and many
of the sea-fights, till Napoleon was captured and sent to
St. Helena, may be attributed partly to a lack of knowledge
of, or belief in, the peace, partly to the ill-feeling which had
not died down, partly to the lack of control—there were
no telegraphs or steamships in those days, and the men in
the ships were pretty much a law unto themselves—and
partly to the tendency to indulge in a fight whenever the
opportunity presented itself. There was a good deal of
truth in the old saying at that time that there was no
law south of the equator or east of the Cape. After it
became generally known and accepted that peace really

prevailed, the East India Company's ships continued to carry guns, but, especially on the homeward voyage when space was wanted for cargo, the guns were consigned to the hold and the gun deck or 'tween deck was used for stowing cargo.

When Napoleon resumed his war activities, hostilities between the French and the Company's ships were renewed. The Company's ships generally, but not always, came off best. The Company throughout its career was almost in a chronic state of war with somebody or other in India ; these wars led to increases of territory, but were of little financial benefit to the Company, and it also suffered, as an English trading concern, when England found herself at war with another nation.

The Company's losses seem to have been heavy at times. In the two years, 1808 and 1809, the Company lost four outward bound and ten homeward bound ships, one of which caused the Company a loss of over a million pounds.

The Company lost in the three years 1807, 1808, and 1809 fourteen ships laden with valuable cargoes ; the value of the vessels and cargoes, if they had reached England, was estimated at £1,202, 638. Most of them were lost on the way, wrecked or foundered ; very few were captured. In 1808 a fleet of nine vessels encountered a hurricane in which three of them went down. Another fleet of fifteen ships sailed in February, 1809, from Point de Galle, and in March were struck by a hurricane and the *Jane, Duchess of Gordon, Lady Jane Dundas, Calcutta* and *Bengal* were sunk. According to Hardy's Registry, the East India Company lost in 1800-1813 five ships burnt, eight taken, five taken and retaken, thirteen foundered, and fifteen put down as " lost." As long as the Company ran its ships there was hardly a year in which one or more serious losses were not reported. After 1815, they were chiefly due, not to enemies, but to the " perils of the sea."

Before this, however, the Company's increasing power in India compelled the introduction in Parliament by Pitt, in 1784, after other enactments had been made, of his India Bill, which created a Board of Control to exercise political, military and financial superintendence.

A concession was made by the Company in 1793 that private individuals might trade with India, provided they employed the Company's ships for the purpose. This was not a very great privilege, but it gave those who took advantage of it an insight into the Company's trade, its methods, and the profits that it was making. One result was to stimulate the opposition to the Company's monopoly.

Another of the causes which helped the Company on its downward path was its decision that India built ships should not be permitted to convey goods from India to London, and this unbending attitude was rigidly maintained until 1795. In that year, however, so many of the Company's ships were taken over by the government that the Company issued instructions to its representatives in India to engage locally built vessels, what were known as " country ships," a term applied not only to vessels built in India but later to any owned there. Many of these ships were built on speculation. Lord Cornwallis issued a warning to the speculators that the ships might not be wanted in the number in which they were proposed to be launched, but because some of the ships were taken over by the Company the speculators continued to build ; they had the mortification of finding the vessels left on their hands because after the immediate wants of Government and the Company had been met no more vessels were needed, and as opportunity offered the country ships taken over were returned to their owners. Still, the incident was destined to have an important influence upon future events. Many British merchants combined with the owners of the Indian ships in the agitation against the Company, and the directors were induced to make concessions which helped towards bringing about the opening of trade and the restriction of the Company's monopoly.

Every time an agitation arose, or became stronger or more assertive than usual, the Company issued a statement of arguments to show how necessary it was that it should maintain its exclusive trade. In 1812 a particularly strong attempt was made to create a breach in the Company's trade, and it was pointed out that one of the reasons why people did not ship goods to India in the Company's ships was that the freights charged were so heavy as to be prohibitive. It was not much encouragement to owners of free trade ships to take goods to India at less rates than the Company saw fit to charge, owing to the impossibility of getting homeward cargoes from any ports at which the Company exercised control. The Company blandly replied to the effect that free trade was not necessary, that if it were granted all their clerks and warehousemen would lose their work, and the great expense the Company had incurred in England and India would be to all intents and purposes wasted. Another argument adduced was that the Company's ships already brought over more produce from India than this country could consume, but it did not accept the doctrine that if goods were brought over more cheaply the country could consume more, besides which there would be more for export to the Continental ports. Nothing very definite came of the 1812 agitation, for in 1824 the Company paid shipowners £22 to £27 a ton for the voyage to and from China.

In 1813 Lord Liverpool's measure abolished the India monopoly, and in 1814 the Company's trade was opened to private competition so far as India was concerned, but the Company still clung to its China monopoly. This concession only served to whet the mercantile appetite for more. The agitation increased for the removal of the China restriction, but it was not until 1833 that Lord Grey's Act brought that about and ended the Company's monopoly for ever. The national opinion could not be ignored, and though the Charter was renewed in 1833, it was in a form which obliged the Company to cease from trading altogether, and to confine its energies to the government, in association with the Board of Control, of its possessions in the Far East. In that capacity the Company existed until the Indian mutiny of 1857, when the British government assumed control of Indian affairs.

When the Company ceased to trade, its ships, or such of them as remained, were thrown on the market and sold for what they would fetch. Not many were of the largest and best types, as the building of the best Indiamen had almost ceased six or more years before the smash came. With the freedom of the trade, rates of freight fell heavily, for the competition of shipowners, hitherto shut out from the Company's preserves, all anxious to secure a share of the prize, had its natural result. Some shipowners began to wonder whether the freeing of the Eastern trade was as advantageous a step as they had anticipated it would be. Rates fell to considerably less than half what they had been in the Company's days, and the owners of inferior ships were not always able to make profitable voyages. The good-class ships, including a number of the Indiamen

which had been bought by their commanders, did well.
Several of the ships were sold to native owners in India,
especially Parsees, who employed them in the local trade,
or country trade, in which they were profitable. Of
course such vessels were run more economically than
those which were retained in the trade between England
and India.

No fewer than nineteen of the sixty-one ships sent to
India by the Company in the years 1831 to 1833 were
broken up. All but three of the others found purchasers,
mostly at good prices. For the *Canning*, 1326 tons, Joseph
Somes gave £5,700, and in 1834 she was broken up.
£10,000 was the price paid for the *Lady Melville* in 1832,
and she was handed over to the shipbreakers in 1834.
A similar fate befell the *London* in the same year, after she
had changed hands for £5,900. Others which are said to
have been broken up included the *Lowther Castle*, *Marquis
Huntley*, *Warren Hastings*, *Dunira*, *Macqueen*, *William
Fairlie* and *Farquharson* ; these were mostly vessels of
over 1300 tons and carried from thirty to thirty-five guns
apiece. The *Lowther Castle* is said to have been bought
by Joseph Somes for £13,500. The *Buckinghamshire*,
1369 tons, was built at Bombay in 1816, and at the disposal
of the fleet was acquired by Thacker and Mangells for
£10,550, and continued in active service for some years.
The *Inglis*, a country built ship, 1321 tons, was bought
in ; ten years later she was wrecked. The *Minerva*,
another country built ship, launched at Calcutta in 1813,
found a purchaser in the Templer firm at £9,400, and
lasted until the middle of the century before she met her
fate, being wrecked off the South African coast.

The famous old *Scaleby Castle*, launched at Bombay in
1798, was bought by Templer at the great sale for £6,900,

and after being given all her stores and put in readiness to go to sea, was sold again for £13,500. A London built ship, the *Thames*, 1425 tons, was bought by Chrystall for about £10,000. The *Windsor* and *Waterloo* were each sold for between £7,000 and £8,000 to be broken up. The *Earl of Balcarres*, which used to carry two tiers of guns and found them useful on more than one occasion, was consigned to a more or less peaceful old age as a hulk on the West Coast of South Africa.

The patriarch of them all, however, was the *Java*. She was built at Calcutta in 1813 and even now is doing duty as a coal hulk at Gibraltar. I wonder how many of the passengers on the modern steamers calling there ever thought she was a vessel with a romantic and historic past. Lieutenant Coates describes her as he saw her : " Her shortness, her low bluff bow, and tumbledown sides, her square stern, and the fact of her being pierced by gun-ports on two decks, all pointed to a bygone date. Her decks still had the heavy iron eye-bolts for securing the breechings of the guns. One mast still stood, which being of teak might be assumed to be the original stick. Her windlass seemed massive enough to have held the *Great Eastern*. The old pair of double steering wheels, which used to be under the break of the poop, had been used as the wheels of the hand winch. The upper and main deck beams were supported by massive teak stanchions hand-somely turned." The then P. & O. agent at Gibraltar said he had been told by a French naval officer that the ship when built was presented to a British naval officer under these circumstances : " A girl of birth and position was carried off by savages, and on the British officer landing a party for her rescue, she was found in the bush safe, but in a perfectly nude condition. Her father was so grateful for her deliverance that he built and equipped the *Java* and gave her to the gallant rescuer of his daughter."

On hearing this story the agent had the figurehead brought into the light of day from its resting place under the coal in the hold, and found it to represent a woman with her hands covering her bosom.

It is recorded that when the *Java* was taking coal to Gibraltar, she struck on the Pearl Rock, to the south of Carnero Point, and about a mile from the shore. She got off and went into Gibraltar Bay. The underwriters wished her to be docked in England, and this was done, and it was found that she had made the voyage back to England with a big piece of rock sticking in her bottom, and had it come out on the way she would probably have filled and gone down.

A somewhat similar incident is reported in connection with the *Princess Charlotte*. She sailed from Samarang for Calcutta in September, 1816, with a division of the 78th Regiment, and the following afternoon struck a rock that carried away her rudder. The boats were leaky and useless, and a raft was constructed, but the vessel swung off the rock and was with great difficulty carried into Batavia Roads the second day after she grounded. As she was extensively damaged, the troops were transferred to a 700 ton ship called the *Francis and Charlotte*, under the command of a Captain Acres. Some time afterwards, when the *Princess Charlotte* was being repaired at Calcutta, a large piece of rock was found wedged in her planking near her keel while she was ashore. " Yet in this state had she, subsequently to this disaster, been again employed to carry troops from Java to Bengal, and had encountered two gales of wind off the Sand Heads. Had this piece of rock fallen out, which it is next to a miracle it did not,

she must have instantly foundered with all on board.
To such frail chances have the lives of our gallant soldiers
been too often entrusted." So writes G. W. Barrington
in his " Remarkable Voyages and Shipwrecks."

The unfortunate soldiers were not at the end of their
troubles by any means. Before daybreak on the morning
of November 5th, the *Francis and Charlotte* struck on a reef
a few miles from Preparis Island, sixty odd miles from the
mouth of the Rangoon River. The boats would only
hold about a fifth of the five hundred and forty persons on
board. Some went away in boats from the ship to try and
reach the island, and others sought such comparative
safety as they could get on a rock and on rafts which they
moored to rocks. The captain and a few others, as the
boats did not return, tried to reach the shore in another
boat. There were then three hundred persons on board the
vessel, which was bumping and rolling heavily on the rocks,
and was expected to go to pieces before the next day.
The next day, however, two of the boats returned and
managed to land on the island some of the persons from
the ship after a pull of eighteen miles in a rough sea and
against heavy currents. One or two vessels sighted them
in the next few days, including the *Prince Blucher*, commanded by Captain Wetherall, bound from China to
Bengal. Meanwhile the ship *Po* had rescued some of those
still on the wreck. Others, a day or two later, managed to
pull from the island in their boats to the *Blucher*, a task
which took them the best part of a full day. Unable to
save any more, and being herself damaged, the *Blucher*
left for Bengal. She arrived nine days later and reported
to the authorities the disaster which had befallen the
Francis and Charlotte. Lord Hastings sent two of the
Company's ships with stores to the rescue. The survivors

were found thirty-six days after the wreck, in a very weak
state and almost starving to death. Some died on being
taken on board the cruisers. How many perished through
the disaster is not known.

The Indiaman *Ernaad*, with the 45th Foot, and others,
totalling nearly eight hundred persons, struck in 1826 on
one of the shoals of Preparis while on a voyage from
Rangoon to Martaban, but got off. She had on board a
Lieutenant Smith, formerly of the 78th when it was wrecked
on the island, and now attached to the 45th.

Some of the old country ships lasted for many years after
the East India Company had passed away. Being built
chiefly of teak, they would not decay, and short of being
battered on rocks, or broken up, or used as hulks, or
succumbing to the perils of the sea, there was no reason
why some of them should not have seen the last century
out. There was certainly one of the country built ships
knocking about until a very few years ago. This was the
Success, which it may be remembered visited many British
ports as an Australian exhibition convict ship, three or
four years before the War. It is claimed that she was
built as far back as 1778 or 1779 at Moulmein ; on the
other hand it has been asserted by a writer in the " Nautical
Magazine," that she was the successor of the *Success* built
in 1779 and was not herself launched until the beginning
of the last century. Whichever be the date of her launch,
she was a tough old ship, otherwise she could not have
passed through as many weird experiences as she did.
She was built almost entirely of Indian teak, and massively.
She had the usual bluff bows of the period, and her heavy
square stern had eight windows. She was not a big ship,
even as ships were accounted in those days ; her tonnage
was about 530 gross, and she was 135 feet in length by

29 feet beam. Artistic carving decorated her quarter galleries and gilded scrolls and escutcheons were in evidence from stem to stern on her hull, and a beautiful figurehead represented a woman smiling at nothing in particular.

Her sides at the bilge were two feet six inches thick. It is no wonder she earned a reputation for slowness, and as she was round bottomed it is still less of a wonder that she rolled till her yard arms are said to have touched the water. The sailors' chanty of " Rolling Home," would be peculiarly appropriate in her case. She was intended to hold her own against pirates and privateers, and for that purpose she carried seven guns, the fittings for which remained on her till the present century. Her hull bore shot marks which were said to have been inflicted in a fight with a French privateer in the Bay of Bengal in 1815. Her original teak lower masts have been in her throughout, but her upper masts and all her spars were comparatively new.

The main mast bears a mark where a large splinter was torn from it. It seems that her crew on one occasion mutinied while she was in Calcutta river, and because of a mistake in signals the guns at Fort William opened fire on the *Success* ; a shot knocked off the splinter which killed one man and wounded several others. Her early years were spent in the tea trade between India and China.

In 1829 she appears to have been chartered by the British Admiralty to take emigrants to Swan River, better known now as Perth, Western Australia. Afterwards she was put into the trade between England and India, and in 1847 she is said to have carried emigrants from England to Port Adelaide. In 1849 she took passengers and convicts from Botany Bay to Tasmania. A later voyage was to England, and in May, 1854, she arrived at Melbourne. The

Australian gold fever was then raging furiously. The captain, crew and passengers caught the fever, and the captain, officers and crew deserted her for the gold fields, and the ship's agents and consignees of the cargo had to get her discharged as best they could. She was soon afterwards offered for sale.

Those were lawless times, and bushrangers and others who preferred to live by robbery and sometimes murder were making themselves uncomfortably conspicuous. A few of the worst desperadoes, after arrest, succeeded in breaking out of the stockade or prison, and as it was necessary to find a stronger and safer place for the detention of the more dangerous prisoners, the government bought the old *Success* and two other vessels to serve as convict hulks. Seventy-two cells are reported to have been fitted in her, from her keel to her deck, and altogether she could accommodate about a hundred and twenty involuntary guests. The discipline on board was tyrannical. Punishments were frequent. To wear an iron chain round the waist with a 72lb. weight attached was one ; others included gagging, the cat-o'-nine-tails, leg irons, spiked collars, body irons, necklets, handcuffs, strait-jackets, etc. The worst cells were those in the bottom tier, to which daylight and fresh air scarcely penetrated, and to these the worst characters were sent. The well-behaved prisoners had cells in the 'tween deck. These were allowed to be sent ashore to work in chain gangs, and the breakwater in Hobson's Bay was constructed by them. The ship carried twenty-seven warders, who were always armed when on duty, and had orders to shoot at sight any prisoner attempting to escape. As the prisoners always wore their fetters, any attempt to escape was bound to fail ; if they attempted to swim ashore the weight of their irons would sink them, and if they had managed to keep afloat for a few yards the sharks, which swarmed in Hobson's Bay, would certainly have got them. In March, 1857, Inspector-General Price who was very much of a martinet, was in charge, with other officers and some warders, of a chain gang of fifteen convicts sent from the ship to work ashore. All the prisoners were heavily fettered. A dispute arose, and the prisoners attacked Price and other officers, and killed Price and wounded some of the others, using their shovels and such heavy stones as they could throw at them. Seven of them were hanged for their share in the crime. This tragedy accentuated the agitation for the abolition of the convict ships, and as the reports of murders on board lost nothing in the telling and could not always be denied, the government at last determined to yield to the agitation.

One of the most noted bushrangers, Frank Gardiner, was a tenant of a cell in her for some time ; he finished the rest of his term of imprisonment ashore, and was pardoned in 1874, and is then reported to have gone to San Francisco where he became a saloon keeper. George Lovelace, who was transported from England for joining a trade union in violation of the law of 1834, was also on the *Success* for a time, but was pardoned before he had served his sentence of seven years. Later the *Success* was used as a prison for refractory seamen, then as a women's prison, later as a reformatory ship for boys, and later as a store hulk. Many a time I have seen the old ship swinging at her moorings in Hobson's Bay ; even on a calm day she rolled. The government ordered all the old convict hulks to be sold and broken up, but the *Success* escaped in some way, and in 1890 she was bought by speculators who fitted her up as an exhibition convict ship. Australian public senti-ment was against this, but the promoters persevered, and it

was while she was on show at Sydney that she was wilfully
scuttled. She was raised in a few months, and after visiting
other Australian ports left Adelaide for London in 1895.
She made the passage under her own sail in 165 days. Her
then captain told me she rolled her gunwales under whenever there was a good sea on, and that in rough weather
lifelines along the deck were indispensable, and also that
her rudder kicked so severely that it often took two men to
steer her. She visited a large number of British ports and
was visited by a great number of persons. Her gruesome
attractions included the alleged armour Ned Kelly, the
last of the bushrangers, wore in the fight with the police
which ended in him being wounded and captured ; there
were about half a dozen sets of Kelly's only suit of armour
in existence within a few months after his gang was broken
up ; further, Kelly was never a prisoner on the *Success*.

Next the *Success* went to America. Her voyage thither
from England was as deliberate as her voyage from
Australia. She left Queenstown on May 12th, 1912, for
New York. Sixty-six days later the Cunarder *Franconia*
was in wireless communication with her—it seems curious to
think of an old Indian country ship carrying wireless in
her very old age—and Captain Scott, her master, reported
that she had been blown on her beam ends and her yard
arms had touched the water. The liner instructed her
to make for Boston instead of New York.

The " Liverpool Journal of Commerce " reported in
July, 1912, that a passenger on the *Franconia* was said to
have received a private wireless from the *Success* that
there was trouble with the crew who thought the vessel
was haunted, and that the captain had to resort to stern
measures. When the *Franconia* arrived at Liverpool in
July she reported that the only messages she received from

the *Success* were greetings, and not requests for assistance or provisions. The *Franconia* passed the *Success* on three successive trips across the Atlantic, and on the last occasion her master received from Captain Scott the following message : " Greetings for the third time. You are passing · the old ship *Success*. We expect to arrive July 13th. Regards."

The last I heard of the *Success* was that she was somewhere up the Mississippi, and had gone ashore.

NOTE.—Messrs. Smith, Imossi & Co., the owners of the *Java*, have written stating that " her condition is as good as ever. As a matter of fact it is better than it was, as we had her drydocked a few years ago, and we had the part damaged by striking the Pearl Rock repaired with teak. As a result she makes no water at all now." She may easily last another century.

CHAPTER III

Growth of American Shipping—Buccaneers, Privateers and Pirates of the West Atlantic and Spanish Main—The American Packets.

BOTH before and after the revolution of 1776 the British government did its best to stifle the small but growing and vigorous mercantile marine of the Americans. Fortunately the British government did not succeed. Had the attempt been successful, a very different history might have had to be written of the last one hundred and fifty years of the sailing ship industry. Stern necessity drove the dwellers on the western side of the Atlantic to build vessels for themselves. For many years their vessels showed no originality in design, but by degrees types were evolved as the Americans gained experience, which in their highest development out-classed completely anything the Old World had to show or seemed able to produce or emulate till long afterwards. The Americans were not hampered by tradition or custom in the design of their ships, as British and European builders were. British shipowners ultimately saw the superiority of the American ships, and began to purchase them in increasing numbers, until the best sailing ships under the British flag were practically all built in American yards.

In the latter part of the seventeenth century the East
India Company called attention to the New England shipbuilding facilities, and its chairman protested that " there
is nothing more prejudicial, and in prospect more dangerous, to any mother kingdom, than the increase in shipping
in her colonies, plantations and provinces."

Earlier in that century certain London shipbuilders
complained that so many men had gone to the New
England yards that there were not enough left in London
to do the work. They suggested that American ships be
shut out from all trade except with Great Britain and her
colonies, and that the Americans should not be allowed to
build ships above a certain size. This rather absurd request
was rejected, and the Americans continued to build ships
and send them where they would. Although as many as
389 vessels were launched on the Atlantic coast in 1769,
they averaged only about fifty tons.

In the eighteenth century France was the leading country
in the designing of ships, and some of the best frigates in
the British navy were modelled on those captured from the
French. It was from the French frigates and luggers which
visited America after the treaty of 1778, between the two
countries, that the best American frigates and privateers
originated. American privateers were built in great
numbers, and being as a rule much faster than the British
vessels captured a great many of them.

The early New York privateers seem to have been an
unscrupulous lot of ruffians, judging by such records as
have come down to us. In the seventeenth century, long
before the war of independence, mistakes could easily be
made, and doubtless were, as to the nationality of any
vessel which seemed likely to be a profitable capture. New
York, by its geographical situation, was an ideal place for

privateers' headquarters, and New York, with American thoroughness, did its best.

"After the dull and unprofitable quiet of Lord Bellomont's too-moral rule—when an honest sailor man could not take a quiet turn off soundings without having the Governor hot upon him with a whole string of impertinent questions on the very moment of his return—the joy of going cruising with the openly avowed intention of hunting prizes was exceedingly keen. Therefore it was with all the goodwill in the world that our people made the most of their lucky geography by getting quickly away to sea ; and presently a fleet of more than twenty sail had cleared the Hook and had stood away to the s'uth'ard with the first favourable slant of wind—for there was little worth fighting for afloat in the St. Lawrence region, while the French and Spanish craft to be had for the taking in West Indian waters were, of a sort, usually, to set a man's mouth watering merely to think about them as made prize." [1]

One of the most conspicuous of them seems to have been a Captain Renier Tongrelow—his name was spelt in various ways—who after one or two insignificant exploits, bought a 200-ton ship with eighteen guns, and fitted her out as a privateer with a crew of 160 men. Another privateer sailed in consort with him in December, 1705, but beyond a few small prizes being taken for some months, nothing happened until midsummer when Tongrelow's ship took a French brigantine—cut out of a convoy—with 400 hogsheads of sugar, and also took a prize from France with claret. When more than one vessel was sighted Tongrelow usually attacked the biggest, and generally captured it. Once he tackled a French ship of thirty or thirty-six guns,

---

[1] T. A. Janvier in "Harper's Magazine" for Feb., 1895.

and after four hours' fighting concluded he had enough,
and sailed away. Only three months later the governor of
Havana, being anxious to rid the seas of such a nuisance as
Tongrelow, sent two privateer sloops to take him. They
came, they met and fought, and he conquered the two of
them. Then the Spanish governor sent a ship, a brigantine,
and a sloop after him. This was too much even for Tongrelow to fight. His sloop, the *New York*, was missing for
several days and it was feared she was taken, but she
managed to outsail her pursuers. After this, the adventurous captain stayed ashore. Captain Tom Penniston,
who commanded Tongrelow's consort, also had a fancy for
taking the biggest when opportunity offered. His vessel
was much smaller than the *New York*, but the last fight
reported of him is that he boarded two ships together, one
of eighteen and the other of twenty-four guns, but was
beaten off with the loss of his arm and nine men killed, and
as many wounded.

Another New York privateer, the brigantine *Dragon*,
attacked simultaneously two French privateers off Porto
Rico ; they ran, and his ship was too damaged to follow.
Another impudent exploit was the cutting out of a sugar
laden barque in Cartagena Roads in sight of a strong
French fleet, by Captain Zacharias. Tongrelow's tender,
a sloop of six guns and with a crew of twenty-seven men,
attacked a 600 tons Spanish ship off Cuba, and according to
a news-letter of 1706 fired six shot at her, one of which
blew up the round-house and killed the captain and five
men, and another damaged the main mast which fell over
the side. The sloop found the ship too strong for her and
went to tell Tongrelow, who could not find her. The sloop,
however, found her ashore on the Cuban coast, and the
Spaniards, after a little fight, agreed to hand over the wine

and brandy on board on condition the privateers would not burn the rest of the cargo or the ship.

Fighting men afloat, they seem to have been equally pugnacious ashore. " Considering what a terror afloat they were to their enemies," Mr. Janvier writes, " it is no great wonder that these privateersmen of ours should have been also a bit of a terror to their friends ashore. New York seems to have gloried in their deeds and to have stood in awe of their persons—as well it might, in view of their broadly impartial tendency to get drunk on anybody's premises, and thereafter to fight everybody who came along."

After the arrival of the sloop with its wine and brandy the privateers men began a riot in New York, and murdered one of two British army officers whom they met, and grievously wounded the other. The fight between the party led by the sheriff, reinforced by sailors from the British warships in the harbour, and the privateers, ended in the defeat of the privateers, one of whom was killed. The man who killed the British officer with the sword of the other was afterwards hanged.

American privateering had an easier time for several years until France went to war again in 1744, when it revived with much of its old energy. Most of the privateers' ships were little vessels of from 120 to 200 tons, of various rigs, and well armed, with crews that seldom exceeded a hundred men, and many prizes were taken. They were not always polite to the fair sex. It is recorded that a woman stowaway was found on a privateer. The crew ducked her three times from the yard arm, and then had her tarred and feathered, and says the historian, " the poor woman was very much hurt and continues very ill." Another short peace in Europe which caused a temporary stagnation in active privateering by the Americans was used by them to get ready for the good time they foresaw when France and England or any other nations should be at war once more. This time New York sent out 130 privateers before peace was again made. By January, 1758, the New York fleet captured eighty prizes.

The pirate has always been the Ishmaelite of the ocean, his hand against everyone and everyone's hand against him. It is hard to draw the distinction at times between a pirate and a privateer. Lord Nelson held the opinion that all privateers were no better than pirates. Privateers held letters of marque, or licenses to capture ships belonging to an enemy, but when once a privateer was well out at sea he was a law unto himself, and the privateer's interpretation of what constituted an enemy lacked nothing in breadth, besides which it was so easy to make a mistake, especially when it might prove a profitable one. Still, privateers were protected by the law of the country of their allegiance; pirates were outlaws, and behaved as such. No laws protected them, and they respected none, not even among themselves. Might was right with them, and as to their human victims they acted on the motto that dead men tell no tales. Some of their captives had to walk the plank; others, not so often, were strung up to the yard arm. Some were turned loose in small boats at sea without water or provisions to die of thirst or starvation.

Groups of islands have generally been the favoured haunts of pirates, provided that the islands were not too far from a convenient market where the stolen goods could be sold and questions were regarded as a troublesome superfluity. Even the islands round the British Isles have known their pirates. The Scilly Islands, Shetland and the

Hebrides are all reported to have been their headquarters. One notable exponent of the trade was a Captain Avery or Every, who is supposed to have been the original of Defoe's " Captain Singleton." It is told of Avery that he shipped on a large merchant vessel, organised a mutiny among the crew, obtained control of the ship, and then sailed her to Madagascar which was a notorious haunt of pirates in the Indian Ocean. After a rest there he sailed for the Indian coast and captured a " large and valuable ship belonging to the Great Mogul and his subjects," and returned to New England to sell his spoil. He afterwards came to England, but managed to evade arrest though several of his men were taken and punished.

Piracy in eastern seas became so prevalent, and the losses in the Indian Ocean so serious, that it was decided to suppress piracy there if possible. Captain William Kidd, of all persons in the world, whose exploits were already being talked about, was selected for the work. He is supposed to have been born in Scotland. He served with distinction against the French in the West Indies, and came to London with a sloop of his own in 1695. Possibly he was chosen on the principle of set a pirate to catch a pirate. A galley called the *Adventure*, of 275 tons and carrying thirty guns, was fitted out for him and he was granted a commission to rove and bring to trial all pirates, and his commission also gave him permission to indulge in reprisals against the French. He sailed from Plymouth for New York, where he filled up his crew with more desperadoes and took on board stores, and sailed. Madagascar was reached in 1697. Instead of routing the pirates out— probably he found them too numerous—he fraternised with them. Possibly he also saw that there was more money to be made by turning pirate than by trying to suppress piracy; anyway, it might be less risky. He associated with a notorious pirate named Culliford, and reports of his exploits reaching England and America, he was recalled. From the West Indies he sent a letter by one of his prizes to Governor Lord Bellomont at New York saying he could justify himself; he also sent the governor a gift. However, he was arrested, sent to England, and with some of the members of his crew he was tried and convicted for piracy and hanged at Execution Dock in May, 1701. As usual pirates were supposed to have accumulated and hidden on some island vast treasures, and as Kidd has been no exception to the rule, various expeditions have been organised to find his ill-gotten hoards, and they have been uniformly unsuccessful.

Some pirates had crude notions of religion, and would pray for good booty and plenty of spoil, or sing a *Te Deum* in a church in a city they had sacked. Protestant and Catholic pirates often quarrelled, and the English protestants demonstrated their views by shooting at statues in Catholic churches; the Catholics, finding no protestant churches to attack, made matters unpleasant for the too-enthusiastic protestant reformers, some of whom died in the discussions. One pious Catholic leader noticed a follower to behave in what he considered an unseemly manner during the celebration of mass, and thereupon shot him.

Such was the peculiar moral outlook of the time that some pirates claimed to be social reformers. A curious community was established by them in Madagascar under the leadership of a Frenchman and an Italian, which lived by piracy, and promised all its members, negroes included, liberty, equality and fraternity.

The later buccaneers of the West Indies seem to have

been as unsavoury a lot of ruffians as could be found anywhere, notwithstanding the cloak of romance with which some writers have seen fit to envelope them. They appear to have originated through the Spanish incapacity to rule its possessions. The Spanish government had shown how not to govern its oversea colonies, even more thoroughly than England afterwards did in regard to New England. But whereas the British government merely reached the limit of sheer tactlessness, and goaded the New Englanders into rebellion, the Spaniards indulged in a policy of deliberate cruelty and oppression, and having a very different problem to deal with from that in New England, soon found that they had stirred up a hornet's nest beyond their powers to suppress. Trading and unfair monopolies were at the bottom of the trouble. The Spaniards on the island of Santo Domingo were deprived of their markets, and accordingly English, Dutch and French vessels smuggled goods into the island on a large scale. One of the island industries, in which French settlers excelled, was the preservation of the flesh of the native cattle at establishments called boucans, whence the term buccaneering arose. Spain refused to allow other nations to trade with the West Indies, of which she claimed to possess the whole ; the other nations therefore traded without her permission, and their vessels being armed fought any Spanish vessel that interfered. They went further, and when possible levied tribute on the Spaniards —levying tribute being a euphemism for collecting all they could ; the English were the chief sinners in this respect. Singeing the Spanish King's beard was a favourite pastime or occupation for adventurous Britishers from Elizabethan days up to the eighteenth century.

Buccaneering, or dealing in meat, became a highly

profitable speculation, and as the trade developed enormously, a place of storage, more secure from the Spanish
government than Santo Domingo, became necessary.
The little island of Tortuga was chosen. This did not suit
the Spaniards, who eight years later seized the island and
killed all the settlers they could find. This united the
buccaneers against the Spaniards as nothing else could have
done. For one thing they were of various nationalities,
and however much national animosities might have been
shown among themselves, they were all agreed in a thor-
ough detestation of the Spaniard. They formed an organis-
ation known as the Brothers of the Coast. Adventurers
from many European countries joined them, and for three
quarters of a century they were a terror to Spanish-
American trade. For their own protection they flew the
flag of any nation with which Spain happened to be at
war, but did not acknowledge allegiance to it.

English traders established themselves in Tortuga.
The French captured the island and expelled them. Then
the Spaniards recaptured it from the French, who after
a time retaliated and expelled the Spaniards.

The buccaneers as such were not concerned with the
quarrels of the European nations, but they were open to
hire if the pay were good enough. Both France and
Spain employed them in their attacks upon Tortuga.
The British Commonwealth fleet found the buccaneers
very helpful in taking Jamaica.

Spanish possessions ashore or property afloat were not
their only victims ; any ship of any nationality was fair
game. But that was in their later days.

Some extraordinary and daring exploits were perpetrated by the buccaneers when at the height of their
power. One, in which they were led by a man named

Morgan, an adventurous spirit if ever there was one, and joined by all the rifraf of the Caribbean Seas, was the attack on Porto Bello. As a lawless enterprise it was sufficiently serious to be one of the inducements of Britain and Spain to make peace in order that this sort of thing might be stopped. The then governor of Jamaica, acting on his own initiative, granted Morgan a commission to attack the isthmus of Panama, this being the route by which the gold and silver from the South American mines were taken to Porto Bello to be shipped to Spain. The atrocities perpetrated by Morgan and his followers during this expedition are too well known to need recapitulation. Morgan was recalled to England, and imprisoned. In 1674 he returned to Jamaica as governor. He had robbed his former followers in the Panama expedition, and as his unpopularity was great he set to work to try to suppress the buccaneers.

The years 1671 to 1685 were the time of their greatest daring, prosperity and power. At last they made their way overland to the Pacific. Three of them, whose names are given as Sawkins, Sharp and Watling, ravaged the coast from Panama to Peru. Some of them returned by way of Cape Horn to the West Indies. In 1683 an expedition of buccaneers under John Cook left for the Pacific by way of the Horn. Cook died on the voyage and was succeeded by a man named Edward Davis, who has been described as " the greatest and most prudent commander who ever led the forces of the buccaneers at sea." They met a Captain Swan from England, and the combined force became a perfect curse to Spanish trade in the Pacific. More buccaneers went by land to Panama, and the great expedition was undertaken, and was marked by great cruelty and vice. In 1685 the French and English buccaneers in the West Indies parted. In 1688 Davis returned to the West Indies by the Horn, and Swan in his ship, the *Cygnet*, sailed as far as Madagascar where she was abandoned as unseaworthy. England and France were at war again in 1689, and the French and English buccaneers took sides and fought each other. The buccaneers were never again united in strength, and sank into piracy, which was not finally suppressed until early last century. One of their favourite haunts was a small island in the Virgin Islands ; it was known as the " Dead Man's Chest," from the amount of booty taken there for division. It is referred to in one of the grimmest poems I have ever read, " Fifteen Men on the Dead Man's Chest," in which the result of a fight among the crew of a pirate is described, and ten of them lay stretched out dead. R. L. Stevenson mentions the island " The Dead Man's Chest " in one of his books.

Some of the pirate captains were rather dandified, and most of their followers followed suit. It was not surprising that rough, vicious, ignorant men, obtaining all the necessities and most of the luxuries of life by plunder, should seize upon the best clothes of their victims and wear them till another ship came along to be robbed and probably sunk ; they simply displayed the love of personal decoration common to all savages, whatever their colour or nationality. One pirate captain, Bartholomew Roberts by name, liked to dress the part. His fighting costume included a red feather in his hat, a gold chain with diamond cross pendant round his neck, and crimson damask waistcoat and breeches. When his wardrobe permitted, his shirt—or that of a victim—was white, likewise his stockings, at the beginning of an action. His pistols were hung on a silk ribbon round his neck, and came as low as his waist or hips, to be handy if he should want to use them quickly. He is stated to have taken more than four hundred prizes before he was himself taken in an engagement with H.M.S. *Swallow* off the West African coast in 1722. Roberts first distinguished himself as a filibuster ; he was persuaded to turn pirate by a man named Howel Davis. Roberts is said to have been the " nearest approach to the pirate of romance, conscientious and brave, and not without touches of generosity," known in the annals of the sea-outlaws. His exploits show that there was another side to his character.

Dressing the part, but to accentuate his natural repulsive appearance, was a weakness of the notorious Captain Edward Teach, more widely known as Blackbeard. He wore his long, thick black beard in four or five curls, cultivated a ferocious moustache, and added to his ugliness by tying round his head a piece of match cord, such as was used to ignite the powder in the touchholes of his guns, and lighting it before he went into action. Possibly he did this to make his victims think, from the smoke rising from his locks, that he was associated with the devil, with whom, indeed, many pirates did claim to have personal relationship. He seems to have been a particularly bad specimen of humanity, even for a pirate. At one time, he and a number of other pirates of the Spanish Main took advantage of an amnesty or offer of pardon to settle ashore on the American coast on promise of behaving themselves. When his money was getting low he returned to piracy, and his depredations became so serious that the governor of Virginia sent an expedition to capture him in 1718. There was a tough fight in which Blackbeard and his crew boarded the American ship, and in the hand to hand conflict Blackbeard was killed. Disheartened by the death of their leader, his crew were speedily subdued.

The victorious Virginian ship returned to port with Black-beard's head decorating its bowsprit. The Americans discouraged piracy in the West Atlantic and Spanish Main. They captured scores of pirates and hanged them wholesale.

Both before and after the peace of 1815 piracy continued in the Spanish Main, combined very often with the running of slaves from Africa. Every merchant vessel either had to be armed for self protection, or to sail in the convoys. The pirates, though not possessing the reckless bravery of the old buccaneers, were daring at times, but as a rule their enterprises were conducted with more regard to their own safety than their predecessors had shown. The cutting out of a vessel from a convoy under cover of darkness was one of their favourite exploits, nor were they averse from attacking any lone merchantman they might sight. One result was that ships from British and European ports sailing to the West Indies carried guns and crews to work them. Vessels sailing by themselves might be attacked by two or three pirates, who would probably be victorious unless the selected victim was able to fight them or outsail them, as occasionally happened. There are very few reliable accounts of encounters between pirate vessels and merchant ships in which the latter were beaten, as the pirates generally left no one who could tell what had happened, and preserved a discreet silence concerning themselves. On the other hand there are several short accounts of fights with pirates, which almost invariably state that after the exchange of a few shots the pirates drew off and would not continue the engagement.

The south coast of Cuba was one of their chief haunts, and they made themselves such a nuisance that the British and American governments combined to suppress them.

7

The Spanish authorities of the islands did not look kindly upon this interference from outside with one of the established habits of the islanders and sources of income, but the vigour with which Americans and British carried out their work compelled the Spaniards, to avoid international trouble, to take at least some steps to deal with the evil.

New Orleans and the delta at the mouth of the Mississippi constituted the last of the pirates' haunts on the American coast. It might perhaps be more correct to say that their haunts were in the delta, and that their sympathisers in New Orleans provided the market. An interesting article by George Washington Cable on " Plotters and Pirates of Louisiana," which appeared in the " Century Magazine " in 1883, describes the district of the delta known as Barataria, with its numerous intricate channels known only to pirates and slavers. Guadaloupe and Martinique, in the West Indies, had been the headquarters of the French privateers till the British conquest of those islands in 1810 made them as " homeless as Noah's ravens." To the delta they came, in spite of American opposition, and fortified the small island of Grande Terre. Here they " built store-houses, sailed away upon the Gulf, and re-appeared with prizes which it seems were not always Spanish. . . . The Baratarians had virtually revived, in miniature, the life of the long-extinct buccaneers." There was no attempt at concealment in New Orleans of their trade, where they found an excellent market. British merchantmen were among the vessels that suffered ; they were captured in the Gulf, and sold behind Grande Terre.

" The English," says the article, " more than once sought redress with their own powder and shot. On the 23rd of June, 1813, a British sloop of war anchored off the outer end of the channel at the mouth of La Fourche and sent

her boats to attack two privateers lying under the lee of
Cat Island ; but the pirates stood ground and repulsed
them with considerable loss." Other records show that the
British were sometimes successful.

In 1814 the nest was broken up by the Americans, and
after order was restored and New Orleans had settled down
from the other troubles that had afflicted her, the pirates'
leaders, the brothers Lafitte, and their assistants settled
down too for a time. What happened to the two brothers
is a matter of doubt, but one or two of their assistants went
into local politics. One of the brothers, John Lafitte, had
not abandoned freebooting altogether. He transferred his
activities from New Orleans to Galveston, Texas. An
American ship was robbed of a certain amount of specie on
the high seas. Shortly afterwards Lafitte's ship arrived at
Galveston with a similar quantity on board. Explanations
were demanded, and not forthcoming. One of Lafitte's
schooners, brought from New Orleans, took a prize, and
" was met by the revenue cutter *Alabama*, answered her
challenge with a broadside, engaged her in a hard battle,
and only surrendered after heavy loss. The schooner and
prize were taken into Bayou St. John, the crew taken to
New Orleans, tried in the United States Court, condemned
and executed." For a time Lafitte sailed as a privateer
with a Colombian commission, but when this expired he
became an open pirate.

" The end of this uncommon man," Mr. Cable wrote,
" is lost in a confusion of improbable traditions. As late
as 1822, his name, if not his person, was the terror of the
Gulf and the Straits of Florida. But in that year the
United States navy swept those waters with vigour, and
presently reduced the perils of the Gulf—for the first time
in its history—to the hazard of wind and wave."

A vivid account of the wastefulness of pirates is given in a description of the adventures of Captain Snelgrave, of the *Bird* galley, in 1718, off the West Coast of Africa. On the *Bird* arriving at the river of Sierra Leone, three pirates anchored in the river sent their crews to board her, and owing to the treachery of the mate they were allowed on the ship. After maltreating the captain, the pirates wantonly injured several of the crew. Next they helped themselves to the provisions on board. Fowls, ducks, geese and turkeys were beheaded and their wing feathers drawn, and with a sow the pirates killed and several Westphalia hams, were boiled altogether. One of the pirates took the captain's gold watch, and saying it would do for a football kicked it along the deck. After being taken on one of the pirate ships Captain Snelgrave was confronted by an old schoolfellow, turned pirate, who saved his life more than once. Next day ten of his crew joined the pirates. A Captain Glynn, who lived at Sierra Leone, was on good terms with the pirates, and thanks in some measure to him Snelgrave was allowed to return to his own ship. He found it had been looted, and what the pirates had not wanted they had thrown overboard. One man whose name is said to be Kennedy dressed himself in a suit belonging to the captain, so his comrades drenched him with claret, and in half an hour he took the clothes off and threw them overboard ; he ended his days at Execution Dock.

At last the pirate captains gave Snelgrave a ship they had captured—not his ship, which they wanted to keep as she was a good sailer—and a lot of goods taken from other prizes, and one of the pirate captains, Davis by name, invited him to go and dine on the *Bird*. A negro went into the hold with a naked candle to draw some rum, and set a cask of spirits on fire, and as there were some thousands of pounds weight of gunpowder on board, together with barrels of tar, the ship was expected to blow up. Snelgrave aided some of the pirates, led by a man named Taylor, who, pirate though he was, acted like a hero on this occasion, to cope with the fire. Taylor and fifteen of his associates placed a pile of blankets and rugs against the powder room bulkhead, and drenched them with water under Snelgrave's direction, and did not desist until they had subdued the fire. Taylor and his fifteen men were all badly burned. The help Snelgrave had given disposed the pirates in his favour. They returned some of the things stolen from his ship, and allowed him to buy back others, With these he hid in the forest until the pirates sailed away, after which he loaded a vessel with what goods he could, and with six captains whose vessels the pirates had taken, and sixty passengers, he sailed for Bristol, arriving safely in August, 1719. During his enforced stay among the pirates he found that ten English ships had been captured, in addition to a French ship they brought in while he was there.

The only part of the world where piracy now survives is the China Seas, and there it is carried on in a very different fashion from what it was a hundred years ago. The Chinese method now is to board in force some steamer, as passengers, and when the vessel is well out to sea to over-power the officers and crew and seize and loot the vessel. As soon as they learned that the innocent-looking wireless aerials might be the means of calling assistance, the Chinese made it their first duty to render the wireless useless. Their plans are always well laid, and are often successful. Sometimes the steamer officers who resist are killed; sometimes they are compelled at the point of the revolver to take the vessel where the pirates wish for looting purposes.

II

After the revolutionary war the American merchants sent their best ships abroad in larger numbers and to more foreign ports than ever before, and there were not many ports which could be entered where American ships were not to be found. Naturally this cut to some extent into British shipping, and complaints followed. The Americans used to do a great deal of trade with the West Indies, but after the war American ships were no longer of British nationality and were classed as foreigners, and as such were excluded from the British West Indies. Probably this step did Britain more harm than it did America. For one thing it is stated that fifteen thousand slaves died in the British West Indies between 1780 and 1787 because the American vessels could no longer take them food to replace the hurricane-wasted crops.

Looking back, one can only wonder at the extraordinary state of affairs which existed at the beginning of the last century, and the contrast to trading conditions prevailing now. Then the East India Company had a monopoly and was protected by its charters, and for years and years excluded all other British ships from the ports under its control. In the last hundred years of its existence the Company became less a trading concern than an enterprise for extending its aggrandisement in India until it controlled a great part of the peninsula. Even when the fateful writing appeared on the walls, it shut its eyes, and tried to persuade itself the writing was not there. It is not surprising that the owners of the free trade ships, as all other British vessels were called because they were free to trade where they liked or could outside the Company's monopoly, looked longingly and lovingly at the Tom Tiddler's ground from which they were debarred, and at the Company's immense profits into which they could not dip.

After the Americans in 1776 attained their independence of British rule and unfair laws they began to trade with India and contended their ships had a right to do as those of an independent nation. " So early as 1789, the merchants of Boston and Salem," W. S. Lindsay writes in his " History of Shipping," " sent various ships direct to the East Indies and China, and many years before the ʻfree traders ' of Great Britain could enter this trade, then monopolised by the ships of the East India Company, so far as regards Great Britain, the merchants of Massachusetts supplied not only their own people with the bulk of the teas, spices, silks, sugar and coffee from the East, as well as with nankeens and other cotton cloths, but reshipped them from Boston to Hamburg and the northern ports of Europe in their own vessels, thus deriving large profits from a trade with our possessions, from which the great bulk of our ships were excluded by the stringent restrictions of a pernicious monopoly."

It would serve no good purpose to describe the retaliatory measures adopted by this country and America against each other with a view to hampering each other's shipping and benefiting their own. The measures, like many expedients to restrict trade, generally did as much harm as good to their individual authors. Probably the impositions of Britain on American shipping induced the Americans to look for other avenues. Certain it is that they did so, and it is equally certain that their activity helped to break down the Company's monopoly.

One of the earliest American ships, perhaps the earliest,

to reach the Far East, was the *Empress of China*, which under Captain Greene, made the round voyage from New York to Canton and back between February, 1784, and the following May. In December, 1785, Elias Hasket Derby, of Salem, one of the most prominent men in the history of American shipping, sent his *Grand Turk* to the Isle of France, India and China, and by 1789 several American ships were engaged in that trade.

One of them was a little sloop of eighty tons ; Captain Clark in his " Clipper Ship Era," calls her the *Experiment*, and Marvin, in his " American Merchant Marine " calls her the *Enterprise*. Presumably they refer to the same vessel, as both say she was built at Albany and was commanded by a man named Dean. It is also asserted Dean served on a privateer during the revolution. Her crew numbered fifteen. Small though she was she carried six guns, beside muskets and other weapons ; she went from New York to Canton and returned in safety, and it is said she made a profit on the trip. She contrasts oddly with the *Massachusetts*, built in 1789 at Quincy, of 600 tons and the largest launched up to that time in America ; she was intended by the two enterprising Americans who owned her to inaugurate an American East India Company. She had two decks and was armed, and is said to have been a very fine and well-proportioned vessel. Unfortunately she was built of white oak timber newly cut and wholly unseasoned, and before she had finished her first voyage she was rotten.[1]

The Americans were not slow to profit by the lessons of their shipping enterprises, not all of which were by any means successful. America had no navy worth speaking of after the war, and American ships probably had to run

[1] (W. L. Marvin: The American Merchant Marine).

a greater number of risks than the ships of any other nation, particularly from pirates and privateers, for the sea-robbers knew that no warships could be sent against them. The Barbary corsairs, for instance, were well acquainted with American weakness in this respect, but they were not well acquainted with the American habit of remedying a weakness as soon as possible when necessary. The corsairs captured many American traders, one of their squadrons of four vessels seizing ten American ships in one cruise. The American government of the day attempted to bribe the corsairs into letting the American ships alone, but this only whetted the corsairs' appetite for more booty. A change in the American government was not understood by the Moors. A caution having no effect, and the American government having provided itself with a few new warships, it sent one of the best to the Barbary Coast, and a little gun practice and a strict blockade taught the Moors that it was best not to interfere with American ships.

The adventurous spirit of the Americans was extraordinary. One or two instances may be given. The ship *Columbia* and a smaller vessel, the *Lady Washington*, sailed from Boston to the north-west coast in 1787 to get furs. They sailed via Cape Horn and parted in the Pacific. The *Columbia* obtained her cargo of furs and took them to China, where there was a good market, and sold them, and loaded up with a cargo of tea with which in August, 1790, she returned to Boston where it was sold at a good profit. She returned by way of the Cape of Good Hope, being it is said, the first American ship to sail round the world. Captain Gray, her master, took the vessel to the northwest coast on another fur gathering expedition, in 1792, and this time discovered the mouth of the great river of Oregon, which he named the Columbia, and thus added the Oregon territory to the American possessions.

Far more venturesome was young Richard Cleveland. Indeed, the adventures of some of the American mercantile marine officers would tax the powers of credibility of people in these times were they not authenticated. Cleveland, a member of an earlier generation of the same family as President Grover Cleveland, entered at the age of fourteen the counting house of Elias Hasket Derby to learn the business. At the age of eighteen he made his first voyage, as captain's clerk, under Captain Nathaniel Silsbee, aged nineteen, in a ship bound for the Cape of Good Hope and Mauritius. The first mate, Charles Derby, was not so old as the captain, but a little older than Cleveland, who became second mate. The voyage of these youthful mariners brought to the owner of the ship about four times the amount of capital he had invested. By 1797, when he was twenty-three years of age, Cleveland had already made a voyage as commander. Being at Havre that year without a ship, he acquired a small coasting sloop, and started for the Cape and Mauritius. The vessel was blown ashore within a few hours, but Cleveland got her off, repaired her, and set forth again. He had an American lad as mate, and the rest of his crew consisted of a cook, one sailor, and two boys. Shortage of water was experienced before he arrived at the Cape in 1798, after a passage of three months. He sold the sloop there for about £1,000, and made his way to Batavia and Canton, intending to enter the north west fur trade.

Not having enough money to buy a ship, he obtained another sloop and shipped a tough crew, mostly of deserters from warships and Indiamen. Before long part of the crew mutinied, so Cleveland loaded his two 4-pounders, trained

them forward where the mutineers were, armed the faithful members of the crew, and cowed the rebels. Ultimately
he put the worst of them ashore somewhere to look after
themselves, and sailed on without them. Somehow that
little vessel of only fifty feet in length accomplished a five
thousand miles voyage across the North Pacific in winter.
He loaded her with furs, and returned to China where he
sold his cargo at a profit, and the sloop as well. At Calcutta he bought a pilot boat of thirty-five tons, and sailed
her to Mauritius. Here he made the acquaintance of a man
named William Shaler, and with him went to Hamburg
where they bought an American brig, the *Lelia Byrd*, of
175 tons. They tossed up who should be captain, and
Shaler won. They had as guest a Polish nobleman, Count
de Rouissillon, who had been a supporter of the Polish
patriot Kosciusko. They sailed the brig to Valparaiso,
and were imprisoned by the Spaniards who seemed to
think that American ships only went there to be robbed,
and acted accordingly. They escaped from Valparaiso,
and went to Mexico, where the Count left the party, and
then to San Diego in California, which was then Spanish,
and the Spaniards pursued their usual tactics. Cleveland
and Shaler resented this, and decided to run for it. Accordingly the brig opened fire on the fort with her guns, and
gave the Spaniards a bad time and a fright, and sailed away.
The brig was headed for the Sandwich Islands, and then
for Canton, and Cleveland left her at the latter place. It
was a trading trip throughout, and Cleveland and Shaler
made a good deal of money out of it. Cleveland returned
to Salem, and after living ashore for a time returned to the
sea, but had a run of misfortunes after which he settled
down to a shore life again. It is recorded of him that he
never took alcohol in any form, and never smoked.

As already stated, American shipbuilders adapted the finer lines of the French vessels which visited their ports, and their ships, besides being lighter than those of their British rivals were also larger and faster. When peace at last came in 1815, the Americans with their usual commercial acuteness saw that the opportunity had come to establish a number of lines in the trade with Europe, and the New York and Liverpool packets began their work in the following year. The first of these enterprises was the Black Ball line, which must not be confused with the English Black Ball line. It started operations with four ships, and ten others were soon added to meet the demands of the trade ; they were between 300 and 500 tons each, a tonnage that contrasts oddly with that of the giant steamships of the present day on the same route. Their eastward passages averaged twenty-three days, and the westward passages forty days. One of them, the *Canada*, is credited with having made the voyage to Liverpool in 15 days, 18 hours. Unlike most of the ships of their size, and they were reckoned big vessels, though not equal to the stately East Indiamen which they could have outsailed, they were flush decked ; they had no raised forecastle or poop, and as few deck obstructions as possible. They kept up, summer and winter, communication between Liverpool and New York, and in the matter of speed were driven for all they were worth. Two sailings each way a month were made. In passenger accommodation they were far in advance of any of the older merchantmen.

So successful was the enterprise that in 1821 another line was started, called the Red Star line, which began with four ships, and the same year saw the appearance of the Swallow-tail Line, so called because of its house-flag, with four packets, and these lines between them maintained a

regular weekly sailing each way between New York and
Liverpool. Thus was the famous packet service begun,
which continued to hold its own for thirty years. The
Black Ball and the Swallow-tail lines added to their
fleets from time to time, and the rivalry between them
could not have been more intense had one been British
and the other American, instead of both being American.
Captain E. K. Collins joined in the competition with the
celebrated Dramatic line. The names of many of these
packets are still well known to readers of sailing ship
history, and the names of their captains will never be
forgotten as long as their ships are remembered. The more
recent additions to the Swallow-tail Line included the
Roscoe, under Captain Joseph C. Delano, of New Bedford;
the *Independence*, Captain Ezra Nye; the *George Washington*, Captain Henry Holdredge; and the *Pennsylvania*,
Captain John P. Smith, all master mariners of the highest
repute. Not less well known were the ships and masters of
the Collins Line : the *Shakespeare*, Captain John Collins;
the *Siddons*, Captain N. B. Palmer; the *Sheridan*, Captain
F. A. de Peyster; the *Garrick*, Captain Alexander Palmer;
and the *Roscius*, Captain Asa Eldridge. The Swallow-tail
Line owners replied to this rivalry with the *Patrick Henry*,
of about 1,000 tons, about the same size as the *Roscius*, and
placed her under the command of Captain J. C. Delano,
who proved that she was an unusually fast sailer; she
made more money for her owners, for her tonnage, than any
other vessel belonging to them. The *Ashburton*, 1215 tons,
and the *Henry Clay*, 1250 tons, followed, to compete with
the Collins Line. The *Henry Clay* was a three decked ship,
and so great were the crowds that went to see her that
" no admittance except on business " notices had to be
displayed. Then came the *New World*, of 1400 tons, the

largest American vessel afloat in 1846. She was built by
the famous Donald McKay, of East Boston. The Irish
famine prevailed about this time, and the freight on a barrel
of flour rose to five shillings from New York to Liverpool.
More than one cargo of food crossed the Atlantic three
times, owing to food speculators, before it reached the
hungry Irish peasantry.

Woodhull and Minturn's line passed into the hands of
the Swallow-tail Line, the owners of which were Messrs.
Grinnell, Minturn and Company. The *Constitution*, the
largest of the four vessels thus acquired, was of 1400 tons
and was described as the finest ever built up to that time.
She was commanded by Captain John Britton, who afterwards became American Consul at Southampton. In 1823
the firm opened a packet line to London, the ships being the
Corinthian, *Cortes*, *Brighton*, and *Columbia*. They were of
about 400 tons. Captain Delano had the last named.
About a score of other vessels were added to the fleet for
this route. It is interesting to note that the famous flag
was regularly borne between New York and London until
1883. The last to carry it was the *Ne Plus Ultra*, of about
1300 tons, of which Captain Borden was master. For years
past the sailing ships had ceased to carry passengers.

Another line to London, which began to operate soon
after the others, was that of John Griswold. It was
afterwards the Morgan line. By 1837 its fleet numbered
twelve ships ; one of them, the *Philadelphia*, was built by
that remarkable man, Christian Bergh, in 1832, and a New
York newspaper said she was sumptuously fitted and had a
piano.

There were also other lines between American ports and
British and French ports, all the ships of which were
commanded by men well known as hard sailors. The

Orient, of Spofford and Tileson's line to Liverpool, was commanded by Captain George S. Hill, who at one time had the *Henry Clay,* and afterwards became the secretary of the Marine Society of New York. The French government chartered the *Orient* to take a cargo of wheat from New York to Havre, about 2100 tons. Her French pilot let her swing across the entrance to the harbour and go ashore. She was refloated and towed to Liverpool for repairs.

Three winter voyages were made from Havre to New York by Captain John Johnston, of Fox and Livingstone's Havre line, in the *Isaac Bell,* in less than eighteen days each. Johnston was a master for seventeen years. He wrote afterwards : " In all my career I never knew the wind to blow but twice." Once was in August 1839, when his ship the *Rhone* had every sail blown away in a hurricane. Another master in this line was Captain James A. Wotton, whose daughter became the wife of Lieutenant de Long, of *Jeannette* Arctic exploration fame.

It would be an easy matter to fill this book with nothing but details about the packets and their captains and crews. The captains, without exception, were hard men as sailors, and their crews of " packet rats " were a hard lot who rather gloried than otherwise in their hardships. They were good enough for the work they had to do on the comparatively short transatlantic voyages, but the few who essayed long or deep-water voyages were seldom much good as sailors. The real sailors on, for instance, ships bound round the Horn or to Australia, or the Far East, had a profound contempt for them. They were good at going aloft and setting or reefing or taking in sail, but there were many other things on board a sailing ship that had to be done which these " packet rats " could never do. They were a turbulent set of men, many of them gaolbirds, who could only be kept in control by severe methods. "The packet mates," Captain Clarke writes, "having no social duties on shipboard to distract their attention, were able to devote their time and energies to improving the morals and manners of the crew, and it was on board the Black Ball liners that 'belaying pin soup' and 'handspike hash,' so stimulating to honest toil, were first introduced for the benefit of mutinous or slothful mariners." Which is a polite way of saying that the conditions prevailing on board some of the packets earned them the reputation of being "hell ships."

Reference to the packets would indeed be incomplete if no mention were made of the *Dreadnought* and her master Captain Samuel Samuels. Probably a greater controversy has arisen about this ship and a record voyage she is said to have made across the Atlantic than about any other American packet. She was built by Currier and Townsend at Newburyport, Massachusetts, and launched in 1853, and was of 1413 tons register. Her dimensions were: length 210 feet, breadth 40 feet, and depth 26 feet. She was owned by a group of New York shipping men, who put up the money to have her built for Captain Samuels; one of them was David Ogden, who was then running the Ogden Red Cross Line, his other vessels being the *Highflyer*, *Racer* and *Victory*. The *Dreadnought* carried a large red cross on her fore topsail, just as the Black Ball liners displayed a black ball in a similar position.

Most American captains began their sea careers before the mast and worked their way up, but Samuels had a more adventurous career than most of them. His autobiography, "From Forecastle to Cabin," states that he ran away from home at the age of eleven and became a cabin boy on a schooner from Philadelphia to New York.

AMERICAN PACKET DREADNOUGHT

Facing page 112

After serving in two more schooners and the revenue brig
Jefferson, he was shanghaied aboard the Baltimore ship
Belvedere to Liverpool, afterwards sailing in a ship called the
Emily to Galvestone. Then he became a member of the
crew of the frigate *Houston*, and deserted her at New
Orleans, and went on the vaudeville stage as a singer and
dancer. He was shanghaied again, this time on the
Ocmulgee, for Liverpool. After two more voyages he became second mate of the *Henry Pratt*, for Liverpool, and
chief mate of the British ship *Caledonia*, 1200 tons, with
800 emigrants for New York. He was also chief mate of
nine other vessels, and obtained command of the last, a
Dutch ship called the *Angelique*. He was now twenty-one
years of age, so the ten years he spent since he left home
were rather crowded. He first took the *Angelique* up the
Mediterranean, and then brought her to New York.
His record appealed to the Red Cross line people, and when
they decided to build another ship, the *Dreadnought*, they
offered Captain Samuels the command and instructed him
to supervise her building. This he did with such attention
to detail that he used to say he knew every rope and spar
in the ship.

The *Dreadnought* was a full-rigged ship, and rather heavy
for an American vessel. She was built to be driven hard
in bad weather, and Captain Samuels was the man to do it.
I met him more than once during the time I lived in
America, and was never tired of hearing him tell how he
made the old ship go, to use one of his own phrases. He was
a great believer in the saying that if you want a thing done
well you must do it yourself.

" Many a time," he used to say in conversation, and he
says much the same in his book, " I have been told that
the crews of other vessels lying hove to could see our keel

8

as we jumped from sea to sea under every rag we could carry ; she used to be called the ' wild boat ' of the Atlantic." She certainly earned her name. Captain Samuels was not the man to take in an inch of sail if he thought the ship was able to stand it, no matter how hard the gale might blow. He had her for ten years, and in that period she crossed the Atlantic between seventy and eighty times. The system of driving Captain Samuels maintained enabled her to make some fast passages. One of her voyages from New York to the Mersey, in 1854, was made in 13 days, 11 hours, 15 minutes. Another passage eastward in the same year was made in 15 days 12 hours. In her crossing in January and February, 1856, she covered 3116 miles in 14 days, an average of 222 miles a day.

It was in 1859 that her wonderful record run of 9 days 17 hours from Sandy Hook to Queenstown was stated to have been made. Captain Clarke in his book calls it a " mythical tale," and points out that Samuels does not mention the accomplishment in his own book. Clarke further states in his " Clipper Ship Era " that an analysis of the *Dreadnought's* log of the voyage in which the record is said to have been made, shows that the ship was not within 400 miles of Queenstown 9 days 17 hours after she dropped her pilot off Sandy Hook.

On the other hand, the following quotations from an article by Mr. F. B. C. Bradlee, of Marblehead, Massachusetts, show that Captain Clarke's statements are not wholly reliable, and that Captain Samuels did claim to have made the much disputed record voyage :

" I wish to put forward the following facts which I think prove the record of the ship beyond a reasonable doubt : First, the statement of the late Captain Samuels made to the ' New York World,' June 5th, 1905. 'We were off Queenstown in 9 days and 17 hours

(March 1859) when the wind died down and I decided to discharge the mails. It took us three and a half days to beat against the light wind to Liverpool. That run to Queenstown has never been beaten.'

"Captain Clarke, in a letter to the writer, dated December 29th, 1910, admits that the *Dreadnought's* log book for this famous and disputed trip, upon which he lays so much stress in his book, has been lost and cannot be found and that he bases his statements from the log upon abstracts published in the Liverpool papers. So much for the log book.

"For some unknown reason Captain Samuels in his own book makes no mention of this remarkably fast passage, although he speaks of being 13 days and eight hours dock to dock, March, 1859. Probably the fact of simply communicating with the pilot boat off Queenstown in nine days 17 hours had not sufficiently impressed him at that time, when not nearly so much interest was taken in shipping matters as there is to-day."

Mr. Bradlee quotes John H. Morrison, author of "History of New York Shipyards," as stating in that book that Captain Samuels told him he made the passage.

I have also in my possession a photograph of a letter sent by Captain Samuels, and written I understand by his daughter, a month before he died, to Mr. Morrison who had asked as to the passage. The letter states :

194, Clinton Street,
April 2, 1908.

Dear Mr. Morrison,

You ask me for the record voyage of the Dreadnought. We discharged the pilot at 3 p.m., Feb. 27, 1859, off Sandy Hook. We were off Queenstown at the end of nine days seventeen hours, when we sent our mails ashore by a Cork pilot boat. The wind then became variable and died down. In thirteen days eight hours we were abreast of the North West Light Ship at Liverpool and one hour later anchored in the Mersey—March 12, noon. The following will give you an idea of the character of the ship and the time she made during the above. In 1854 she made the same passage in 13 days 11 hours, and six times made the passage in succession under sixteen days, including one run of fourteen days and one of fifteen days.   Yours,

S. S.

E. M. S.

The *New York Herald* on April 1st, 1905, published an interview with Captain Samuels in which he states that the passage was made.

I therefore think it may be accepted as a fact that Captain Samuels really did accomplish the record sailing ship passage across the Atlantic.

When the *Dreadnought* had a strong wind in her favour, nothing, not even a steamer, ever passed her, but she passed the steamers more than once. While on a return voyage from Liverpool to New York in 1862 the *Dreadnought* was swept by a big sea, which almost took her captain overboard. He was rescued by some of his crew as he was hanging over the bulwarks on the other side of the ship, and when he came to his senses in the cabin he found he had a gash in the head and a broken leg, with the broken bone protruding through the flesh. The captain proposed to amputate the limb himself, as there was no one else on the ship competent to attempt it, and instructed the mate and steward to help him and revive him if he fainted. They induced him to postpone the operation, and managed to pull the leg straight, but could not keep the broken bones in the proper position, though they bandaged it as well as they were able. For some reason the helmsmen left the wheel and the steering gear became disabled and the ship lost her rudder. Injured though he was, and in excruciating pain, Samuels gave instructions to make a new rudder. When it was ready and was being lowered over the stern, the tackles gave way and it fell into the sea. It being impossible to sail or control the vessel properly, Samuels, still on his back on his wet couch in his wet cabin —the cabin had been flooded by the same sea that nearly carried him overboard—decided on one of the most daring pieces of seamanship ever attempted.

" If Samuels had not done it, I should have said it was impossible," a well-known New York ship master said to me when we were talking about it, and that seemed to have been the general opinion when the feat became known. The ship was about 280 miles from Fayal, and he sailed her backwards that distance. Shortly before reaching Fayal Samuels succeeded in getting his second rudder shipped, and she entered the harbour fourteen days after the disaster. He was carried ashore to a hotel and doctors were sent for. They wanted to amputate his leg, but Samuels replied that he could have done that himself two weeks before, and that as he had come into the world with two legs he intended to go out of it with the same number. The Fayal surgeons did not reset his leg properly, and Captain Samuels was lame for the rest of his life and had to walk with the aid of a stick.

Captain Samuels was a man of remarkable personality. " Any one can sail a ship in the day time," he used to say, " but I was always on deck at night." He had a little shelf constructed in the after companionway of the cabin, upon which he could recline, but it was not long enough to allow him to stretch at full length, so that if he stretched to fall asleep he would wake up. Thus he could rest, but would know if any change were being made on deck. He would never waste time. Whatever he wanted done had to be done with a jump, or he wanted to know why ; this was how he got the reputation of being a hard man to work under ; a man who knew his work, and did it, had nothing to fear from Captain Samuels.

The *Dreadnought* was wrecked in July, 1869, off Tierra del Fuego ; Captain Samuels said he thought her new master must have let her run away with him.

CHAPTER IV

NAVIGATION LAWS, UTILITY SHIPS

THE captains and officers of the best British ships were as good as those of America, as good navigators and seamen, but they had not an equal chance of showing their ability as the British ships were heavy and slow in comparison with their American rivals. The lower class of British ship was often a very inferior vessel. Some ships were a disgrace to the men who owned and sent them to sea, and the owners of them were a disgrace to their profession. There were no Lloyd's Rules in those days to control shipbuilding, or surveys to determine whether a ship was fit for sea service or not, or examinations of officers to ascertain whether they were competent. So owners of that type were able to overload rotten ships which ought to have been condemned years before, and send them to sea, secure in the knowledge that whatever happened they, thanks to insurance, would make a profit. What happened to the unfortunate officers and crew did not matter.

Anybody who could raise the money could own a ship of some sort, and let her go to sea with officers and crew worthy of the ship. The losses of ships and men were appalling. The better class of owners saw that their vessels were kept in really good repair and were commanded by competent men, with competent officers and reliable crews. But with no standard, except such as the shipowner chose to impose, of competence, it is little wonder that some ships were sent to sea in charge of men who should never have been entrusted with the responsibility. Suggestions of reform were opposed by interested parties. " Leave shipowners to mind their own business," was the cry.

Apart from shipowners as a class, though there were some notable exceptions, the view widely held among the general public was that though the Navigation Laws might protect the British shipping industry to some extent they maintained restrictions which prevented the extension and development of that industry, and of commerce generally. It was also contended that the Navigation Laws really placed foreign nations in a position of superiority. It was found, says Lindsay, that neither the ships nor the crews kept pace, during the first half of the last century, with those of foreign nations, " till at length it became necessary to add measures not merely for the improvement of the condition of our ships but for raising our seafaring population by means of a sound education to such a position as would enable them to compete successfully under all circumstances with the ships and seamen of other states."

Changes had often been recommended in the Navigation Laws, and a few had been effected, but shipowners as a whole were opposed to their repeal. Still, the repeal was bound to come. The whole conditions of sea trade had changed. One monopoly after another was broken down, and the phrase, " the freedom of the seas," began to take on another meaning and to stand for the freedom and unrestricted nature of ocean carrying in peace.

Lord Palmerston saw in 1847 that changes were necessary

in the Navigation Act. The Navigation Laws, as they stood in 1847, when they were suspended, contained certain vexatious stipulations. They should be read carefully, in order that some idea may be obtained of the onerous conditions under which British shipowners endeavoured to carry on their business. These stipulations were :

1.—Certain enumerated articles of European produce could only be imported into the United Kingdom for consumption, in British ships or in ships of the country of which the goods were the produce, or in ships of the country from which they were usually imported.

2.—No produce of Asia, Africa or America could be imported for consumption into the United Kingdom from Europe in any ships, or in ships of the country from which they were usually imported.

3.—No goods could be carried coastwise from one part of the United Kingdom to another, in any but British ships.

4.—No goods could be exported from the United Kingdom to any of the British possessions in Asia, Africa or America (with some exceptions with regard to India) in any but British ships.

5.—No goods could be carried from any one British possession in Asia, Africa or America to another, nor from one part of such possession to another part of the same, in any but British ships.

6.—No goods could be imported into any British possession in Asia, Africa or America in any but British ships, or in ships of the country of which the goods were the produce, provided, also, in such case, that such ships brought the goods from that country.

7.—No foreign ships were allowed to trade with any of

the British possessions unless they had been specially authorised to do so by Order in Council.

8.—Powers were given to the Queen in Council which enabled her to impose differential duties on the ships of any foreign country which did the same with reference to British ships ; and also to place restrictions on importations from any foreign countries which placed restrictions on British importations into such countries.

Lindsay says : " In the regulations respecting the trade of Europe, the restrictions only applied to imports. Exports were not affected ; so far as the Navigation Act was concerned foreign ships might export any goods from this country. Certain states had navigation laws before we had, and would not have our goods except in their own ships, so necessity, not wisdom, compelled us to make this allowance."

This seems to be an excellent illustration of the practical application of the principle of safeguarding of industries to shipping.

There followed in due course the introduction by the Board of Trade of examinations for masters and mates for British ships, and the application by Lloyd's of rules dealing with scantlings, measurements, and materials, and numerous other points which had to be taken into consideration in the designing and construction of ships.

These three events, the throwing open of the Indian trade and afterwards of the China trade to the shipping of all nations, the rise of American shipping to the leading position in the world, and the repeal of the British Navigation Laws, may be said to have prepared the way for, and made possible, future developments in the sailing ship that were equally as extraordinary as anything that had gone before, though in a different way. The packets which ruled the Western Ocean in the early part of the last century, and continued in evidence until the 'eighties, were the forerunners of the famous clippers. Many of the later packets were semi-clippers so far as shape went. They were also the forerunners of the great multitude of British and American sailing ships which carried the world's commerce till the steamers drove them entirely out of it, a consummation that was not reached until after the Great War. The British clippers, to which reference will be made later, were of a different type.

The best British ships had characteristics of their own, which were as marked in their way as those of the American packets. The best shipbuilding and ship-owning firms, such as Wigram, Green, Smith of Newcastle, to mention only three at random, besides those gentlemen who were owners only, who included Joseph Somes, John Willis, Duncan Dunbar, George Thompson, etc., and others, had the best of the British ships. But for the most part such importance was attached by them to safety rather than to speed, in which the American ships excelled, that in some trades, notably that with India, British ships had a preference for the conveyance of certain classes of goods over their American competitors. Speed, however, told, as it was bound to do, and American ships gradually obtained the cream of the trade in every route on which they sailed. Most of their early mistakes in shipbuilding were remedied. For one thing they had to make their vessels stronger—not all were built to defy wind and sea like the *Dreadnought*— because the cost of frequent repairs made too great an inroad into the profits, and because merchants complained that their goods were damaged in transit. Their later ships were more strongly and heavily built. They were also larger than most British vessels, and were designed and constructed both for carrying capacity and speed. Their masts and yards were longer than those of British ships in proportion to their size, and were lighter, and their cotton sails were correspondingly larger, and also lighter and were so shaped as to be as flat as possible, instead of bellying out in the fashion thought suitable for British ships. This made their sails easier to handle, especially if it became necessary to take them in in a strong wind. American captains earned and lived up to a reputation for carrying sail when it seemed impossible that masts, yards and cordage could stand the strain. Occasionally the strain was too much, and then the last stage of that ship was worse than the first.

Scores of times American ships, carrying almost everything below their royals, and sometimes with their royals set, have passed or been sighted by British ships snugged down to reefed topsails. If there was one part of the ocean which compelled American masters to shorten sail, it was that off Cape Horn, and even American vessels in trying to beat round the end of South America into the Pacific against the terrible winter gales and the heaviest seas in the world, have taken three weeks to accomplish the task and have been glad to set as little canvas as any British vessel. I remember seeing a big American trying to beat round the Horn, with only a reefed lower fore-topsail and a reefed main staysail, and she was making dirty weather of it. She was well handled, and the way she suddenly swung to the starboard tack, and the rapidity with which her yards were altered, showed that she had a good crew, and she probably had a bucko mate or two who kept the men to their work. A few days later, after we had left the Horn well behind and were in the Atlantic, we sighted another big American wooden ship bowling along

towards the Cape of Storms under her courses, topsails, and
to'gallants, and some fore-and-aft sails. She was a fine
lined vessel, with a long bowsprit and longer jibboom,
evidently built on the clipper model, and she tore along
through a smother of foam, from wave to wave, with
indescribable buoyancy, beauty and speed. I was never
able to ascertain the identity of either of these vessels.

American anxiety to retain the leadership of the shipping industry was one of the causes which led to their
undoing. They built at last more large ships than they
could run successfully and profitably. Steamships were
slowly but none the less surely establishing themselves in
the North Atlantic trade. The packets often beat the
steamers in time, and they undercut them in their charges
for freight, and were themselves undercut in freight charges
by the slower British and ordinary American ships. The
steady improvement in the size and power of the steamers
in the North Atlantic trade soon had its effect, and their
voyages were performed with greater regularity. Not only
did they take more cargo, but the numbers of their passengers increased, and the packets suffered accordingly.
The then chairman of the Liverpool Shipowners' Association, produced a return showing that in 1857 no fewer
than 74,890 passengers embarked for North America
in foreign vessels, and only 13,661 in British ships. The
great majority of the foreign vessels were Americans.

Britain could not compete against the Americans in
building good wooden ships at the price at which the
Americans could turn them out. British timber resources
had long been exhausted to meet the needs of the royal
navy, and the cost of importing suitable timber from the
Continent or India would have made the ships too
expensive. British owners at first took to chartering or

buying American-built ships, and some remarkable and historic vessels were acquired. But England had an immense reserve of coal and iron in her mines in close proximity to her shipbuilding yards, especially those of the North. Ships of iron, small at first, were constructed, and as these showed their worth, and gradually but surely overcame the prejudice with which they were greeted at first, larger ones were built. This was a field in which the Americans could not compete, especially as the iron ships could be produced more cheaply than theirs. Thus they lost the British market for ships, and Continentals began to buy second-hand British iron ships in preference to American wooden ones. Scandinavians bought any second-hand tonnage available, as long as it was cheap, and have been buying them ever since. Most of the few sailing ships still afloat are owned by Scandinavians. Steel ships followed iron ones.

The preponderance of first-class American ships and the repeal of the Navigation Laws helped to bring about an extraordinary period of depression among shipowners in Great Britain. Some sighed in vain for the return of the days when shipowning was a protected industry—" safeguarded " would be the word in these days—but the public had already begun to experience the benefit of cheaper and more varied imports, with a corresponding increase in exports, and public opinion was against any such reimposition.

The building of iron ships in Britain made considerable progress, and the only wooden ones launched were little vessels intended for the coasting trade. The Americans continued to build wooden ships, for which they had ample material, and because of their peculiar geographical situation they were able to use them in their coasting trade, and in such international trade as presented itself. Geographically, a voyage from Boston or New York to San Francisco was and is a coasting trade, and as Americans have always kept their coastal trade a close preserve for American vessels they had no competition to fear. Now a coastal voyage may start at New York, and include San Francisco, Hawaii, and the Philippines before a return is made to New York.

The Civil War in America played havoc with the American merchant service, and very few of the vessels lost were replaced. For one thing, it was found that American ships with their higher scale of pay for their crews and their better scale of food, could not be run so economically as British ships, and certainly not so cheaply as some European owners ran theirs. Americans therefore concentrated rather on the development of their coastal service, though they constructed a few very fine wooden and steel ships. The finest three-master I remember visiting was the *William H. Lincoln*, named after her owner, and captained by his brother. I think she was ultimately burnt in Sydney Harbour, N.S.W.

Among the splendid wooden ships built in America of late years, were the *Great Republic*, and some years later the *Shenandoah* and her sisters the *Roanoke* and *Susquehanna*. The *Great Republic* was McKay's masterpiece. The McKay brothers, headed by Donald, attracted attention by the splendid packets they built for Enoch Train's well-known line of packets between Boston and Liverpool, whose owner confidently expected them to beat the Cunard steamers, which they often did. When the California rush came, McKay launched a series of vessels for it, of which particulars will be found in another chapter, which established his reputation as one of the leading

AMERICAN SHIP GREAT REPUBLIC
From negative owned by F. C. B. Bradlee, Marblehead, Mass., U.S.A

shipbuilders of America. The McKays had their building-yards at Newburyport, and afterwards at East Boston. It was in honour of the McKay family that Longfellow is said to have written his famous and beautiful poem, beginning :

> "Build me straight, O worthy Master!
> Staunch and strong, a goodly vessel,
> That shall laugh at all disaster,
> And with wave and whirlwind wrestle."

To what vessel these lines especially applied, I cannot say.

The *Great Republic* merited the description, if ever a ship did, when at last she was launched. She was built at East Boston in September, 1853. Her dimensions were : length 325 feet, width 53 feet, and depth of hold 38 feet. American ships hitherto had been three masted ; the *Great Republic* was four-masted ; she was square rigged on the fore, main, and mizen masts, and fore-and-aft rigged on the spanker or jigger mast. Without entering into too technical details of her rig, it may be said that her topsail yards were on what was known as the Forbes system, after its designer, Captain R. B. Forbes, to obviate or lessen the difficulty of handling the immense single topsails then the rule. They were often the largest sails on the ship. The Forbes method was superseded by that of Captain Howes, which is practically the same as the divided topsail system of the last fifty or sixty years. When built she had four decks, the uppermost or spar deck being flush and protected by a rail. An engine of 15 horse power was carried on deck to hoist the yards and work the pumps, this being the first time an engine was shipped for these purposes. Hitherto all such work had been done by man power, but with such big yards and sails as the *Great Republic* was to have, an exceptionally large crew would have to be carried if there were no mechanical aids of this sort.

Her fore and main masts were 44 inches in diameter, her mizen mast 40 inches, and their lengths 130 feet, 131 feet, and 122 feet respectively. Her masts, according to figures published at the time and since, were over 250 feet high, and the fourth mast 150 feet. Her yards were in proportion, the fore yard being 110 feet, the main yard 120 feet, and the crossjack 90 feet ; the other yards were correspondingly long. Her rigging was of a substantial character to match her masts and yards.

It was intended to put her into the Australian trade, to compete against the best British ships then being built for that service. She was rigged and loaded for Liverpool at New York, and when almost ready for sea she was partly destroyed by fire. It broke out in a building some distance from where she lay, but the wind carried blazing fragments and sparks and dropped them on the ship, and on two other vessels, the *Joseph Walker* and *White Squall*. She was soon ablaze, her rigging and sails catching first, and it was not until the foremast was cut away and allowed to fall over the side into the water that the firemen were able to attack the flames. After some hours work in the night they overcame the fire on deck and left the vessel. When the burning foretopmast came down it crushed into the deck, and it was afterwards found that the cargo had been set alight. It then became necessary to scuttle the vessel as she lay in order to extinguish the flames. She burned herself out almost to the water's edge. Both the *Joseph Walker* and *White Squall* were destroyed by the fire.

The wreck was sold by the underwriters, to whom it had been abandoned, and they sold it in turn, and the Low

Brothers bought it. She was rebuilt, but her spar deck was not restored, nor were her masts and yards as large as before. Her sail plan was cut down also, and she was given divided topsails on Captain Howes' system. In her new guise she registered 3,357 tons, and required a far smaller crew, having now sixty-five all told.

She made her first voyage in February, 1855, running from Sandy Hook to Land's End in thirteen days. At one time she was chartered by the French Government to take troops to the Crimea, and during the American civil war she had another spell of trooping for the North. A Liverpool firm, the Merchants' Trading Company, bought her in 1869, and changed her name to *Denmark*. She made some good passages, as it was expected she would do seeing who her builder was, but she did not prove herself the fastest ship afloat. Perhaps she might have done so, had it not been for the fire and the consequent reduction of her sail area.

Great regret was expressed in American maritime circles when it was learnt in 1908 that her owners had decided to sell the four-masted barque *Shenandoah* to the United States Government to be used as a coal hulk at San Francisco. A New York paper wrote of her as the " last of the famous wooden vessels created in a Maine shipyard, and one of the proudest craft that ever graced the American merchant marine." It has been stated that she was the biggest wooden ship ever built in America, but a comparison of her dimensions with those of the *Great Republic* shows that the latter was considerably larger. She was 299 feet in length, 49 feet beam, and of 3407 tons gross. She was built in 1890, by her owners, Messrs. Arthur Sewall and Company, of Bath, Maine. She had no fewer than eighteen square sails, including three skysails, besides staysails, headsails, spanker and two spanker topsails, spreading altogether over 11,000 square yards of canvas. She was not built specially for speed but her fine lines, for in this respect she was like other American ships, and her immense spread of sails enabled her to hold her own against all sailing competitors. One peculiarity was that unlike most American ships, she had a long steel bowsprit but no jibboom. She was built of oak. The experiment of building a large wooden vessel to compete against the steel sailers of Great Britain was watched with a good deal of interest on both sides of the Atlantic. She is said to have " made a regular business of whipping British, French and German ships that attempted to compete against her on long voyages."

During the Spanish-American war she showed the Spaniards what she could do. In July, 1898, while she was loading coal at Liverpool for San Francisco, Captain James F. Murphy, her master, received cabled instructions from the owners to increase the insurance lest she should be captured by the Spaniards. Captain Murphy thought that guns would come cheaper, and bought two four-inch rifles, one of which he mounted forward and the other aft. When four days out from Liverpool and off the south-west coast of Ireland, a Spanish gunboat appeared abeam and fired across the ship's bows as a signal to her to heave to. Captain Murphy hoisted the Stars and Stripes and replied with two solid shot from his guns and held his ship on her course. She had a good wind and all sail set, and was logging fifteen miles an hour, and outsailed the Spanish gunboat, but it took her four hours to get out of sight of her.

When she first appeared at New York and moored in East River, to load for San Francisco, there were then in port at New York 117 steamers, 43 ships, 79 barques, and 19 brigs, besides several schooners. When she was last at New York, in 1907, there were in port 131 steamers, seven ships, 27 barques, and two brigs. In 1878 brigs and brigantines under the American flag numbered about 700 ; by 1908 the number had sunk to eleven, of which seven were on the Pacific coast and four on the Atlantic coast. This will help to show how steadily and rapidly the number of ships had been diminishing.

Other exploits of the *Shenandoah* were when she went from the Golden Gate to Sandy Hook in ninety-six days, a performance which was within a few hours of the best authentic clipper record ; her victory in a sea race from San Francisco to Havre against five other vessels, none American, which she won, doing the voyage in the excellent time of 109 days ; and her match against the Belfast built ship *California*, when she overtook the latter, after giving her 10 days' start, and arrived first in a voyage from San Francisco to the United Kingdom. Ship captains sometimes boasted about the capabilities of their vessels, and the captain of the *California* is said to have asserted that he never saw the wind that would make him take in his royals. The *Shenandoah* overhauled her one Sunday morning off the Irish coast, and found that the *California* had taken in her royals, though the *Shenandoah* was still carrying hers and had a main skysail up as well. Captain Murphy afterwards said that may have been the only time the *California* had to douse her kites, but he caught her napping. Whether she was a profitable ship her owners alone know. In her short, active career she sailed between New York, Liverpool, Baltimore, San Francisco, Yokohama, Port Gamble, Port Blakely, Port Pirie, Newcastle, N.S.W., and Sydney, N.S.W., and once put into Melbourne

and once into Valparaiso for repairs. On all of her fastest
runs Captain Murphy had her ; he was always accompanied
by his wife, who was called his mascot. Altogether Captain
Murphy rounded the Horn over fifty times in his career
as master and mate. Not many " Cape Horners " have a
record like that.

Shipping Illustrated of New York records that " It was
an ordinary thing for the *Shenandoah*, with her canvas
spread to the last inch of even fore and main lower stunsails to log upwards of 300 knots in a single day. When
the *Shenandoah* raced the five foreign ships, three of which
were British, she had 5,300 tons of wheat as cargo, the
biggest shipment ever taken to France from San Francisco
in one vessel. Several days during the voyage the Maine
ship reeled off 298 knots, and for 20 successive days her
average was 278.

As to her sisters, both were lost at sea.

The Americans also built some very fine steel ships, one
or two of which are still to be found laid up at San Francisco.

American ship builders, on both the Atlantic and
Pacific coasts, specialised in fore-and-aft schooners, and
turned out some remarkable and beautiful vessels. Not
that all were schooners, however. The barque was trans-
formed into a barquentine, which had all the advantages
of the barque and some of her own. The brig became the
brigantine or hermaphrodite brig, but whether the Americans originated her is a point not always credited to them.
Both barquentine and brigantine were very easily handled,
and they required smaller crews than barques and brigs.

Schooners at first were small, mostly from 50 to 100 tons,
and were two-masted and carried square topsails, such as
most British coasting schooners do to this day. In time

the Americans found that the fore-and-aft schooner was preferable to any other rig for their coasting trade, and the square sails were dispensed with. The limit of size of such vessels was about 250 to 300 tons ; above that, their spars were too heavy to be handled well, and even 300 ton schooners earned the ugly name of " man-killers." The biggest two-masted schooner is said to have been the *Oliver Ames*, 456 tons, a New England collier. The three-masted schooner had these advantages over the two-masted of equal tonnage : her canvas was divided into more sails which were therefore easier to handle, and her spars were lighter, and she could therefore be worked with a smaller crew. The three-masters grew in size until the *Bradford C. French* appeared, of 968 tons. A three-masted schooner much smaller than this was very unwieldy, and schooners with four, five and six masts were built. One four-master, the *Haroldine*, 1361 tons, launched in 1884, went to China and Australia. The first five-master was the *Governor Ames*, of 1778 tons ; she went round the Horn from New York to San Francisco. The biggest five-masters were the *John B. Prescott*, 2454 tons and *Nathaniel T. Palmer*, 2440 tons, both launched in 1898. Six-masted schooners appeared in 1900, the principal being *Eleanor A. Percy*, 3401 tons, of Bath, and the *George W. Wells*, 2970 tons, of Boston ; there were very few six-masters. These were all wooden vessels, as wooden vessels could be built far more cheaply in America than steel ones of equal size. Only one seven-masted schooner has been built, and her life was comparatively short. This was the *Thomas W. Lawson*. She was designed by Mr. B. B. Crowninshield, of Boston, who also designed the six-master *W. L. Douglas* and several other of the largest schooners. At the time the *Thomas W. Lawson* was launched, it was stated that her masts were 195 feet high, of which 135 feet was a steel lower mast in each case, and that the wooden topmasts were each sixty feet in length. Mr. Crowninshield, when asked to give the exact figures, replied : " The *Lawson's* spars were very similar in dimensions to those of the other large colliers. When loaded it was 160 feet from the water to the level of her trucks, 112 feet to the upper caps on the mast heads, and 101 feet to the trestle trees. Her masts were stepped 48 feet apart. She was 404 feet over all, 50 feet beam, and 33 feet deep. When fully loaded she drew 28 feet of water, and when sailing light with water ballast tanks full, 12 feet. Seven lower sails and three jibs measured 25,900 square feet ; with topsails, staysails and two outer jibs, her area of canvas was more than 40,000 square feet." The *Lawson* was built of steel.

She was lost in 1908 near the entrance to the English Channel.

Scores of American full-rigged ships were sold foreign, mostly to German and Norwegian owners, and were generally given fresh names. I saw two of them, then known as the *Wolf* and the *Fidelio*, in the Regent's Canal dock a few years before the War. There was no mistaking them, though they had been turned into barques ; the *Fidelio* was formerly the *Winona*, and was built at Newburyport as far back as 1862. Her captain, who permitted me to go over her, and acted as guide, told me that she was still a fast vessel, but that on account of her age he could not press her to get the speed out of her that she used to show.

While the Americans confined their attention to wooden vessels the British developed the iron shipbuilding industry to such an extent that they began to monopolise a very large share of the sea-carriage of the world. The British Islands owned thousands of handy little ships and barques,

AMERICAN SEVEN-MASTED SCHOONER THOMAS W. LAWSON

(By courtesy of " Syren and Shipping ")

Facing page 134

some of the latter being of no more than five or six hundred tons ; they went everywhere it was possible for a sailer to push her nose into, and except for protected coastal trades in various parts of the world, there were no trade routes and no ports where they were not to be found. Take it all round they earned good money, too. The new Board of Trade rules had come into force, the ships were well equipped, the old " coffins " that were a disgrace to their owners and the nation had disappeared because they could not stand the test of a survey for seaworthiness, and the ships were captained and officered by men who had passed their examinations, and had crews mostly of Britishers and Scandinavians with very few dagos or Southern Europeans.

The builders put good work and plenty of material into the iron ships of those days. Calculations had not been made to ascertain the minimum of material that could be employed in a ship of a given size, and the ships and barques were as strong and staunch as could be wished. They were practically all clipper bowed with fine lines, though not so fine as the Americans liked to have their vessels ; not many, too, were given skysails and other handkerchiefs to wave in the clouds. After the tea races from China were ended the practice of carrying stunsails gradually declined.

The French tried subsidies to bolster up the French mercantile marine, but without much success. One result of the attempt was that a French vessel could go round the world, and call at two or three ports, and come home without having earned her expenses, but the voyage, owing to the subsidy, would show a profit. In all other European maritime countries, the sailing ship tonnage showed a decline in the fourth quarter of the last century but so late as 1910 the French sailing fleet stood practically where it did in the 'eighties. British sailing tonnage dropped from 3,851,045 tons in 1880 to 1,101,494 tons in 1910, and that of Germany dropped from 965,757 tons in 1880 to 506,837 tons in 1910. The French, however, had 541,539 net register tons of sailing ships in 1880, and 636,041 tons in 1910. The subsidies were to be paid in respect of each vessel for a certain number of years. As soon as the subsidies began to stop the ships were sold. Various arrangements were tried to keep alive the French sea-going merchant service. As the law stood when the war broke out, a sailing ship of 2,500 tons, working three hundred days in the year, would receive an annual sub-vention of 22,500 francs.

In regard to the *France*, the largest sailing ship in the world, little was heard of her during the war. When peace came she was put in commission again. In 1919 she was chartered to take coal from the Tyne to America, and left early in December of that year in tow of tugs. Having got her clear of the land, the tugs left her, except the big French tug *Joffre*, which was to take her as far as the Lizard. A few hours after she left the Tyne it was reported that she and the tug had parted company, through the tow-ropes carrying away in a gale off Flamborough Head. She was then stated to be on her beam ends, but this was an exaggeration. As nothing was heard of her for some days, it was feared that she was lost together with her crew of fifty-five men besides the captain and his wife. However, she was sighted some thirty miles south of Flamborough Head, making bad weather of it. The next heard of her was when she arrived in the Firth of Forth a week later, for repairs. These having been effected, she made another start, and this time made a good voyage.

FRENCH FIVE-MASTED BARQUE FRANCE

Photo by R. A. Fletcher

Facing page 136

The *France* attracted a great deal of attention when she visited London a few years ago. There was a steady stream of persons interested in shipping, and of others who did not know the bow of a vessel from her stern, to the Surrey Commercial Docks, to see this wonderful ship. I visited her twice. One thing that impressed me was the thoroughness of her equipment, the owners having installed everything they could to add to her efficiency. Her captain told me her engines had been removed. She was lost a year or two afterwards, shortly after leaving New Caledonia with a cargo of iron ore for Europe ; the winds and ocean currents in that part of the world have an unpleasant knack of varying suddenly, and it is supposed that she was piled up on a reef by one of these currents. She was a vessel of 5633 tons gross register, and 418 feet in length. She carried on four of her five masts divided topsails and divided topgallants, but had no royals.

Up to the middle of the last century, the Germans had no merchant service of their own worth speaking about, though Bremen and Hamburg and one or two of the Baltic ports had a few small ships. When the Germans decided to develop their mercantile marine they began by buying American and British ships, especially the British iron ones. With these as models they began to build for themselves, and ultimately owned some of the finest sailers afloat. By their laws, German ships had to have German crews. Nearly the whole of their trade was between German ports and foreign ports and back again to Germany. The German ships were not ocean tramps in the sense that many British ships were, picking up a cargo wherever they could. The German built ships were chiefly intended for certain trades, and were equipped accordingly. Those of the famous

" P " line, so-called because their names began with that
letter, owned by the Laeisz firm of Hamburg, most of
which were constructed in Germany, were employed chiefly
in bringing nitrate from the West Coast of South America
to Hamburg. Not infrequently they went out in water
ballast, which brought them down to first-class sailing
trim, and they were far better able to beat round Cape
Horn than the average British vessel laden down to
her Plimsoll marks or in ordinary ballast, in neither case
able to avoid having a rough time in beating round the
Horn into the Pacific. The German ships were specially
built to contend against the westerly gales of that part of
the world, and those British writers who tried to make out
that the German ships and sailors were better than the
British ought to have taken all the circumstances into
consideration.

The *Preussen*, the largest of them all, was a very fine
vessel. She was built of steel, and had five masts, and was
square-rigged on all five. She was built in Germany in
1902, and was of 5081 tons, with a cargo capacity of about
8000 tons ; her length was 438 feet, breadth 54 feet, and
depth from deck to keel amidships 33 feet 9 inches. On
all five masts she carried double topsails and double topgallant sails. The masts, yards and bowsprit were made of
steel. She carried no fewer than forty-five sails, without
counting spare sails. Her lower yards were 102 feet 6
inches in length, and her main royal yard 50 feet. The
greatest diameter of the lower masts was 36 inches, of
the lower yards 25 inches and a half, and of the bowsprit
36 inches and a half. It is interesting to compare some of
these figures with the corresponding spars of the great
American ships. The total length of the cordage employed
in the rigging of this ship was over eighteen miles. She had

six anchors, the largest of which weighed four tons, and the anchor chains and anchors weighed altogether sixty-six tons. She carried two steam boilers in a house on deck, to be used for pumping out the water ballast tanks, and working the anchors, winches and steering gear. She made her two voyages out and home a year between Hamburg and the west coast with great regularity until 1908, when her route was changed and on March 10th of that year she sailed from Hamburg for New York to load case oil for Japan.

Another remarkable sailing ship, also German, is the *Potosi*, sailing under the Laeisz flag ; she is five-masted, but is fore-and-aft rigged on the fifth mast, and is known as a five-masted barque, and by the Americans as a five-masted shipentine. She was built at the same yard as the *Preussen* but in 1895, and is of slightly less tonnage, being 5026 gross. Her length is 366 feet, her breadth 49 feet, and her depth 28 feet. She is, I believe, the only five-masted sailing vessel to carry square rig, unless one may count a vessel having an auxiliary engine as a sailer. In this case the German five-masted barque *R. C. Rickmers* must be included ; she was built in 1906 at Bremerhaven by the Rickmers firm, and has a gross tonnage of 5548 as a steamer and 5400 as a sailer, and in that case is the largest sailer in the world. The German government also gave financial help to its shipbuilding industry.

In the early days of iron shipbuilding, the industry flourished in many ports round the British Isles. Then most of the vessels were small, from three hundred to five or six hundred tons, but as the demand grew for larger ships only the larger yards could compete for the orders, and the smaller yards gradually became deserted. This process continued until the building of the largest iron and steel ships was confined practically to Liverpool, New-castle, the Wear, the Clyde, Belfast, Londonderry, South-ampton, Aberdeen and Dundee. Orders fell off, and the builders devoted attention to steamers.

The number of firms who became owners of sailing ships was legion. Some of the owners made enough out of their little sailing ships to sell them and to retire—for those were the days when freights were remunerative even for small ships. Foreigners bought hundreds cheap. As larger ships proved more remunerative, and the science of shipbuilding improved, still larger vessels were constructed, but freights began to decline, and the demand for the smaller vessels dropped until there was little employment to be obtained for them at a price which would pay.

Iron ships, in spite of their greater durability and the greater facility with which they could generally be repaired, were stated to be subject to accidents to a greater extent than wooden vessels. The many disasters led to a report by the Chief Surveyor of Lloyd's and his assistants on a letter received from Lloyd's Agency at Melbourne on the dismasting of iron sailing ships. The report, dated December 14th, 1874, stated that of nine vessels dismasted within the last twelve months, nine were new vessels on their first voyage, and built by experienced builders in different parts of the country, including Liverpool, the Clyde, the Tyne, and the Wear. Seven were bound for Australia, one for San Francisco, and the others for ports in the East. The nine on their first voyage were the *Loch Ard*, 1693 tons (twice dismasted) ; *John Kerr*, 1864 tons ; *Cambridge-shire*, 1766 tons ; *Chrysomene*, 1835 tons ; *Loch Maree*, 1657 tons ; *British Admiral*, 1808 tons ; and *Norval*, 1503 tons, all built in 1873, and the *Rydal Hall*, 1864 tons, and *Duchess of Edinburgh*, 1766 tons, both built in 1874.

The other two in the list were older vessels, the *Dallam Tower*, 1499 tons, built in 1866, and the *Rooparell*, 1097 tons, built in 1868.

The causes assigned by the Melbourne surveyors were :

That the vessels were overladen.

That the stowage of iron was too low, thus making the vessels too laboursome.

That the vessels were overmasted, the masts being too taut, considering the spread of rigging and weight of yards.

That sufficient care had not been taken in staying the masts, or in the strength of head gear.

That the masts were not stiff enough at the deck, and in one case that the material was defective.

The Melbourne agent did not indicate to which ship each of these opinions applied. Dealing with the third clause, Lloyd's Surveyors reported :

" The fact that these modern iron sailing ships possess sufficient strength and stability to carry very great areas of sails and attain high speed has led to the masts and yards being much increased in length and consequent weight. The fitting of double topsail and topgallant yards has added still further to the topweight, and from their great height materially increased the strain. At the same time, instead of the greatest possible spread of rigging being obtained to compensate for these additions to the strain, the shrouds are secured on the inside of the vessel, whereas formerly in large sailing ships (and in the Government service still) guard boards or channels were fitted, which admitted of the shrouds passing outside of the rails. . . . It is greatly to be feared that many recent disastrous cases show that additional strength is needed generally in the masts and standing rigging, as well as greater care in the fittings, to enable vessels of this magnitude to pass successfully through the heavy gales to which they are sometimes exposed."

The report, after making several recommendations, says in its concluding paragraph : " Much will still depend upon the skill and judgment of those in command of these large vessels to prevent accidents. The inducement to make quick passages is fostered where so many similar ships are engaged on the same voyage, and there can be little doubt that a spirit of emulation often induces captains to carry on with a full spread of sail long after it is safe and prudent to do so. Formerly a limit was provided to the amount of sail that it was considered right to carry in any particular weather, by the straining, as well as by the heeling of wooden vessels. In a modern iron ship no such straining is visible, and if the vessel is excessively stiff and does not heel much no direct warning is conveyed until something gives way aloft, or until it has become so late that, with the limited number of men available, sail cannot be shortened in time to relieve the masts and rigging."

From this last passage it would appear that insufficient crews were not unknown on sailing ships even in those days.

Probably this report had some effect, for the number of such disasters in the years following seems to have been rather less.

Though it is impossible to mention a hundredth of the ships which were employed in the sea-carrying trade in the middle and later parts of the last century, a reference to a few of them may be interesting, as tending to show what the conditions of their employment were like, and what they were like themselves. As already stated, the most successful ships were those which made the best voyages with the fewest incidents. Ships which earned a reputation for carrying away masts or yards, or straining themselves, or delivering cargo in a more or less damaged condition, were not popular with shippers or passengers ; and it did not take much in the way of accidents to put intending passengers off going on a vessel which had experienced one or two mishaps. Cargo, however, was a different matter. Unless there was something special about a consignment, shippers would accept the most suitable vessel and protect themselves by insurance.

Some proprietories had extraordinary good luck, and others the reverse. It was the same with ships ; some had one or more accidents every voyage, and some never had a serious accident throughout their career. Carrying away a sail or two, or losing a yard were not reckoned serious, but the loss of a mast might easily result in grave injury. An apparently trivial accident, or what to a landsman might appear trivial, might endanger the ship. The carrying away of the bobstay, or of the foretopmast stay, thus depriving the bowsprit of part of its support, or the breaking of the foretopmast stay, depriving the foretopmast of its support, might bring about the fall of the topmast and all the yards above it, and there have been many instances where this has happened and it has caused the maintopmast to come down too, leaving the ship little better than disabled—and all through the snapping of one rope to begin with. The various parts of the rigging of a ship are all mutually supporting, and no one can suffer without imperilling others. This was unquestionably the case in the old wooden ships with their hempen rigging ; when iron and steel ships came in, with their steel rigging, the danger was the greater, because these vessels were often heavily laden, and were stiffer, and in their rolling had a greater tendency to come back with a jerk and possibly carry something away. As metal shipbuilding improved, however, many of the defects were remedied ; experience taught both designers and builders, and every effort was made to produce ships as safe and strong as it was possible to make them. Some of the later Mersey and Clyde built four-posters were not so heavily " top-hatted " as their predecessors, that is, they had not such long spars in proportion to their size, and they were all the better in consequence. Nor were the vessels built so narrow in proportion to their length.

Take the Liverpool three-masted ship *Glenlui* and her experiences. She was built long and narrow, after the fashion of 1884, and was heavily sparred, carrying double topsails and double topgallants on every mast. Captain R. C. Scott, a most able navigator and seaman, was in command. When she was towed into Port Chalmers, New Zealand, in May, 1907, on her way from Adelaide to England with wheat, all her boats had been washed away, except two, one of which was smashed to pieces and lay stove in on the skids, and neither was of any use whatever. The ship was deep in the water, and her decks were littered with rubbish. Sea after sea had swept over her, carrying away the rails and binnacle from the flying bridge, the poop ladders had been torn away together with portions of the deck where they were attached, the steering wheel was smashed, the poop rails were bent or broken away, furled sails were blown out of the gaskets (or ropes which bound them to the yards), cordage was snapped in all directions, and the topsails were blown out of the bolt-ropes and torn to shreds.

When the gale first struck her, on a Sunday, the *Glenlui* ran before it. Enormous waves broke over the stern.

At 10 p.m. two men were lashed to the wheel, and soon afterwards a tremendous sea washed over the stern, washing half the wheel with a man lashed to it, to the top of the cabin skylight ; when released it was found he had broken his hand. . The next sea that came over broke away the other half. The wheel being gone, two men steered with the tiller, and Captain Scott managed to bring the vessel to the wind. Several more accidents followed, and it was thought the ship was sinking. Seas swept over her from forward and rushed along the deck and stove in the doors leading to the cabin, filling the whole place with water, which reached to the skylight and nearly drowned the occupants. The second mate was twice washed out of his bunk, a top one. The steward was caught near the door when the waves smashed it in, and carried along the passage, through the saloon, and bumped against a bicycle hanging at the extreme end of the saloon. The smashed doors were buttressed up from within, and other repairs effected, and the wheel was replaced by a contrivance consisting of iron bars ringed with wire rope.

When the gale was at its worst, notwithstanding that everybody gave up the ship for lost, they all worked their hardest to bring her through if possible, under the direction of Captain Scott and his officers, and it is owing to their splendid seamanship that the vessel was saved. On the Monday the foretopmast staysail sheet parted, and the mate and boatswain went forward and succeeded in furling the sail. They had nearly gained the comparative safety of the poop when a huge sea came over the starboard quarter, and carried the mate over the side. Lines were thrown to him, but they fell short. One of those on board, describing the scene, says : " His face under his sou'wester was visible for a little with a look of pathetic despair, and then he sank. He was clothed in heavy seaboots and oilskins, which fettered his movements. Nothing could have been done to save him." He was a Carnarvon man, named Evan Hugh Jones, and was only 29 years of age. He joined the *Glenlui* at Adelaide from another vessel. Captain Scott, a Liverpool man, had at that time thirty-eight years' service in sailing ships.

That the perils of the sea are not confined to dirty weather was proved by the American ship *Eclipse*. She had about as uncanny an experience as can befall a ship when she was taking coal from Newcastle, N.S.W., to Honolulu. After losing the trade winds she went into one of those scorching hot calms for which the Pacific is notorious. Every available sail, even to three skysails, was set, and the sea was so smooth that it seemed to be asleep. At noon all hands were sent to dinner. About a quarter of an hour later there was a report like a cannon shot ; the mizen royal was split from head to foot. The mate ordered a man aloft to stow the sail and to be "lively." John Nicholson, who had the reputation of being the first aloft and the last at meals, went up the rigging, and the mate returned below to finish his interrupted dinner.

The captain would not believe that the sail had split. "In a calm like this ? What split it ? " he demanded incredulously, and not being satisfied with the mate's explanation, started to go on deck to see for himself. When he was about half way up the companion ladder leading to the poop, the ship shook convulsively, accompanied by a tremendous bang and a noise like the cracking of wood, and the captain found himself shot backwards to the cabin floor. He was not hurt, and jumping to his feet and with the two mates, rushed on deck with the steward at their heels. The main royal mast was broken at the hounds or cap, and dangling with the royal and skysail yards. Steel shrouds and stays were severed all over the ship as though made of string, braces, sheets, and halliards were snapped, and no fewer than thirteen sails were reduced to ribbons, and a great deal of other damage was done. The ship was filled with water to the bulwarks. John Nicholson had vanished. The only explanation offered is that the ship was struck by a waterspout which formed suddenly alongside, but this is only conjecture. At the New York Maritime Exchange it was remarked that John Nicholson was the only man who saw what happened, and he had not survived to tell. It is a curious coincidence that the *Eclipse* was lost about the end of 1907, within a hundred miles of the spot where she went through this experience, and that her crew only reached Honolulu in January, 1908, after great privations which caused the death of three of them.

Probably the longest direct voyage which any sailing ships made in the ordinary course of commerce was from British Columbia to England ; to do this they had to sail the length of the Pacific, round Cape Horn, and then up the Atlantic. There have been such voyages when not a ship has been sighted and no land has been seen from the time she left port until the English Channel has been reached, a period of five months' loneliness. A common round voyage for many ships which took goods from Britain to Australia, was to go thence with coal to San Francisco or the west coast of South America, and there load with a fresh cargo for this country. The regular traders to Australia, however, generally took out a mixed cargo and several passengers, and returned to this country with Colonial produce, mostly wheat or wool, and some passengers, making the homeward voyage either by the Cape of Good Hope or by way of Cape Horn, in the latter case giving the passengers a taste of running down the eastings when the ship got into the high latitudes of the 'forties and 'fifties, where the westerly gales sweep uninterruptedly round the world.

CHAPTER V

OPIUM AND TEA CLIPPERS

THE first so-called clippers were probably the schooners and other small vessels launched at Baltimore prior to the war of 1812. They were of a distinct type of hull, with raking masts, and carried an enormous spread of canvas ; they were particularly useful to the Americans as privateers, because they were fast in all weathers, and could be heavily armed, and many did good service as privateers, and others bad service as pirates and slavers.

While it may be admitted that the opium trade in China was a disgrace to those who carried it on, there is no denying that the vessels employed in it were splendid craft of their kind, and admirably suited to their purpose, and were superbly handled. They were small vessels ; there was only one fully ship-rigged vessel among them, the remainder being brigs and schooners, with a few small barques. They carried double crews.

The trade was conducted with four sets of vessels, three of which were specially designed and constructed for the purpose. Fast clippers took the drug at all seasons and in all weathers from Indian ports to certain rendezvous, where the cargo was transferred to receiving ships, mostly old Indiamen, which were heavily armed ; from these it was carried to the Chinese coast in small fast sailers, and again transferred to other fast vessels for distribution. This was the riskiest part of the work, for the little vessels had to navigate unknown waters and inlets, with the ever-present danger of being attacked and looted, if opportunity arose, by the very Chinese with whom they were dealing. That, and the necessity of being able to repair damage at sea, rendered it necessary for very large and thoroughly competent crews to be carried.

The *Falcon* was once a yacht belonging to Lord Yarborough, commodore of the Royal Yacht Squadron, and carried several guns ; she was of 350 tons. She took part in the battle of Navarino in 1827. Her owner sold her to a firm who sent her to India, where she was sold again to Jardine Matheson and Company, who refitted her for the opium trade.

The American opium clippers were probably the fastest employed in this nefarious trade. The real rivalry between the English and Americans over the clippers began in the opium trade with China, and the vessels engaged in it may be accurately described as the first of the clippers. The British, who were the first in it, soon found the need of much faster vessels than they had been employing. Three English schooners, the *Jamesina*, 382 tons, formerly the naval gun brig, *Curlew*, the *Sylph*, of 305 tons, built at Calcutta and owned by a native firm in the opium trade, and the *Lord Amherst*, were active in the opium trade as early as 1831. The *Jamesina* is credited with having sold £330,000 worth of opium at Chinese ports in one year, which showed an enormous profit.

Seeing there was money to be made, the Americans joined in, sending a 90 tons schooner, the *Angola*—the name is also given as *Anglona*—from New York to Hong Kong for Russell and Company, of that port, in 1841.

The following year the schooners *Zephyr*, 150 tons, *Mazeppa*, 175 tons, and *Ariel*, 101 tons, came from America, and being very successful became known as the opium clippers. The brig *Antelope* arrived on the scene in 1843. When the *Ariel* arrived she raced the *Angola* and beat her by seventeen minutes, winning a wager of a thousand dollars.

The *Antelope* was attacked on one voyage when she was among the Ladrone Islands, by Chinese. Two long mandarin boats, heavily manned, rowed out towards her, and the Captain of the *Antelope* let drive at them with his " Long Tom," whereupon they retired. Later the *Antelope* was becalmed, and the Chinese, strongly reinforced, came out in four boats, there being perhaps three hundred of them. A shot or two from " Long Tom " did no harm, and the pirates advanced and fired their swivel guns at the vessel without causing injury. The crew of the *Antelope* triced up the boarding nettings, which delayed the pirates who had not expected this obstacle, and " Long Tom " sent a shot through a boat and injured some of the men in her. The crews of the other three boats tried to climb on board over the bows, but the sailors greeted them with a volley of pistol shots, and about a dozen fell back into their boats. Then the invaders were met with pikes, and a stiff hand to hand fight followed. A section of the pirates drifted in a boat to the stern of the ship and attempted to board her, but the cook repulsed them with a bucket of boiling water. The captain seized a bucket of boiling water and went forward and threw it among the Chinese there, who did not like it, and retreated and were driven off the vessel. The wind rose, and the *Antelope* was able to sail out of danger.

On her next passage the *Antelope* was again attacked. This time her captain ran down two of the mandarin boats and left their crews to do the best they could for themselves, and sailed his ship into Macao roads with a Chinaman dangling at each yard arm as a warning. The smuggling of the opium cargoes into China before the receiving ships were established was seldom accomplished without a fight with the Chinese under the control of the mandarins.

The superiority of the American opium clippers over the British induced the owners of the latter to have some vessels specially built for this trade. One of them, the *Torrington*, was built in 1846 by Alexander Hall and Company, of Aberdeen, who gave her a bow of the shape for which Hall's clippers were famous in later years. This was the first British opium clipper in those seas. Several other schooners followed, including the *Wild Dayrell*, of 253 tons, and the *Eamont* of a little over 200 tons, both built by White, of Cowes, for Dent and Company. They were all well armed. They all earned a lot of money for their owners. About 1850 steamers began to share in the opium trade, and in a few years took the places entirely of the sailers.

Up to 1834, when the China monopoly of the East India Company was ended, John Company's ships were alone allowed to convey tea and other Chinese produce from Chinese ports to Britain. They were painfully slow. Just before the charter expired the Company built a few ships which displayed a good turn of speed. The *Thames*, for instance, left Canton on November 18th, 1831, and arrived in England after a passage of 115 days. The *Buckinghamshire* and *Waterloo* left Canton on October 31st, and were both off the Lizard on February 9th. For many years the tea trade was not a large one, but as more treaty ports were opened tea for export became available in larger quantities. The Americans put several ships into the China trade which were larger and faster than any British vessels, and out-sailed them every time. The superiority of the American ships gave them almost a monopoly of the trade.

One remarkable vessel was the *Ann McKim*, in which an attempt was made to embody the shape of the fast Baltimore clipper schooners in a full-rigged ship. She was of 493 tons, and measured 143 feet in length, 31 feet beam, and 14 feet depth, and was considered a big ship in those days. Her sails included skysails and royal stunsails on every mast. As a sailer she was very fast, but her carrying capacity was small. She was certainly put in the China trade, but it cannot be claimed for her that she started the clipper ship era, though seeing that she passed to the ownership of Messrs. Howland and Aspinwall, of New York, who later ordered the first extreme clipper, the *Rainbow*, she may have had some influence on the design of that vessel.

The real American clipper bow is said to have been designed by John W. Griffeths, a naval draughtsman of New York. He proposed many improvements in ship design. Among them he urged that the stem should be carried well forward in a curve, instead of being nearly upright. His proposal meant the lengthening of the bow above water, which involved a finer entrance, the bows being wedge-shaped instead of bluff ; he went further and introduced long hollow lines and placed the greatest breadth of the vessel further aft than had been the custom. He also modified the shape of the stern, by rounding it, instead of maintaining the old heavy square transome.

The first vessel of the extreme clipper type to be built on these lines was the *Rainbow*, of 750 tons. She was constructed by Messrs. Smith and Dimon, of New York, to the order of Messrs. Howland and Aspinwall, and launched in 1845. Notwithstanding that the many innovations in her had been freely criticised, and that there had been not a few prophesies that she would not be able to sail well, she proved a satisfactory and fast ship. Captain John Land, her master, asserted she was the fastest ship in the world. The *Rainbow*, when under Captain Hayes, left New York for Valparaiso in 1848, and was never heard of again.

In the middle 'forties the Americans built a number of ships for the trade with China. One, the *Paul Jones*, of 620 tons, launched in 1842, had Captain N. B. Palmer in command on her first voyage and went from Boston to Hong Kong in 111 days. A few years later she went from Java Head to New York in 76 days. The *Houqua*, 706 tons, launched in 1844, sailed on her first voyage from New York to Hong Kong in 84 days, and in 1850 she is said to have done the passage from Shanghai to New York in 88 days.

Two vessels began to make remarkable sailing ship history. The *Natchez*, a former New Orleans packet, built in 1831, had a reputation for being a slow sailer. As she was built for the New Orleans trade, she was flat-bottomed and shallow, so as to be able to cross the bar which existed at the mouth of the Mississippi before Captain Eads showed how the obstruction could be dealt with. This vessel was placed by Aspinwall under the command of Robert H. Waterman, later notorious as " Bully Waterman," one of the most extraordinary men who ever trod a deck. With this unpromising vessel Waterman laid the foundation of his reputation as a shipdriver. With Waterman in command the *Natchez* went from New York to the west coast of South America, and thence to Canton to load tea for

GROUP OF SAILING SHIPS IN REGENT'S CANAL DOCK
Photo by R. A. Fletcher

New York. The passage from China was made in 94 days, and the round trip occupied less than ten months. Her second voyage was also remarkable for her fast times, and on her last voyage under Waterman she went direct from New York to Hong Kong via Cape Horn in 104 days, and back in 83 days.

These performances induced the owners of the *Natchez* to build a ship especially for Waterman, which should surpass the *Rainbow* herself. This was the famous *Sea Witch*, built by Smith and Dimon. Her tonnage is variously given as 890 and 907. She was 170 feet in length, 33 feet 11 inches beam, and 19 feet deep, and her cargo capacity was 1,100 tons. All the details of sails, spars and rigging were superintended by Waterman personally. She had skysails, royal stunsails, and square lower stunsails, with swinging booms, besides such fancy canvas as ringtail and watersails. Her hull, as was the custom with American ships, was painted black, her masts had considerable rake, and her figurehead was a great Chinese dragon carved and gilded. Her officers and crew, several of whom had sailed with Waterman in the *Natchez*, consisted exclusively of picked men.

She sailed from New York on December 23rd, 1846, and at once encountered a north-west gale in which her behaviour convinced those on board of her sea-going qualities. She ran to Rio in 25 days, and reached Hong Kong 104 days after leaving New York. On the homeward voyage she ran from Canton to New York in 81 days. Her second voyage from New York to Hong Kong occupied 105 days, and the return run from Canton to her home port was made in 78 days. On her third voyage she went from New York to Valparaiso in 69 days, from the Chilian port to Hong Kong in 52 days, and from Canton to New York in 79 days. After this voyage she was under Captain George Frazer, who was mate under Waterman, and was not so speedy ; possibly she was feeling the effects of the hard driving Waterman had given her. On her fifth, sixth and seventh voyages she ran from New York to San Francisco in 97 days, 110 days, and 108 days, but the homeward voyages from China to New York were not equal to those when she was under Captain Waterman.

Other famous American clippers of those days in the China trade were the *Samuel Russell*, 940 tons, built in 1847, and the *Memnon*, 1068 tons, built in 1838.

British owners had the mortification of seeing the larger and speedier American ships securing the bulk of the China tea trade, and obtaining freight rates which were far higher than, and sometimes nearly double, those they could get for their " tea-wagons." It was not altogether the fault of British shipowners that they were so beaten. Certainly they were a conservative lot, and opposed to any changes in methods or policy, but they were also handicapped by the shipping laws and their effects on ship design.

After the repeal of the Navigation Laws British shipowners were very despondent. American vessels for some years had more than rivalled British ships in speed, size and comfort. British owners lamented the fact, but they were loth to follow the American methods of design and construction, and much preferred to retain the characteristics in their vessels with which they were familiar, notwithstanding that experience had taught them the superiority of the American ships. Not all owners and builders were of this conservative type, though they seem to have preferred to try to combine the British and American characteristics in ships, with the result that they improved the British ships and did not equal the Americans.

Still, the new vessels were a distinct improvement. These
included such well-known ships in their day as the *Baring,
John o' Gaunt, Euphrates, Foam,* and *Monarch.* These
ships were put into the China trade, and are asserted to
have been the equals of any of the Americans then in that
trade.

The Americans in 1845 put in the trade between New
York and Boston and China some ships of a new type
which again proved better than anything the British had
to offer. These vessels had low hulls, great beam, and very
fine lines, and could set more sail area in proportion to their
tonnage than any vessels then afloat.

At the time the American ships were having it all their
own way, the *Oriental* sailed from New York to Hong Kong
in 109 days, and home again in 81, and on her second voyage in 1850 did even better, with the result that she was
chartered to carry tea to England at a price nearly double
that which the best British ships could command. The
Oriental was the first American ship to bring tea to England
after the Navigation Laws were repealed.

Alexander Hall, the Aberdeen ship builder, had
introduced about ten years before this voyage, the kind of
bows with which nearly all Aberdeen built vessels were
fitted. These bows were not similar to the American
clipper bows, but were long and sharp. Vessels thus
equipped made some remarkably good passages.

To compete against the *Oriental* two vessels were ordered
from Hall, the *Stornoway* and *Chrysolite.* Compared with
the American ships, they were of less tonnage, and narrower
in proportion to their length. The *Stornoway* was placed
in command of Captain John Robertson, who made his
reputation in the *John o' Gaunt,* and the *Chrysolite* under
Captain Anthony Enright, both of whom were favourably

known in the tea trade, and it was expected that if anyone could make these ships hold their own against the Americans they could. The *Chrysolite* made her first passage from Liverpool to Canton in 102 days, beating the *Oriental's* record by eight days, and she made the homeward voyage to Liverpool in 103 days from Whampoa. The *Stornoway's* passage out and home was equally satisfactory. No other British ships equalled these two, and the Americans continued to secure the bulk of the trade.

Mr. Richard Green, of Poplar, in a speech at a dinner in the City in 1851, at which a member of the American Legation was present, and largely attended by shipowners, asked why they should allow themselves to be beaten by the Americans. His question was received with applause. Mr. Green was a man who believed in deeds as well as words.

So confident were the Americans to build better and faster ships than the British, and so elated by the feats of their clippers and by the victory of the *America* schooner at the Isle of Wight, when she " lifted that cup," that the American Navigation Club issued a challenge to British shipowners and builders suggesting that each country should build a vessel of between eight hundred and twelve hundred tons, American measurement, which should race with cargo from an English port to China and back with another cargo. The prize was to be £10,000. There being no takers, the American Navigation Club offered to double the prize, and to allow the British vessel several days' start. The challenge was not accepted.

In fulfilment of Mr. Green's promise made at the meeting a new tea clipper was built at his yard at Poplar. She was called the *Challenger*, and was of 699 tons. She was owned by Mr. W. S. Lindsay. She was sent to China in

1852, and after loading tea at Shanghai she sailed for London. She called at Anjer, and found the big American ship the *Challenge* there, bound for London with tea from Canton. This was a new vessel, one of four built by William H. Webb in 1851 to solve the problem of speed, capacity and strength. She was about 2,000 tons, American measurement, and was the largest clipper launched in New York up to that time; two others of the four, which succeeded her, were slightly larger. She was owned by N. L. and G. Griswold. The smaller British vessel actually beat her big rival into dock in London by two days from Anjer. What became of the *Challenge* is not known. The story that she was forfeited as the prize is not substantiated. Nor is another story that she was bought by Messrs. Green and renamed the *Result*. There was a ship of that name, but she is said to have been a very different ship from the *Challenge*. Several other vessels have been confused with her as they have borne the same name.

This victory put heart into British shipowners, and at last successful efforts were made to capture the China trade.

The American clipper ship *Witch of the Wave* made the best passage from China to London in 1852, taking only 90 days. She was a vessel of 1494 tons, 202 feet long, 40 feet broad, and 21 feet depth, and when she was launched she was referred to as the newest and youngest of the Salem witches, an allusion to the belief in witchcraft which distinguished the Salem people in the early days of the settlers there.

In that year the *Chrysolite* and *Stornoway* loaded tea at Whampoa and sailed on July 9th. For twenty-one days in the China Sea they were in sight of each other; they sighted one another at various times during the voyage, and by the time they reached England their days in company numbered about forty-six. The *Chrysolite* had the luck of the winds at the end, and docked at Liverpool 104 days after sailing, three days before the *Stornoway* got to the Downs. For the second time in his career, Captain Enright was given a special reward by the owners of the ship for bringing her in first with the new season's tea.

Notable passages were also made by the American ships *Surprise* and *Nightingale*. The latter was named after Jenny Lind, the famous Swedish singer. Messrs. Sampson and Tappan, of Boston, the owners of the latter vessel, believed she was as fast as any afloat, and they issued a challenge to all and sundry, Americans as well as British, for a race from England to China and back, for £10,000 a side ; there were no takers.

In that year also a beginning was made with the building of the *Cairngorm*, a ship which was destined to make history, at Messrs. Hall's yard at Aberdeen ; she was a clipper of about 1,000 tons, and was intended to compete against the Americans on something like equal terms in the matter of size. She has been described as the first real British clipper to prove herself a match for the hither-to all-conquering Yankees. She joined in the races in 1853.

The much smaller *Challenger* was the next to get to London in 1852, beating some American clippers including the famous *Nightingale*. There were a few other vessels in the race in that year, and victory was claimed on behalf of every one of them, and that was why the owners of the *Nightingale* issued their challenge.

In 1853, a little American clipper, the *Architect*, entered the lists ; she was of 520 tons, and was built about 1847 at Baltimore. Her master was Captain George A. Potter.

The *Architect* found herself one of the group of clippers at Canton, and having finished her loading when they did she left Canton river with them. That was the last they saw of her, and the captains of some of her larger opponents were inclined to think her chances in the race were small. Others, who knew Captain Potter, were inclined to think that there was something in the circumstance that the *Architect* was not in sight the next day. Like the others she started against the monsoon, and unlike the others she made her voyage to London in 107 days ; she sold her cargo of tea before any of the other ships arrived. The *Hero of the Nile* was the next to appear. Her captain inquired of the pilot if he had seen anything of a little American ship from Canton, and was told she was already in London and had discharged her tea. The *Architect* returned to New York with a light cargo, received a cargo of flour and cotton goods, and sailed again for China. Owing to the speed she had displayed on her previous voyage she was chartered to take a cargo of tea to London at £8 per ton, as against £6 on the other voyage. English vessels, it is said, were accepting as low a rate as £3 to £4 a ton.

The first iron vessel built for the tea trade was the *Lord of the Isles*, by Messrs. Scott of Greenock, and owned by a Mr. Martin. She was of 770 tons, and under Captain Maxton did some excellent work. In that year, too, there entered the China trade the *Northfleet*, one of Duncan Dunbar's frigates, built at Northfleet on the Thames, and the *Crest of the Wave*, built by Pile of Sunderland.

The chief event of 1854 was the race between the *Chrysolite* from Foochow, and the American *Celestial*, of 860 tons, built by W. H. Webb and Sons at New York, from Whampoa. Both sailed on July 14th, and the British ship was off Deal in 108 days, a day earlier than the other. The best passage from Shanghai was made by the *Cairngorm*.

In 1855 the Americans began to drop out of the China trade, so far as rivalry against the British clippers in the trade to England was concerned, though they still carried teas direct to America. For one thing, freights were beginning to decline ; there were no more cargoes at £8 a ton to be had. For another, many of the American ships began to show unmistakable signs of the strain and wear and tear of being driven from New York to San Francisco, and thence to China, and then back to New York, and the cost of the necessary repairs was often so great as to make a large hole in the reduced profits. Besides this, British clippers were proving they were as fast, and that they delivered their cargoes in better condition than many of the American ships sometimes did.

The *Nightingale* made the last passage of note by an American ship when she ran in 1855 from Shanghai to London in 91 days. Some of the Americans found it paid them better to stick to the California trade.

After 1855, the rivalry was chiefly between British built ships. The *Kate Carnie*, Steele's first tea clipper, appeared that year and was the forerunner of a series which included several of the most noted ships that ever took the water from any British yard. From 1860 the number of clippers intended for the tea trade, launched yearly, began to increase until 1863.

The *Lord of the Isles* was known among sailors as the Diving Bell, because she used to cut through the waves instead of going over them. Captain Maxton did not care whether she was wet or dry as long as she made a good passage. With the advantage of the north east monsoon in the early part of the voyage she ran from Shanghai to London in 1855 in 87 days. The next year she had as her opponent the American ship *Maury*, under Captain Fletcher, and both sailed from Foochow to London with the new teas. A premium of £1 per ton on the freight was offered for the first ship home during the season, regardless of the length of the passage. The *Lord of the Isles* sailed four days before the other, and both reached the Downs the same day and passed Gravesend with only ten minutes between them, the *Maury* leading, but Captain Maxton had secured the better tug and got his ship into dock first ; so the *Lord of the Isles* was adjudged to have won the prize. The *Maury* is described as a pretty barque of about 600 tons, owned by Messrs. A. A. Low and Brother, of New York, and built by Messrs. Roosevelt and Joyce. The same builders were responsible for the barques *Fairy*, *Penguin* and *Benefactor*, which also were in the China trade.

The American ships *Celestial* and *Ringleader* were in this year's sailing, but did nothing to add to their fame.

The *Chrysolite* sailed from Whampoa at the same time as the *Lord of the Isles* and had the bad luck to lose some of her spars in the China Sea, and her crew thought this an opportune moment to refuse duty and complain of the food. Captain McLeland, her then commander, was unsympathetic. One of the crew threw a bone at him. The captain promptly pulled out a pistol and shot him in the arm. It is not surprising that the voyage lasted 144 days ; the crew would certainly do nothing to enhance the Old Man's reputation under such circumstances.

The recurrence of war between England and China in 1857 and 1858 interfered a great deal with the tea trade; and as Canton was closed to the tea ships they went to other ports, and it was not until the latter part of 1858 that Whampoa again saw the tea ships.

The next vessel of note was the *Chaa-sze*, about 550 tons ; she was built by Hall of Aberdeen in 1859, and was originally intended for a whaler. Her figurehead represented a Chinaman with tea-chests, tea-pots, cups and saucers, and a tea shrub. This design was chosen because her name was stated to be the Chinese for tea-taster.

The first *Fiery Cross* was built by Challoner at Liverpool in the middle 'fifties, and made some good passages. She is reported to have come from Anger in 1857 in 74 days, arriving off Dartmouth, but did not reach London until some days later. She was under a Captain Dallas, who was one of the driving fraternity. In the following year she sailed from Foochow to London in 115 days, as against the *Chrysolite's* 140. The *Robin Hood* made the shortest run that year between those ports, being 101 days ; the *Kate Carnie* did the journey in 122 days ; and the *Stornoway* in 136. The sailings from Shanghai included the *Challenger*, 115 days, and the *Lord of the Isles*, 89 days. The *Cairngorm* and *Lammermuir* from Whampoa were 92 and 93 days respectively.

John Willis had the *Lammermuir* built by Pile of Sunderland in 1856, and as she was not an out-and-out clipper, but a first-class all-round ship her making such a good voyage may be attributed to the fact that she was a new vessel and was superbly handled. Moreover she was under Captain Andrew Shewan, the elder, which meant a lot.

Among the vessels at Whampoa were many well-known British clippers and five American ships ; two of the latter had negro crews but white officers. The prospects of the various ships were eagerly discussed, but the *Cairngorm* and *Lammermuir* were the favourites, especially as they were known to be fast vessels and were captained by men experienced in the China trade. It is curious that so many of the English ships should have had Scottish captains, the little port of Peterhead in Aberdeenshire alone contributing three. The shippers offered a substantial money prize to the officers of the first ship to arrive. Captain Ryrie was in charge of the *Cairngorm* in place of Captain Richard Robinson. Two of the smallest ships got away first, and the *Cairngorm* sailed from Whampoa on November 6th, and her Sunderland built rival on the 8th, and the remainder followed at short intervals. A north-east monsoon favoured them. A few stunsail booms were carried away, but the only serious mishap seems to have been that the *Lammermuir* lost her main-top-gallant yard. The *Cairngorm* went through the Straits of Banca, and the *Lammermuir* through the Gaspar Straits ; they found themselves in company in the Java Sea, and, the wind being very light, Captain Ryrie invited Captain Shewan to dinner on the *Cairngorm*, and he had a boat lowered and went.

This fine weather suited the *Lammermuir* much better than it did the *Cairngorm*. While the two captains were at dinner, Mr. Moore, the mate of the *Lammermuir*, thought it was a fine opportunity to display the sailing qualities of his vessel, he being in charge in the captain's absence. Accordingly he tacked his ship and sailed across the bows of the other. Presently he tacked again, and so performed what sailors call the feat of sailing round her. What Captain Ryrie thought of Moore's exploit may be imagined, as for a sailing ship to sail round another in this way was to inflict a terrible indignity and cast untold reflections upon her speed. In the Indian Ocean the *Cairngorm* got her own back, for in the strong south-east trade winds she secured the lead and maintained it to the end of the voyage, arriving forty hours before the other.

There was an amusing incident when the *Lammermuir* was passing Anjer, in the Straits of Sunda. Malay boats came alongside with natives, who were ostensibly peaceful traders but would as soon have looted the vessel as not, had opportunity offered. The mate, by the captain's instructions, bought some eggs from one of the men, a well-known character, who for some reason did not wait for his pay. The next day the ship's cook found that the eggs were very antique, and they were consigned to the sea. The following voyage the same native came aboard with more eggs to sell. Mr. Moore, remembering the last purchase, bought a lot and handed them to the men of his watch who pelted the Malay with them till he was glad to escape to his own boat without waiting for his money.

Owing to the difference in the times of departure of the two vessels, the *Lammermuir* made the passage in six hours less than the *Cairngorm*, and so appreciative were the consignees that they made a gift to the master and officers.

After 1859 the Americans left the tea races alone so far as the run to England was concerned, but their vessels continued to take tea to American ports. The American *Sea Serpent* from Foochow for London was expected to win that year, especially as she was commanded by Captain Whitmore and had a double crew. But both the *Ellen Rodger* and *Fiery Cross* arrived before her. From then until the tea races ended Foochow was the chief tea port for the racing ships. This was the *Fiery Cross's* last voyage, as she was wrecked that year. The second *Fiery Cross* was built in 1860. Captain Dallas, who had been so successful with the first ship of that name, had her for her maiden voyage, after which she passed under the command

STERN OF CUTTY SARK

Photo by R. A. Fletcher

Facing page 166

of Captain Richard Robinson. " Carry-on-and-go-ahead Dick Robinson," as he was generally called, was an active man who was apparently never tired, and could do with a minimum of sleep or none at all for days on end, and never spared his ship, his crew, or himself. He was the most daring ship driver of all the captains. It was said he had phenomenal luck ; if so, he had the genius to see his opportunities and turn them to his advantage. Other outstanding drivers were Captain Innes, of the *Serica* ; Captain Shewan, senior, of *Lammermuir* and *Norman Court* fame ; Captain Keay, of the *Ariel*, and until he grew old, Captain Ryrie.

The following years were remarkable for several new clippers and their wonderful races. The rivalry between the various British builders was keener than it ever was between the British and American builders, and was fully as intense as it was among the American builders when they were turning out their ships for the California trade, which is described in a later chapter. The east and the west coasts of Scotland were the homes of the chief British builders, or perhaps to put it more correctly, the Scottish builders represented the methods of the firms on the two coasts. Steele and Connell were the chief clipper ship builders on Clydeside, and Hood and Hall were equally prominent at Aberdeen. Other builders included Pile of Sunderland, whose *Maitland* did not prove the success anticipated ; Green, of Blackwall, whose *Highflyer* did not show the turn of speed expected ; Scott and Linton, of Dumbarton, who produced the *Cutty Sark ;* her great rival the *Thermopylae*, came from Hood's yard. The *Ariel*, considered by many to be the fastest clipper ship ever built, was one of Steele's ships, and that firm also was responsible for such fliers as the *Serica, Taeping, Lahloo, Sir Lancelot*, and *Titania*. All the clippers, from whatever yard they came, were remarkable for their exquisite symmetrical beauty ; no two of them were quite alike, and the differences gave rise to much discussion among their several admirers, not only as to their perfection of form but as to the effect those differences would have upon their sailing qualities and how they would be coped with by this or that commander.

Many of the later British ships in the tea trade did not distinguish themselves, but that was not so much the fault of the ships as of the captains, for there were not enough men of the dare-devil racing clipper type to go round. Consequently some ships, of which great things were expected, did badly ; their captains either did not know how to drive them or were afraid to do so and run the risks which a real racing captain regarded as part of the day's work. Some ships did badly under one captain and well under another, but those which were able to be driven, and were lucky enough to get captains and officers who knew how to drive them, and were not afraid to do so, and did it, made some remarkable passages.

In this connection it may be mentioned that the clippers *Belted Will* and *Black Prince*, which came upon the scene in the 'sixties, were expected to prove themselves very fast vessels. As there were no captains of the racing, driving sort to be had, their owners had to put up with men of different temperament. Captain Inglis, who had the *Black Prince*, would have been an excellent commander of one of the slow easy-going East Indiamen ; he erred through excess of caution, and never gave his ship a chance of showing what she could do. Captain Braithwaite, of the *Belted Will*, was another easy-goer. This ship made one good voyage in her career, and did nothing worth speaking about at any other time. Even more unfortunate than either of these was the *Sir Lancelot*, which, on her first voyage with a Captain MacDougall in command, had a remarkable series of accidents, attributable in more or less degree to her master's mistakes or lack of nerve. On her homeward voyage she was so badly handled that the passage lasted 122 days. Mr. James MacCunn, the owner of the *Sir Lancelot*, dispensed with the captain's services soon after his arrival.

Captain Dallas, after the maiden voyage of the second *Fiery Cross*, left her, and she was handed over to Captain Dick Robinson, who had her until 1866, and, says Lubbock in "The China Clippers," "under these two famous skippers she proved well-nigh invincible, receiving the premium for the first vessel in dock on no less than four occasions, and being only twenty-four hours behind in 1864 and 1866."

The *Flying Spur*, when under Captain Ryrie, was not driven as hard as he used to drive his old ship. He was pressing her on one occasion, however, and when that happened she was rather wet, and like all the clippers would go through the seas rather than over them; a sea came over her and washed the cook and the contents of his galley along the main deck.

After the tea race of 1861, in which the *Fiery Cross* under Captain Dallas sailed from Foochow to London in 101 days, beating by several days the *Ellen Rodger* under Captain Keay, the *Robin Hood* under Captain Cobb, and the *Falcon* under Captain Maxton, all three of which sailed from Foochow on June 11th, and the *Flying Spur* which sailed on June 14th, the same day as the *Fiery Cross*, Captains Dallas and Maxton gave up going to sea, the former retiring into private life and the latter going into business. In this capacity he kept up his connection with shipping and became a clipper owner, or a partner in a firm which owned clippers. The *Flying Spur*, of which great things were expected, took 124 days to Falmouth.

The shortest passage from Foochow to London in 1862 was that of the *Ellen Rodger*, 116 days, with the *Flying Spur*, 119 days, and the *Whinfell*, under Captain Yeo, 120 days.

The masters of four of the clippers had the surprise of their lives in this race. The *Robin Hood*, *Falcon*, *Ellen Rodger*, and another (the last being bound to Liverpool) were becalmed in the doldrums, a few miles north of the equator, in the Atlantic, with a little Blackwall frigate, the *Kent*, in their midst ; the *Kent*, which was bound from one of the colonies for London, was a favourite passenger ship in her day, and belonged to Money Wigram. She was one of those vessels which could get along with the slightest puff of air, and when at last a moving current of air from the fringe of the northeast trades was felt, her abilities in these conditions enabled her to leave the four clippers behind. When the wind freshened it was the clippers' turn to leave the *Kent* behind. Captain Clayton did not see why his ship should not be in the race with the best of them, and he drove the *Kent* as hard as he could. He did not, however, get a sight of the clippers. On arriving off Dungeness he learned that none of the three bound for London had arrived. At that moment there were sighted from his ship two vessels coming up the Channel, and still some distance astern, under such a spread of canvas as the racing clippers alone showed. Captain Clayton promptly made up his mind to beat them. He signalled for a tug. By the time the tug had arrived and the tow rope had been made fast, the clippers were less than four miles away. They were the *Falcon* and *Robin Hood*.

They were also signalling for tugs. Captain Clayton at once ordered another tug, and with two tugs doing their best he got the *Kent* into the East India Dock half an hour before the *Robin Hood* with the *Falcon* just behind her. That an ordinary Blackwall frigate, not built for speed, should have been able to outsail two of the chief racing tea clippers of the day, was a feat which if it had not been accomplished would not have been believed possible ; it was not forgotten for many a year in shipping circles, and is often mentioned even now when sailing ship men meet and discuss old times.

None of the passages made in the race of 1863 were phenomenal, but the leaders maintained their reputation.

The year 1863 was chiefly remarkable because of two new ships launched in it. These were the *Serica* and *Taeping*, both of which were built by Steele of Greenock. The former left the ways in August of that year, and was consequently in time to participate in the tea race of 1864. The *Serica*, Captain Innes in command, beat the *Fiery Cross* from Foochow to London by five days, making the journey in 109 days and was awarded the premium for being the first ship to dock with the season's teas. The *Taeping*, which was launched on Christmas Eve, did not reach China in time to join in the race of 1864. She accordingly loaded at Shanghai instead of Foochow. In the China Sea when homeward bound she received such injury in dirty weather that she had to put into Amoy to repair.

The favourites from Foochow in 1865 were the *Serica* and *Fiery Cross*. They were towed to sea together, and set sail together, and were often in company during the voyage, and reported themselves together when coming up the Channel. The *Serica* was two miles ahead when they were off Beachy Head, but the *Fiery Cross* secured the only tug available at the time, which enabled her to win the race.

It was a favourite contention that Steele could not improve upon the clippers he had yet launched, so perfect did they seem, but in 1865 the famous builder showed that he could. He produced the *Ariel* and the *Sir Lancelot*, the former for Shaw, Maxton and Company, and the latter for Mr. MacCunn. The *Ariel* was of 1058 tons. She was commanded for three voyages by Captain Keay. The *Sir Lancelot*, which was a few tons measurement larger than the *Ariel*, carried much the same canvas ; there was little to choose between them in this respect. It is authoritatively stated that the *Sir Lancelot* spread nearly 33,000 square feet under all plain sail.

One of the most famous and wonderful races of the tea clippers was that of the year 1866 ; in some respects it was perhaps the greatest of the whole series of contests in which the clippers were engaged. The following vessels took part in it that year : *Ariel, Sir Lancelot, Serica, Fiery Cross, Chrysolite, Taeping, Taitsing, Ada, Chinaman, Coulnakyle, Black Prince, Falcon, Flying Spur, Yang-Tse, Pakwan, Golden Spur, Belted Will,* and *White Adder*. Though all were good and speedy ships, naturally enough some were speedier than others ; some were fortunate in their commanders, a few were not. The race was to be between the first five vessels to get away from Foochow. The *Ariel* was the favourite, though some of the others had their fanciers ; she was the first to finish her loading, and during the afternoon of May 28th she dropped down the river in charge of a tug, the *Fiery Cross* being twelve hours behind her. Then came the *Taeping* and *Serica*, and a day later the *Taitsing*. The *Ariel* had difficulty with her tug

CLIPPER SHIP ARIEL.   *From oilpainting in Author's possession*

Facing page 172

and pilot, and it was not until the morning of May 30th
that she got going again.

The *Fiery Cross* in the meantime had gained fourteen
hours. At last the *Ariel's* troubles were ended, and she and
the *Taeping* and the *Serica* began to pile on their canvas
and they made a good start for London together. The
Taitsing, the last of the first five to leave, started from the
Min river on the night of May 31st, and the other tea
ships followed at short intervals till, before the end of
June, all were on their way. None of the later departures,
however, had a ghost of a chance of overtaking the leaders.

The *Ariel* was under Captain Keay, the *Taeping* under
Captain McKinnon, and the *Serica* had Captain Innes as
master, all three being men who could be depended upon
to get the utmost possible speed out of their ships. A fine
tribute was paid by Captain Keay at a " blue water "
evening a few years ago at Liverpool to his rivals, when he
declared that " both were splendid commanders," a compli-
ment which certainly would have been paid by both to
Captain Keay. So beautiful and graceful were the ships
that they might easily have been mistaken for ship-rigged
yachts, and it was no wonder that their voyage to London
was spoken of as an ocean yacht race.

The four leading vessels sighted each other at intervals
as far as Anjer. The first to pass that port was the *Fiery
Cross*, on June 18th. Two days later the *Ariel* passed, with
the *Taeping* six hours behind her, and two days later still
the *Serica* passed. Another few days elapsed before the
Taitsing passed on the evening of June 26th. It is well to
notice these dates in view of the extraordinary sailing of
ships during the homeward voyage. Thereafter the
run was across the Indian ocean to the neighbourhood of
Mauritius, and the ships bowled along with the generally

strong and reliable south-east trade wind on their quarter for which they set every available square inch of canvas that they could find room for. In unchanged order the five ships crossed the longitude of Mauritius. By the time the *Fiery Cross* was passing the Cape of Good Hope, the *Ariel* had reduced the lead of the *Fiery Cross* from two days to a few hours ; the *Taeping* was only half a day behind the *Ariel*. The first to pass St. Helena was the *Taeping* on July 27th, with the *Fiery Cross* a day behind her. The *Serica* on the 29th, was the third to pass the island, having sailed from the Cape in ten days, or three days less time than the *Fiery Cross*.

The winds are by no means uniform, even in the trades. First one vessel and then another seemed to have what sailors called the luck of the wind, especially in the doldrums, and *Taeping*, *Fiery Cross* and *Ariel* all crossed the line on August 4th, with *Serica* two days behind, and *Taitsing* six days behind her. The *Taeping* and *Fiery Cross* had one another in close company, or at least in sight, for about a week, and parted when the *Taeping* was fortunate enough to get a fresh breeze which enabled her to leave the other ship becalmed and pass beyond the horizon in a few hours. North of the equator the *Serica* and *Taitsing* improved their positions.

By the time Cape Verde was reached the *Ariel* had secured a day's lead on the next three, and was a week ahead of the *Taitsing*. The *Ariel* was still ahead when passing the Azores, with the other three only just behind her, and the *Taitsing* only two days astern, having reduced the *Ariel's* lead by no less than three days, a remarkable piece of sailing.

This was the prelude to the great finish to the race between the *Ariel* and the *Taeping*. At daybreak on September 5th the two ships were at the mouth of the Channel, with only a short distance between them, with a strong west-south-west wind, and every sail set from water-sails to royal stunsails that they could carry; the *Ariel* was slightly leading. By daybreak the following morning, after a night of tearing up Channel, *Taeping* was so close behind the *Ariel* that Captain Keay, in order to prevent his rival getting the lead, sailed the *Ariel* in front of her and thereby compelled her to heave to; both vessels at the time were signalling hard for pilots. As soon as each vessel had got her pilot she continued for the South Foreland, and when off Deal signalled for tugs. The *Taeping*, which was about a mile astern of the *Ariel*, secured the better tug and arrived off Gravesend nearly an hour before the other. The *Ariel*, on reaching Gravesend, took another tug alongside, and as soon as the tide permitted, both vessels pushed for their respective docks. The *Ariel* arrived outside the East India dock at 9 p.m., and had to wait. The *Taeping* had to go to the London docks, a mile or two further up the river, and reached them at 10 p.m., and as she drew less water than the *Ariel* she was able to enter at once, and passed through the lock gates and docked twenty minutes before her rival.

But this was not the only extraordinary feature of this exciting race. The *Serica* had been rushing up the Channel nearer the French side, unseen by the other two, and she entered the Thames on the same tide and passed into the West India dock at 11.30 the same evening. The *Fiery Cross* was only a day behind, but in that day the wind strengthened to a gale, and she had to anchor, and could not enter London dock until September 8th. The *Taitsing* reached London the next day. A more remarkable race than that of these five vessels was surely never sailed.

Three of them covered the passage from China in 99 days, and the other two in 101 days. The *Black Prince* was the last of the whole fleet to arrive ; this exploit earned for her the nickname of the " Whipper-in."

The *Ariel* left Gravesend on October 14th, 1866, and after a marvellously short passage of 83 days from anchorage to anchorage ended her run at Hong Kong. She beat all previous runs by several days, and established a record which has never been equalled.

Messrs. Shaw, Maxton and Company were so pleased with the *Ariel* that they ordered Steele to build for them another vessel, but they asked that she should not be so tender as the *Ariel*. Tenderness, by the way, in greater or less degree, was a characteristic of all the racing clippers. Messrs. Steele, accordingly, gave the new ship, the *Titania*, a little more beam in proportion to her length. The *Titania* was 199 feet long as compared with the *Ariel's* 195 feet, but her beam was 36 feet as against the *Ariel's* fraction under 34 feet. The depth of hold, 21 feet, was the same in both vessels. The *Titania* was of slightly larger tonnage. On her maiden voyage the *Titania* had two serious mishaps, and did not get to China in time to join in the racing.

Captain Robert Deas was in charge of the *Titania* on her first voyage, when she was dismasted. One reason why so many accidents of this character befell the tea clippers was that they had to be sailed in certain circumstances in a way that was entirely contrary to the accepted rules for ordinary vessels, owing to their narrowness, or lack of beam, in proportion to their length, and the fineness of their " entrance " or bows and of their counters, and it was not until a man had learned by experience how a clipper should be sailed, and the risks that could and could not be run, that he was able in some measure to avoid such accidents. Further, an 800-ton tea clipper would have spars equal to those of a 1,200 ton ordinary trader.

The *Sir Lancelot*, after her disastrous first voyage, amply made up for her mishaps in the next three voyages. In 1869 she sailed from Foochow to Gravesend in 89 days, against the monsoon, thereby establishing a record. Shewan says : " One great point that contributed to *Sir Lancelot's* marvellous success was that her captain had the nerve to take short cuts, through groups and reefs of islands like the Paracels, when a shipmaster would have to trust solely to a good look-out and his own judgment. By doing so it would be possible to obtain a week's sail over more cautious commanders, who would lose days in circum-navigating such risky localities. Such vigilance was a great asset in making quick passages, but there were not many shipmasters who cared to put their seamanship to such a test."

On her second voyage, the *Sir Lancelot* was under Captain Robinson. A few days after leaving London she was caught in a squall, early in December, 1866. The bowsprit snapped, and the fore topmast and main mast broke also, the main mast making a great hole in the deck ; and then the mizen topmast went. Throughout the night all hands worked their hardest to relieve the ship of the wreckage ; during the morning they managed to fit her with a jury rig, and at night she reached a south coast port. Here Mr. MacCunn had her completely re-rigged, and she was given wooden masts instead of iron ones. She sailed again for China at the end of January.

The arrangement was made in 1867 that the winner should be, not the vessel getting into dock first, but the one making the best time. Thirteen vessels got away from

12

Foochow between June 1st and 18th. The first to go, the *Maitland*, a new ship, did not prove herself the fast sailer expected. The *Serica*, under Captain Innes, sailed on the 2nd, the *Taeping*, under Captain Dowdy, on the 4th, and the *Fiery Cross*, now under Captain Kirkup, on the 5th. Captain Robinson had left the *Fiery Cross* to take the *Sir Lancelot*, which did not sail from Shanghai until the middle of the month. The *Sir Lancelot* tore along in Dick Robinson's usual way, with the fullest sail possible, and overtook the *Flying Spur* near the Cape. Captain Ryrie recollected what he used to do in the way of driving, and sent the *Flying Spur* along in company with the *Sir Lancelot* in fine style on the run to St. Helena. On this run they overtook the *Maitland*, whose master, Captain Coulson, had boasted before sailing of what his ship was going to do ; she did not do it. The *Maitland* had every sail up that she could set, even to skysail stunsails and moonsails near heaven, and watersails near the ocean.

" I shall be forced to leave you if you cannot make more sail," Captain Robinson signalled as his vessel passed her (Lubbock reports), and Captain Ryrie simply sailed the *Flying Spur* round her before continuing to chase the *Sir Lancelot*.

Meanwhile, the *Ariel*, which when going to Foochow to load had met the *Serica*, *Taeping* and *Fiery Cross* homeward bound, loaded at Foochow and sailed on the 13th. She overtook the *Serica* on July 10th, and others at intervals, till on September 15th she found herself in company with the *Fiery Cross* and could not get rid of her for five days. The *Ariel's* passage was spoilt by poor winds in the Indian Ocean, but her record from the Cape to port was wonderful ; had she only had as good winds in the Indian Ocean as on her previous voyage, she would have arrived several days earlier than she did. As it was, she took 102 days from Foochow. The *Sir Lancelot* won the race in the short time of 99 days, arriving on September 22nd.

Four new competitors were built for the China trade in 1867. These were the *Spindrift*, built by Connell, which was of abnormal length in proportion to her beam ; she had a great spread of sail, and was very fast in certain weather ; she was built for Findlay. The *Lahloo*, a somewhat im-proved version of *Taeping*, was of 985 tons ; she was placed under one of the drivers, Captain John Smith, and was owned by Mr. Rodger. The *Leander* was built for Mr. Joseph Somes, and in her case she suffered through her skipper's shortcomings. The fourth was the *Undine*, by Pile of Sunderland, and a capital little ship she was. Additional interest therefore attached to the race of 1868. There was some very exciting sailing between the various ships at one time and another. The race ended in *Ariel* and *Spindrift* docking on the same tide, both being 97 days on the passage, but the *Ariel* got in first. All the new vessels acquitted themselves well. The *Black Prince* had two unusual experiences that voyage. One was that she was rammed by a swordfish which left several inches of bone sticking in her side ; the other was that just as she was reaching the English Channel she sighted the *Ariel* which had discharged her cargo and reloaded and was outward bound again.

The tea clipper racing was approaching its end, but it may be said to have finished in a blaze of glory. The concluding years saw the great contests between the *Thermopylae* and the *Cutty Sark* and two or three of the best of those which had already come on the scene. The *Thermopylae* was the first of the two to appear. She was built by Walter Hood at Aberdeen for Thompson's Aberdeen White Star Line, and launched on August 19th, 1868. She did not go to China direct but to Melbourne, leaving Gravesend for that port in November. She was commanded by Captain Kemball, who had previously had the *Yang-tse*, a tea clipper which was not one of the fastest, but he managed to make her get along so well on one voyage that the performance attracted the attention of the White Star firm, and they offered him the command of the *Thermopylae*. Her first voyage was made to Port Phillip in 63 days, a record, she anchoring in the harbour on January 9th. Thence she went to Newcastle, N.S.W., and left that port on February 10th for Shanghai, and on the way passed the *Golden* which had already been 59 days from Sydney on her way to the same port, and herself arrived at Shanghai, pilot to pilot, after a passage of 28 days, the fastest on record. From Shanghai she went to Foochow to load tea.

The *Thermopylae* displayed at her mainmast head a gilded cock, an emblem of victory. This especially upset the crews of those ships which had won races or distinguished themselves as tea ships, whereas the *Thermopylae* had not. A plot was hatched to remove the offending emblem. The opportunity arose when some function was being held on the *Thermopylae*, when her officers were below. A sailor, said to belong to the *Taitsing*, swam to her, climbed aloft, and secured the bird and returned to the deck undetected, goodness only knows how ; and then went overboard and swam back to his ship with his prize. It was never recovered. A substitute was set up in its place. But great was the indignation on board when the theft was discovered.

The *Ariel* was the first to leave Foochow, sailing on June 30th, followed by the *Leander*, the next day, under

BOWS OF CUTTY SARK
Photo by R. A. Fletcher

Facing page 180

Captain Petherick, and the *Lahloo*, under Captain Smith, the day after. All three arrived at Gravesend on October 12th, their times being 104, 103 and 102 days respectively. They were surprised to find that the *Thermopylae*, which was at Foochow when they sailed, had already arrived ; she sailed on July 3rd and completed her passage in 91 days, on October 2nd. The *Sir Lancelot* made a faster passage still ; she left Foochow on July 17th, and in 89 days was at Gravesend, arriving on October 14th. The *Titania*, now under Captain Burgoyne, a man who believed in making his ship go if she could or would, made a passage which showed her powers, for she did the voyage from Shanghai in 98 days to London.

The next notable ship to appear from the builder's yard was the *Cutty Sark*, in the opinion of many persons the fastest clipper ever built. She was ordered by John Willis with the avowed purpose of beating the *Thermopylae*. Messrs. Scott and Linton, of Dumbarton, had nearly finished building her when they failed, and she was completed rather hurriedly by Denny Brothers. She was almost the same size as the *Thermopylae*, her length being 212 feet 5 inches as compared with *Thermopylae's* 212 feet ; their beam was the same, 36 feet ; *Cutty Sark's* depth, 21 feet, was three inches more than that of her rival, and her gross tonnage, 963 tons compared with *Thermopylae's* 991 tons. These dimensions show that she was a sharper ended ship than the other, and the accompanying photographs of her bows and stern reveal how beautifully proportioned she was. Her first three voyages were in the China trade, and it was during the third, when victory over her redoubtable antagonist seemed certain, that she lost her rudder. Captain Moore repaired her in mid-ocean, performing one of the most wonderful pieces of ship surgery on record, and then raced her home at a pace which seems incredible.

Later ships built for the tea races were the *Black Adder*, one of the unluckiest ships ever launched, the *Hallowe'en* and *Norman Court*. By 1871, so great had been the influx into the trade by the steamers, only three of the racers loaded at Foochow. The *Titania* made the shortest passage that year, 93 days from Foochow.

Though a few of the clippers continued in the trade, the racing days were dying, and with the steamers making much shorter passages by way of the Suez Canal there was no incentive for the clippers to be driven for all they were worth. Several of them went into the American trade, and as the American clippers used to carry tea to British ports, so now the British clippers turned the tables and carried tea to New York and Boston.

NOTE.—For some of the details of the China tea clipper races I am indebted to Basil Lubbock's " The China Clippers."

CHAPTER VI

THE discovery of gold in California caused a rush to that part of the world. Any old tub that would float was pressed into service to convey would-be gold seekers to the fabled land where gold was to be had for the picking up, and to carry the stores which were necessary for the thousands of persons who began to pour into San Francisco on their way to the placer goldfields. To read of gold to be had for the mere washing it out of the dirt, without the labour of deep digging, fired the imagination of tens of thousands of persons in the Eastern United States and of more tens of thousands of persons in Europe, and it may be doubted if five per cent of those who eventually reached the goldfields made a fortune. Prior to 1849, when the rush began, the arrivals of ships at San Francisco barely averaged one a quarter. In the twelve months preceding the gold discoveries the arrivals from Atlantic ports numbered four, besides nine American whalers. California passed into the possession of the United States under the treaty with Mexico in 1848. In that year also the discovery of gold was made in El Dorado County. One result was that in 1849 the clearances from Atlantic ports for San Francisco numbered no fewer than 775 vessels.

Unfortunately many of the vessels which sailed for

California were never heard of after they left port ; they can be added to the list of those missing with all on board. Some had to put into ports on the way, where they might or might not be repaired ; if they were, they made shift to continue their journey ; if not, their passengers and crew had to stay where they were and make the best of it, and get another ship if possible. Others, far from suitable for the Cape Horn voyage, took many months for the passage, and the sufferings of those on board may be imagined.

All necessary stores and requirements of life had to be brought by sea from the eastern seaboard. San Francisco in those days was innocent of practically everything ; she had no more shops than were needed to meet the small primitive needs of her very restricted population, number-ing at the most a few hundred persons. The year 1849 saw the most wonderful change that any port has seen in so short a time. In that year there landed at San Francisco between ninety and ninety one thousand persons. They were not all from the eastern states. Many came from other parts of the world, until it might be no exaggeration to say that nearly every nationality under the sun was represented. Many ships arrived from Europe ; several sailed and did not arrive. The craze to go gold-getting animated all. The number who stayed in San Francisco was small.

No tale of gold discoveries was too tall to be rejected. Speculators in land seized large tracts and spread reports of great finds of virgin gold there, which had no foundation in fact but were merely lures to induce adventurers to buy land and seek treasures which were not there to be had. " Salting," or sprinkling a little gold dust to delude the new comers, was not unknown.

At first many adventurers did not trouble about the

necessary outfits, but set off for the goldfields on foot with no tools but their hands and no resources but what they stood in. Afterwards the shipping firms on the east coast recommended their intending passengers to take their outfits with them. Many east coast merchants loaded ships with the necessary tools and stores, and sold them at San Francisco at fabulous profits.

Ship after ship was deserted by officers and crews; in some cases the sailors did not wait to furl the sails properly. There is excuse for thus leaving some of the ships, for they were unfit to stand the strain of the journey back to the east coast.

There were no railways across America in those days. All overland traffic had to be conducted by means of prairie schooners, as the settlers' wagons were called; they never went, nor were they intended to go, all the way, and there was the probability, so great as to be a certainty, to be faced, that they would be attacked by Indians long before they crossed the prairies and reached the Rockies. The only reliable route to San Francisco was to Central America, thence across the isthmus, and then by steamer to San Francisco. But this route meant two trans-shipments, with all the delay and expense inseparable from such an arrangement, and it was cheaper, and when the clipper ships got going it did not take much longer, to go all the way by sailing ship, even if it did entail a voyage round Cape Horn.

To save time was to save money in those days, and not only to save it but to make it. No one knew how long the goldfields might last, and it was a case of making what money could be made before the decline set in.

The old slow ships were hopelessly inadequate. The great ship builders of the east coast began to build to meet the extraordinary demand. They had the field to themselves, for it was a coastal service, and the United States have always protected their coastal shipping and kept foreigners out of it, and the builders in the eastern states made the most of the opportunity.

The rush may be said to have lasted from 1849 to 1857, but it was not until 1850 that the magnitude of the opportunity began to be realised. It is recorded that in 1850 thirteen clippers were launched for this trade; in 1851, thirty-one; in 1852, thirty-three; in 1853, fifty-one; in 1854, twenty; in 1855, thirteen; in 1856, eight; and in 1857, four. Of these about 39 were launched at New York, and 49 at Boston, and there was hardly a shipyard from Maine to Maryland which did not turn out ships intended for the fast California trade. Most of these vessels were built to order, others as speculations, and those who ordered them, and those who bought them on the stocks, were equally ready to pay good prices for them. Nearly seventy were owned in New York, with Boston a good second.

The desire to participate in the high profits to be made by carrying passengers and goods from the eastern seaboard to San Francisco led many to invest their savings in smaller vessels than the clippers, and many such were built and many old ones bought. It was not unknown for a ship captain and his friends to club their money and build or buy a vessel, and send her to the Golden Gate with the captain in command.

The earliest clippers launched for the trade were comparatively small, but from 1851 onward, they were mostly of from a thousand to seventeen hundred tons, but some of the other ships, old or new, put into the trade were as low as 300 or 400 tons. Besides the American ships others arrived from European and Asiatic ports.

Every American article for use or luxury had to be brought from the eastern states by way of Cape Horn, and prices consequently were fabulous. Gold was obtained from the mines and washings in quantities which seemed at times almost to justify the fantastic reports which had reached the rest of the world as to the ease with which the precious metal was to be secured, and the rush continued. As has happened at other goldfields, speculators who took goods to trade with the miners made quite as much money as did the miners themselves, and in many instances more. Not all gold miners were thrifty, and most traders or storekeepers were avaricious. Anything from £8 to £12 was paid for a barrel of pork, beef or flour, not always in the best condition ; indeed, the quality of some of the food shipped to San Francisco for public consumption, in the certainty that it would be bought for high prices, was worse than some of the stuff served out to sailors on British merchantmen in their worst days. It was not unusual for £1 to be charged for a pound of tea, coffee, or sugar. Whisky, or what passed for it, might be as much as £4 a pint. Wages were correspondingly high, labourers getting as much as £4 to £6 a day, but owing to the high cost of living they were not much better off than they had been in the eastern states. Yet in spite of all this money about, there was often a shortage of necessities, and many a man rich in gold has hardly known where to buy his next meal. As more ships reached California conveying thousands of tons of stores the demand was gradually met and prices began to fall.

Nor did the yield of gold continue unabated. Some gold-fields were dug and re-dug, and the placer diggings washed and re-washed, until not even the patient and persevering Chinaman could find a speck of the metal. As soon as a goldfield showed signs of exhaustion the miners began to troop off elsewhere, and in numerous cases the day came at last when the mushroom camp would be deserted. Then, as my old friend, Eugene Field put it in one of his poems describing western mining life :

"The camp of Blue Horizon busted,
    And every mother's son of us got up one day and dusted."

The first of the clippers launched in 1850 was the *Celestial*, and under Captain Gardner she made the run from New York to San Francisco in 104 days, arriving on November 1st. She was followed by the *Mandarin*, 776 tons, Captain Stoddart ; the *Surprise*, 1360 tons, Captain Dumaresq ; the *Game-Cock*, 1392 tons, Captain Hollis, and *Race-Horse*, 512 tons, Captain King. The last two were owned in Boston and the other three in New York. The *Race-Horse*, from Boston, arrived at the California port on November 24th, after a passage of 109 days, and a similar time was taken by the *Samuel Russell*, Captain Charles P. Low, the *Houqua*, which Low had commanded, being in this race under Captain McKenzie. The *Sea-Witch*, already mentioned in connection with the China trade, sailed from New York in the latter part of April, 1850, and arrived at San Francisco after a passage of 97 days. The *Samuel Russell* was not built for this trade, though she was put in it, but for the China trade, in 1847, and after going in 1851 to Canton she is credited with having made on the homeward journey 6,780 miles in 30 days, her greatest run being 328 miles in 24 hours.

The *Celestial* on her first voyage went from New York to San Francisco in 104 days. The *Surprise*, under the famous Captain Philip Dumaresq on her first voyage, made a remarkable run to San Francisco ; she is stated to have reefed her topsails only twice during the whole passage of 96 days. Then she went to China to load tea, and earned such good freight that by the time she had returned to New York she had covered her first cost and brought her owners about £10,000 net profit. Captain Charles Ranlett, senior, commanded her for some voyages, and was followed by his son. The *Surprise* made six passages in succession from Hong Kong to New York and five from Shanghai to New York, all under 89 days, the best being 81 days from Shanghai in 1857. This splendid and most successful vessel was wrecked off Yokohama in 1876. In her career she made three voyages to San Francisco which averaged 109 days.

The *Sea-Witch* was put in the California trade under Captain George Fraser, who had been mate under Waterman on the *Natchez*, and afterwards on the *Sea-Witch*. Seemingly the relations between Captain Waterman and his mate were not always harmonious. Waterman was one of those men who at sea quarrelled with and domineered over everybody, and gratified this tendency the more because of his position as captain. Fraser once interviewed the captain in the cabin and after placing two pistols on the table announced : " One of us two has got to leave this ship." As the ship was in mid-ocean, this was a challenge to a duel to the death. The captain stared at him, and replied : " You are the only man for whom I ever had any respect," and left him alone after that.

The *Challenge* was built in 1851, and Waterman was appointed to command her, and Fraser to the *Sea-Witch*.

The *Challenge* was the largest ship built up to then at New York, and carried an immense spread of sail. Waterman's record as a ship driver in the *Natchez* and *Sea-Witch* earned him the appointment, just when he had decided to retire from the sea. He had been merciless in his treatment of his crews on both those vessels, though two things must be said to his credit. One is that six men sailed voluntarily with him on every voyage in them, and the other is that he never cost the underwriters a dollar for repairs. Possibly the six men were favoured. Be that as it may, his reputation was such that no good sailorman, apart from the six, would ship willingly with him. So harsh was his treatment that for his personal safety, he used to go ashore by a tug boat before his ship reached her berth.

An article in " Harper's Magazine " in 1884 says :

" Captain ' Bob ' Waterman was one of the most daring of commanders. He did not hesitate to shoot sailors off the yard-arms, and at one time was so sought after by the police that he preferred not to come to New York in his ship, but exchanged her for New Jersey while sailing up the bay."

The *Challenge* had a crew of 56, consisting of most things but sailors ; only six could steer properly and they were made quartermasters and for the most part were kept to the steering. Nearly all the rest of the crew were the offscourings of the port of New York, of many nationalities and various colours, and not all able to understand English; some had professed to be sailors in order to get a passage to San Francisco. Some were diseased. They had all been shipped by crimps. The owners of the *Challenge*, who had gone down New York bay on her to give her a good send-off, saw the kind of crew and suggested that the ship should return and get a fresh lot. Not so, Captain Waterman.

He recognised the opportunity provided for the display of his peculiar abilities. His mate, a big bucko named Douglas, was a man after his own heart, and they determined to lick the crew into shape. The process began that night, after the owners had left the ship, with Waterman cutting the negro steward's head open with a knife. Once Douglas was examining the men's seachests and overhauling their contents. He came upon something which displeased him in the chests of the few English-speaking seamen, and charged them with theft. An old American man-of-war's man went for him and knocked him down, whereupon Waterman jumped among the crew with a navigating instrument and belaboured all in reach with it till he had smashed the instrument.

Captain Clarke, describing in " The Clipper Ship Era " the incident, says Waterman did not use his sextant. " He heard shouts for help from the main deck. He laid down his sextant and hurried forward to find the mate Mr. Douglas, with his back to the port bulwark defending himself with bare fists from four of the crew armed with knives. As Captain Waterman ran along the main deck he pulled a heavy iron belaying pin out of the rail, and using this with both hands as a club, he dealt a terrific blow on the skull of each of the assassins, which laid them out on the deck—two of them dead. Mr. Douglas had received no less than twelve wounds. From that time the officers always carried arms, and there was no further trouble with the crew." It is recorded that Waterman read the burial service over two men who fell from aloft to the deck off Cape Horn and were killed, but " could not bring himself to read the Christian burial service over the bodies of the two men who attempted to murder the chief officer " ; none of the crew would volunteer to conduct the service, so the corpses were taken from where they fell and lowered into the sea.

The ex-naval man disappeared, and the men said he had been lost overboard. Douglas did not believe this, but the man did not reappear and was not found till Douglas discovered him under some boards in the forecastle. When he got him on deck the mate struck at him with a heaver ; the man raised his arm to protect his head, and the limb was broken in two places. He received no medical treatment.

The captain was also fond of the heaver as a weapon wherewith to strike defenceless men. On one night he knocked out three men because their steering did not please him.

The second mate, Cole, was another of the same kidney as his superior officers ; he is credited with having kicked three men off a yard, so that they fell. Two dropped into the sea and were left to drown ; the third fell on the poop alive but badly injured. Douglas had him stitched in a blanket and thrown overboard.

Once the ship's carpenter fell foul of Captain Waterman, or *vice versa*. " You're captain here, but if I had you ashore I'd lick you," he replied to some abuse by the captain. " We'll try it," replied the captain, who was no coward. He pulled off his coat. For once he met his match. It was a hard fight and the carpenter, a big Swede, beat him soundly. The captain did not interfere with the carpenter any more.

The next to fall foul of the captain was the second mate. The captain swore at him, and then jumped from the poop upon him. Cole hit him between the eyes and floored him. The mate flung a belaying pin at Cole, and missed, and ran, pursued by Cole, who knocked him flying. Later, Waterman invited Cole into the cabin under professions of friendship, and gave him a glass of doped spirit. Cole did his best to continue his work, but when the drug had fairly begun to act Waterman hit him over the head with his heaver and laid him out. Cole was then placed in irons and thrown into one of the boats where he was kept a prisoner till port was reached, being fed on bread and water like the ex-naval man.

Other bullying followed by Waterman and Douglas. An old Italian sailor was unable to do his work because his feet had become frostbitten, so Waterman knocked him out with his heaver in the usual way. The man was killed. By the time the ship reached San Francisco there had been several deaths, beside eight men still in their bunks ; of these eight some came aboard ill and could not be cured at sea. Lubbock in his " China Clippers," reports that three men died through being kicked off the yard, and five died in their bunks.

When the *Challenge* arrived at San Francisco, Waterman got ashore before the ship was moored. The crew, however, spread the story of the voyage and the crowd that gathered searched for Waterman and Douglas with the intention of lynching them. By some means the public anger was assuaged. Waterman gave himself up. Douglas was also arrested. They were tried for murder, and although the details of the voyage were testified to on oath during the trial it ended in both the accused being liberated. Justice in those days in San Francisco was a purchasable commodity, and as Waterman was a wealthy man he had no difficulty in getting off. He never went to sea again. One of his apologists in America refers to him as a " humane, conscientious, high-minded man," who really was no rougher with his crews than was necessary to keep a turbulent lot in order.

13

Waterman was perhaps the worst of the " hell-ship "
captains, but nearly all the packet ships (except those that
had Scandinavian crews), and the majority of the American
clippers were more remarkable for the cruelty with which
the men were treated than for anything else. On most of
them there was no watch below during the day, all hands
being kept on deck and plenty of work found for them with
the incentive of the belaying pin or knuckle-duster to keep
them up to it. Some masters had the practice of padlock-
ing the chain halliards to prevent the crew letting them go
at night when the sail was being carried to an extreme that
seemed rash ; Waterman is said to have introduced the
practice.

In justice to the American captains and mates it must be
conceded that they had a rough lot to deal with, and the
officers who could not lick their crew into obedience were
not much use ; but this is no excuse for the deliberate
cruelty which prevailed on some ships, nor for the shaking
of the sails in order to throw a troublesome man overboard
to drown. The mates also had to thrash troublesome
steerage passengers occasionally.

Waterman is stated to have indulged in the tawdry
theatricality of calling for a bucket of salt water at the
beginning of a voyage in order that he could wash off his
shore face, and reveal himself as he was. After he left the
sea he " experienced religion " ; it is a pity he did not get
his experience long before. The story goes that once
in his desire to spread his new-found grace he visited a
ship at San Francisco, and found on board some members of
his former crews who promptly threw him over the bulwarks into the sea ; he was rescued from drowning by the
police. The *Challenge* had an entirely different set of
officers and crew when she sailed for Shanghai to load tea

for England. She was a handsome ship, and her good looks and her evil reputation caused a great deal of interest to be taken in her when she reached London.

A great race was sailed in 1851 from New York to San Francisco by the *Sea-Witch* under Fraser and the *Typhoon* under Captain Salter; the former passed Sandy Hook on August 1st and the *Typhoon* on August 4th; and the *Raven*, under Captain Henry, left Boston on August 6th. The captains of all three knew how to carry sail. The *Sea-Witch* crossed the line on August 30th, and the *Typhoon* and the *Raven* the next day. The *Raven* drew level on the run south, with the *Typhoon* only two days behind. The two leaders beat round Cape Horn, sometimes one and sometimes the other gaining a slight advantage in tacking, and the *Typhoon* steadily reduced their lead till she was less than a day behind. The *Sea-Witch* crossed the equator two days ahead of the *Raven*, which in turn was two days before the *Typhoon*. In the final struggle to San Francisco the *Typhoon* overtook the other two and got into port on November 18th after a passage of 106 days; the *Raven* came in on the 19th and the *Sea-Witch* on the 20th. The *Raven* was the only ship of her size which ever beat the *Sea-Witch* in a sailing match; the *Typhoon* of 1600 tons, was a larger and more powerful ship.

Such passages as these could only be made by driving the ships hard, night and day. Their captains were scarcely off the deck from the beginning to the end of the voyage, but took what rest they could in arm chairs on the poop, weather permitting, and only changed their clothes when they had their baths.

The *Sea-Witch* made only one more voyage to San Francisco and was then returned to the China trade. Fraser, who as chief mate under Waterman, had been a hard specimen of the bucko, may have adhered to his bucko methods as master, for when outward bound from New York to China in 1855 he was murdered by his chief mate, and the *Sea-Witch* was put into Rio where another master was appointed to her. The ship was wrecked the following year off Cuba when carrying coolies from China to Havana.

As a contrast to the rapid passages already mentioned, it may be stated that the *Barrington* and *Franconia*, from Boston, took 180 days, the *Austerlitz* from Boston, and the *Bengal* from Philadelphia, 185 days, the *Arthur* 200 days the *Cornwallis* 204 days, and the *Henry Allen* 225 days, all three from New York; the *Capitol's* voyage from Boston lasted 300 days. These were not clippers; some were old packets, and they certainly were not driven. On the other hand, the little pilot schooner *Fanny*, 84 tons, built at Boston in 1850, sailed in 1851 from that port to San Francisco, by way of the Straits of Magellan, thus avoiding Cape Horn, in 108 days.

A fine race terminating in 1852 was sailed between the *Sword-Fish*, 1036 tons, built by Webb of New York, and the *Flying-Fish*, 1505 tons, built by Donald McKay of Boston. They sailed from their respective ports on November 11th, 1851, the *Sword-Fish* being under Captain Babcock, and the other under Captain Nickels, both of whom were capable ship drivers. The *Flying-Fish* reached the equator in 19 days, and her rival was four days later. They beat round Cape Horn side by side, after which the *Sword-Fish* gradually obtained a substantial lead and anchored in San Francisco harbour a few hours under 91 days from New York, one of the best performances on record. The *Flying-Fish* was eight days behind her. The many splendid passages of the *Sword-Fish* prove her to have been one of the best ships ever launched by her famous builder. One of her runs is the record of 31 days from Shanghai to San Francisco, in 1855, when she averaged 240 miles a day. Her second voyage to San Francisco was made in 105 days.

The *Flying Cloud*, 1783 tons, launched in 1851, commanded by Captain J. P. Creesy, formerly of the ship *Oneida*, ran to San Francisco in the very short time of 89 days. On her second voyage she took 113 days. On this voyage, when off Brazil, she overtook the *N. B. Palmer*, which sailed from New York eight days after the *Flying Cloud* and had gone ahead having had better winds to the equator. When the wind freshened the *Flying Cloud* left her rival behind; she got into San Francisco 23 days ahead. The *N. B. Palmer* had had some trouble with her crew. She put into Valparaiso to land two of them, and this cost her five days, as seventeen men took the opportunity to desert and substitutes had to be shipped in their places. One of the two men landed had shot at the mate with a pistol and wounded him, and the other had knocked the second mate senseless with a marlinspike or some such weapon. For this they were put in irons by Captain Low's orders and tied to the rigging and given four dozen lashes each.

Other record breakers launched in 1851 were the *Comet* and *Northern Light*. The *Comet* was of 1836 tons and was commanded by Captain Gardner, formerly of the *Celestial*, and made the San Francisco passage in 102 days. The next year she was partially dismasted in a gale off Bermuda, but Captain Gardner re-rigged her at sea and she made what must in the circumstances be regarded as the good passage of 112 days.

The eastward voyages were almost always made in better

time than the westward. Going out to San Francisco it was
necessary to beat round Cape Horn against the westerly
gales, which prevail about 360 days in the year, and sometimes more, and this might take anything from a few days
to as many weeks ; for that matter there have been instances when ships have taken two months to get round into
the Pacific. On the eastward passage the ships had the
westerlies behind them and romped past the Horn and into
the Atlantic in grand style. The fastest passage from
San Francisco to New York was 76 days, made by the
Comet in 1854.

The *Northern Light*, 1021 tons, built at Boston in 1851,
under Captain Hatch, and the *Contest*, 1150 tons, built by
Westervelt at New York in 1852, Captain Brewster, had a
remarkable race eastward in 1853. The latter left the
Golden Gate for New York on March 12th, and the *Northern
Light* the following day for Boston. Off Cape Horn they
exchanged signals. The *Northern Light* won the race,
completing the voyage in 76 days 5 hours, and the *Contest*
made her passage in 80 days. The *Northern Light* in 1852
went from Boston to San Francisco in 109 days. The
Contest in 1853 made the westward journey in 108 days,
arriving in February of that year, and after a quick turn
round had a rapid run home. She loaded again for San
Francisco and made her second voyage in the year, this
time in 97 days.

The fastest passage in 1853 was that of the *Flying Fish*,
92 days, and only one day longer was that of the *John
Gilpin*. Altogether 22 vessels made the run that year from
an Atlantic port to California in 110 days or less. The
fastest passage in 1854 was that of the *Flying Cloud*, 89
days from New York. The next best was by the *Romance
of the Seas*, from Boston, 86 days ; other good passages

were made by the *Witchcraft*, 97 days, *David Brown* 98 days, and *Hurricane* 99 days, all from New York. Twenty-one vessels completed the passage that year in 110 days or under.

In the following year the *Herald of the Morning*, from New York in 99 days, put up the best performance; the previous year she had taken 110 days. Sixteen vessels made the run under 110 days.

In 1856 the number of clippers in the San Francisco trade began to show signs of declining. The great profits which had distinguished the early days of the rush were no longer obtainable. The pressure at which many of the ships had been driven had strained them aloft and in hull considerably, and repairs were an expensive item. More new ships were built than the prospect of profitable employment justified. Many were sold to British owners, who found remunerative employment for them in the Australian trade and as transports during the Crimean war and the Indian Mutiny.

From now on, fewer ships were in the California trade from the Atlantic ports, and every year showed a falling off in the number till after the American Civil War broke out, when the number dropped almost out of sight owing to the depredations of the southern privateers.

The famous *Sweepstakes* sailed from New York to San Francisco in 1856 in 94 days, the next best passage being that of the *Antelope* in 97 days.

In that and subsequent years some excellent passages were made, and continued to be made as long as sailing ships remained to sail between the Atlantic ports and those on the west coast, which was well into this century. The performances of the *Andrew Jackson* were somewhat remarkable. In 1857 she went to San Francisco from New

York in 100 days, in 1858 in 103 days, in 1859 in 102 days, and in 1860 in the remarkably short time of 89 days.

After the American civil war several vessels were built for the Californian trade, but it is stated that only twice had the passage from an Atlantic port to San Francisco been made under a hundred days. The *Seminole*, built in 1865, ran from New York in 96 days, and the *Glory of the Seas*, the last of Donald McKay's marvels, made the voyage in 94 days in 1874. The last two of the California clippers in active service were the *David Crockett* and the *Young America*. The latter in 1856 went from New York to San Francisco in 107 days, and in 1859 in 105 days. They were built in 1853 and continued in the trade for thirty years. After the civil war they continued to make good passages. The *David Crockett's* best was 102 days in 1872, and for twelve voyages she averaged 109 days and a few hours. The *Young America's* best was 102 days in 1880, and her best dozen passages averaged a few hours over 110 days. These figures show that they were still capable of a good turn of speed, and as their spars had been reduced in size and their sail area cut down they may be said to have acquitted themselves well.

Other produce than gold was obtainable from the Pacific coast. The Pacific slope was found to be a wonderfully fertile soil for wheat, and in May, 1855, the first cargo of wheat was shipped from San Francisco, 4752 bags, in the barque *Greenfield*, Captain Follansbee. Another cargo was sent by the ship *Charmer*, Captain Lucas, which carried 1400 tons of grain. The increasing crops enabled many vessels to load wheat, and thus secure a paying homeward cargo in addition to the outward cargo. This was very welcome, for the freight rates from the east coast to the California coast were dropping. The carriage of wheat from the Pacific coast ports to the east coast ports and to Great Britain and western Europe, and to some Asiatic ports was the last trade but one or two in which sailing ships were able to earn a living.

Some of the clippers returning to the eastern ports carried passengers, chiefly men who had been successful at the diggings. Most of the returning diggers preferred to travel by the steamship service which had been established from San Francisco to the isthmus, which had to be crossed by vehicle or other means of land transport, and from the eastern side another steamer took them to New York. The scenes on these vessels were extraordinary. Some of the men seemed to have no idea but to waste their money on drink or gambling. A few of the homeward bound sailers were wrecked ; so also were a few of the homeward bound steamers. As there were seldom survivors from the wrecked sailing ships the details of their loss must be left to the imagination. The incidents were probably not dissimilar to those which occurred when the steamship *Central America* was wrecked, in 1857, off Cape Hatteras, with the Pacific mails and passengers and crew and over two million dollars' worth of treasure from California. The passengers had come down the coast from San Francisco to Panama and crossed the isthmus, and then joined the steamship. A vivid description of the wreck was given by one of the few passengers who survived. Loth to lose their store of the precious metal for which they had laboured so hard, perhaps for years, some of the returning miners strapped their fortunes in belts about their waists in the hope that both they and their wealth might be saved. In many instances the weight of the gold caused them to sink at once, never to be seen again. By others their gold was thrown about just before the vessel went down.

" A great number of the passengers were miners," the passenger wrote, " having considerable sums of gold about them, the product of years of toil, but the love of gold was forgotten in the anxiety and terror of the moment, and many a man unbuckled his gold-stuffed belt and flung his hard-earned treasure upon the deck, some hoping thereby to lessen their weight and thus more easily keep themselves afloat, while others threw it away in despair, thinking there was no use for it in the watery grave they were going to. Mr. Chase says he might have picked up tens of thousands of dollars which had been thrown away and lay strewn about the decks ; but he did not think there was sufficient prospect of his surviving to use it, to pay him for the trouble. A Captain Thomas W. Badger, of San Francisco, had twenty thousand dollars in gold in a carpet bag, which, just before the sinking of the ship, he threw into the captain's stateroom. He, however, succeeded in saving himself, being one of the number picked up by the barque *Ellen*."

Prior to the discovery of gold in Australia in 1851 the shipping trade with Australia had been carried on in a leisurely way with some of the splendid sailing ships of the early part of the century, and some which were nothing like so good. The chief owners at that time were Messrs. Green and Wigram, who for a long time were in partnership, and both when a united firm, and afterwards, sent their vessels to Australia, their chief rival being Joseph Somes. The ships of all three were of good class.

Wigram was one of the earliest shipowners in London to enter the Australian trade ; probably his first venture in that direction was with a small barque, the *Emu*, 293 tons, in 1837. The ninety years intervening since then have seen some marvellous changes. What would her passengers have thought of the present day steamships ? And what would the passengers on the latter say if they were offered passages on a little barque like this ? Joseph Somes's ships traded everywhere.

The chief use of Australia in the early days of the last century, the British authorities seemed to think, was as a dumping ground for undesirables in the United Kingdom. Any old ship seems to have been thought good enough for convicts, and seeing the poor rates the government paid to have the convicts conveyed to Australia it is no wonder that certain of the ships would not have been considered fit to carry ordinary merchandise. Many of the convict ships were good vessels ; some were not. Those supplied by Somes were above the average, and were the equal of many he put in other trades. How poor the government pay was for this class of service is shown by the record that for the *Maitland*, 648 tons, the rate was £5 per ton per voyage, out of which all expenses had to be met. The *Asia*, 536 tons, received £5 9s. ; the *Eden* (surely a mis-nomer for a convict ship), 522 tons, £5 13s. 9d. ; the *Lord Lyndoch*, 638 tons, £5 14s. ; the *Mary Ann*, 394 tons, £6 4s. 4d. These sums were paid in 1840. In 1841 the government paid £6 6s. per ton for the *Mexborough*, 376 tons.

The rush to the Australian goldfields was not so severe as that to California in the matter of numbers the first year. As, however, the news spread, and there came reports of large nuggets being dug out of the soil, only a few feet below the surface in some cases, the desire to go to Australia became overwhelming. In 1845 a little ship, the *Rossendale*, of 296 tons, was advertised to sail for Australia, and as an inducement to the adventurous public to go in her she was stated to have " spacious and elegant accommodation." I have seen in two or three of the vessels surviving to the '70's from the days of the gold rush, the accommodation provided for passengers. It could not be called " spacious and elegant," at any time, but rather the reverse ; and especially when packed with passengers who did not care what discomforts they endured so long as they got to Australia and could start, as they anticipated, pocketing the expected gold dust, it could not be pleasant. Their desire to begin amassing a fortune was stimulated by the way, when they got ashore, they could see men throwing about the gold they had obtained, or recklessly drinking and gambling it away, boasting that when that was gone they could go and get plenty more. Some of my relatives who went to Australia in the early '50's used to tell me of the sights to be seen in Melbourne in those times.

The comparatively few miners who took care of their gold were the redeeming feature of the picture. There was another side, in which every form of vice and crime was always present, and robbery and murder were far too common. A few of the ex-convicts, and some who had never been convicts, turned bushranger and " stuck-up," otherwise held up and robbed, mail coaches and passengers with their escorts of armed police—some of whom were murdered by them—or solitary wayfarers. The uncon-victed criminal adventurers who went out to prey on every-body they could victimise, by fair means or foul, seldom went beyond Melbourne or Sydney, unless they ran gambling saloons at the goldfields, or wayside shanties where the vilest drink was sold and the customer could be sure of being robbed ; they preferred Melbourne because there was less authoritative control. The police as a body were not very efficient. However, the gaol was filled with ruffians, and ships in the harbour, deserted by their officers and crews, were requisitioned by the government for the safe custody of the worst of the offenders.

Most of the ships engaged in the passenger trade to Australia at that time were of the slow and stately variety; voyages of 120 days were not uncommon, but when the rush to the goldfields began most of the shipowners in the trade put on the best vessels they had and chartered others, and not a few owners who had not been in the trade before sent their ships into it or bought or chartered others, and the demand was such that there was room for them all.

Speed was all-important. The fastest vessels obtainable were those built in the British colonies in North America and in the New England states. British owners were inquiring all over the place for vessels showing seaworthiness, speed, and the ability to carry cargo and large numbers of passengers.

The *Marco Polo* is stated to have been the first clipper built for the Australian trade. She was of 1622 tons, 185 feet in length, beam 38 feet, and depth 30 feet. She was not English built, but was launched by Smith and Company at St. John, New Brunswick. The statement is often made that she was built to the order of Messrs. James Baines and Company, of Liverpool; certainly she had the distinction of being the pioneer ship of Baines's famous Australian Black Ball Line. She had three decks and was very strongly constructed, had clipper bows, and was as fine in her lines below the water level as many a clipper. She had a square stern, after the fashion of those days, and painted ports, and in some respects suggested a resemblance to the packet ships of the North Atlantic, and in others to the frigates turned out by the Thames-side ship builders, but no one who had seen the frigates or the packets would mistake her for either.

It is also stated that she was sent across the Atlantic with cotton and other American goods to Liverpool, where she was bought cheap by a man known as Paddy M'Gee, a marine store dealer, who sold her to Mr. Baines at an immense profit, and that it was Mr. Baines who had her equipped for the Australian trade. If so, Mr. Baines knew a good ship when he saw it. Wood was cheap in New Brunswick for shipbuilding, but copper bolts were very dear, and some ships built on that side of the Atlantic for British owners were sent over with an insufficient number of copper bolts, and were fully bolted after they arrived at Liverpool. Whether this happened to the *Marco Polo* is not known, and the report that she needed to have her wooden bolts taken out and copper ones substituted needs to be substantiated.

Her voyage across the Atlantic to Liverpool was accomplished in good time, and she gave promise of being the flier she ultimately proved herself. She sailed from Liverpool under the command of Captain J. Nicol Forbes, on July 4th, 1851, with a general cargo, mails, and a great many passengers. One account says she had 648 passengers, but though it was the custom to crowd passengers into a ship until it was difficult to find room for another, this figure has been asserted to be an exaggeration. On another voyage she is stated to have nearly 300 more. She also had £90,000 in specie. On her maiden voyage she beat the steamship *Antelope* to Melbourne. Her run to Port Phillip was made in 68 days, which constituted a record.

The first consignment of gold from Australia consisted of packages of gold dust valued at £81,000, brought by the White Star ship *Phoenician*, which arrived in February, 1852. The *Albatross*, of the Eagle Line of Liverpool,

MARCO POLO

From oilpainting in Author's possession

arrived in the Mersey in the following August with £50,000 worth of gold dust, and, more wonderful still, she had on board some of the crew who sailed on her outward voyage. The *Albatross* had to wait some months at Port Phillip to complete her crew. Her homeward passage of 78 days was the fastest up to that time.

The arrival of these vessels with their large quantities of gold dust, together with the stories told by her successful passengers, seemed to give the whole nation gold-fever ; the out-going passengers numbered thousands, and so great was the desire now of shipowners to share in the Australian trade that there was actually a shortage of good vessels for other trades. It seemed that only the owners of ships in the Australian trade could afford to pay the prices which owners and builders charged for new ships.

The ships in the Australian gold rush had one important advantage over the clippers in the Californian gold rush. Steamers were soon placed on the east and west American coasts, which plied on the one side between the isthmus of Panama and the east coast ports, and on the other between the isthmus and San Francisco, a route which passengers favoured. The voyage between Great Britain and Australia was an ocean voyage throughout ; steamship competition was not experienced till years afterwards.

Prior to the gold discoveries all the ships for Australia were accustomed to take a long route to Australia. Many of them called at the Cape of Good Hope, and then continued in as straight a line as they could to Adelaide or Bass's Straits. They came back the reverse way, thereby completely avoiding Cape Horn, and making rather slow passages, anything up to five months.

About that time Lieutenant Maury began to advocate, as the result of his studies of ocean winds and currents, the adoption of the Great Circle system of sailing. It was partly owing to the adoption of Maury's directions, and partly owing to the fact that the ships put into the Australian trade after the discovery of gold were more or less of the clipper model and were faster and larger, and more able to stand driving in all weathers, that the passages to and from Australia were shorter, by a month each way, taking two and a half months or less in place of the four months which had been the rule. Practically all the ships which participated in the Australian trade, both at the time of the rush and afterwards, returned to England with wool as the principal cargo, and continued to do so for many years ; it was a very profitable trade for the ships.

Some of the voyages were not without exciting incidents. Such crews as were to be obtained at Melbourne or Sydney were by no means the best ; there might be a few real sailors among them, but there were often men who were not sailors at all, but were glad to leave Australia because it had become too hot for them in the criminal sense. It has always been thought that the fine ship *Madagascar*, which had a large consignment of gold on board, and was never heard of after she sailed from Melbourne in 1853, was lost through her crew mutinying and seizing the ship ; she is known to have had some desperadoes among her crew. Some years ago it was reported from New Zealand that a woman who had been living there claimed on her deathbed to have been on board the ship as nurse to a woman who was travelling with two children. Her story was that the crew mutinied when the ship was in the South Atlantic, that the officers were murdered, that the mutineers set the ship on fire, and sailed off in the boats, leaving the ship and those on her to their fate. The boat in which she, another woman, and five of the men were, managed to reach Brazil, but the boat was upset in the surf and the gold dust for which the crime had been committed was lost. After great privations the party arrived at a township and most of them died of yellow fever. Afterwards she went to New Zealand. Her story can neither be disproved nor verified.

The *Madagascar* was commanded by Captain F. Harris, who was not the sort of man to stand any nonsense from anyone, and, if this gruesome story be true, one can only imagine the awful scenes that took place on this lonely ship. She had 68,390 ounces of gold on board. Even before she sailed two of her passengers were arrested for complicity in one of the gold robberies from an escorted mail coach.

Of some of the ships engaged in the Australian trade, both at the height of the gold fever and afterwards, till they were supplanted by steamers, I shall speak in the next chapter.

14

CHAPTER VII

WOOL, WHEAT AND EMIGRANT SHIPS

WOOL, wheat, hides and tallow were the principal Australian exports to the United Kingdom. Wool was packed as tightly as possible in bales, and I have often watched the bales being forced into a ship's hold till it seemed impossible another could be got in. " I think we can get a few more in here," someone in the hold would say, and in they were forced. Or the captain after a visit to the agent might tell the mates who were seeing to the stowing of the cargo " A couple of hundred more bales are coming in the morning ; you've got to shove them in somewhere." Wool was a good cargo if a fast passage was to be made, because it was not too heavy, and a ship with a wool cargo was not down to her Plimsoll lines and was therefore likely to travel well. It depended a great deal on the ship itself whether wool was the only article she should load ; in many vessels it was customary, after a certain amount of wool had been stowed, to fill up with hides and barrels of tallow which were heavier. One reason why wool was packed so tightly was that the tighter it was the less likely was it to develop spontaneous combustion, and the drier and safer it would be.

Wheat was loaded in sacks, and considerable ingenuity was shown in stowing as many sacks of grain as possible into a hull as she would hold, and at some of the small outports neither the captain of a ship taking in wheat there nor the local officials were very particular not to submerge the Plimsoll marks. The dishonest practice was at times resorted to by captains of having a number of bags slit at the sides, after being stowed, to let out part of the grain in them, so that more sacks could be received. Wool and wheat have remained the staple Australian exports to this day.

The London wool sales were held in the first three months of the year, and the ship that made a tedious passage stood a good chance of missing the sales and having to keep her cargo for months unless the consignees were lucky enough to find a purchaser. The supply of wool in Australia was considerable and increasing, and the ships which were known to be slow were always despatched first to give them the opportunity of being in good time for the sales. The *Cutty Sark*, as long as she was under Captain Woodget, was among the last of the sailers to leave, as it was known he would get to London for the sales if driving his little flyer could do it. I don't think he was ever late.

The large soft-wood American-built ships were not popular with shippers of wool. Wool if damp may cause a fire and a good many disasters have been attributed to that cause. These ships were liable to take in a great deal of water through their seams. Nevertheless, at one time they brought home a good deal of wool, until the supply of British ships, especially iron ones, drove them out of the trade.

As it is impossible to mention all the ships, numbering thousands, which have helped to make history in the last hundred years, I propose to mention only a few which have distinguished themselves in one way or another ; many sailed and returned in uneventful fashion, never making notably fast passages or conspicuously slow ones, delivering their passengers, when they had any, and cargo in good condition and loading up for another voyage, until their period of usefulness was over and they were unceremoniously sold foreign or scrapped, regretted by none except a few who had sailed in them. Some attained fame by the regularity of their voyages, or by their ownership, or by their speed, and in a few cases by their lack of it ; or by the disasters which brought their careers to untimely ends.

At first London and Liverpool were the chief British ports in the Australian trade. London catered, with its beautiful Blackwall frigates, for the best class of passengers, and the best available cargo outward and homeward. Liverpool laid itself out for all passengers and cargo obtainable.

When the Australian trade was found to be worth looking after, the later China clippers were sent to Australia, whence they went to China, and thence back to England. Later, direct services between Australia and England were instituted by several lines.

Wigram and Green were in partnership until 1843, and they seem to have owned ships separately and also jointly. Many of their earlier ships have already been mentioned. Both firms had a number of ships in the Australian trade, but they sent their vessels wherever they thought they could be profitably employed. Many of them bore the same names as the East Indiamen of old John Company, and worthily they fulfilled the traditions attaching to them. One of the best of them was the *Alfred*, which carried a crew of 90 persons. A *Monarch* was built in 1833, and another, described as a magnificent vessel of 1,415 tons, in

1844. The second *Roxburgh Castle* was built in 1852, the second *Malabar*, 1,219 tons, in 1860 ; the second *Windsor Castle*, 1,075 tons, in 1857 ; the second *Walmer Castle*, in 1855, the *Wellesley*, 963 tons, in 1844 ; the *Nile*, 1,126 tons, in 1858 ; the *Sutlej* in 1847 ; the *Blackwall*, 674 tons, the *Alnwick Castle*, 1,087 tons, in 1854 ; the *Clarence* 1,194 tons, and the *Dover Castle*, 1,002 tons, both in 1858 ; the *Newcastle*, 1,137 tons, 1859 ; the *Highflier*, in 1861 ; the *Shannon*, 1,272 tons, and the *Lord Warden*, 1,237 tons, 1862 ; the *Childers*, 1,016 tons, in 1863, and many others.

Among Green's iron ships were the appropriately named *Superb*, built in 1866, and the *Carlisle Castle*, 1,435 tons, in 1868, and probably the finest of them all, the *Melbourne*, in 1875, which was better known under her second name of *Macquarie*, and was for many years one of the most popular passenger ships afloat.

Equally well known were the ships of Messrs. Smith, of Newcastle and London. Their earlier vessels resembled warships and could easily have been used for naval purposes. They included, besides the famous *Marlborough* and *Blenheim*, the *Gloriana*, 1,057 tons, built in 1843, the *Hotspur*, 1,142 tons, in 1851, and the *St. Lawrence*, 1,094 tons, in 1861 ; this was one of the last frigate built ships to be launched. The *Marlborough* made the passage to Melbourne in 78 days in 1853 and the homeward in 84. The *Hotspur*, launched after the *Blenheim*, made an outward passage of 90 days and a homeward passage of 91, and is credited with 323 miles in less than 24 hours.

Joseph Somes was another owner whose name was a household word in the sailing ship business of the last century. His fleet included many of the old East Indiamen, and his ships traded everywhere. Among the dozens which might be mentioned was the *Eastern Monarch*,

1,844 tons, built at Dundee in 1856. She was used as a
transport, and as she was completing her voyage home
from India with invalid troops in 1859 she caught fire
at Spithead and was burnt; about 500 were saved and
only eight lives were lost. Somes was a great believer in
keeping his fleet up to modern requirements, selling off
the older and smaller vessels from time to time. Among
the ships he ordered in the '60's were the *Clyde*, the *Star
of India*, 1,945 tons, the *Salisbury*, 1,145 tons, the *Gains-
borough*, an iron ship of 998 tons, and the *Hereford*, 1,593
tons. The firm was afterwards the Merchant Shipping
Company, which ordered the iron ship *Peterborough*, 1,740
tons.

An even more celebrated owner was Duncan Dunbar
of London. His father built up a large business and
Duncan became a partner in it in 1823. When he died
in 1862 his fortune was estimated at a million and a half
pounds. At one time he built a great number of ships
in his own yards at Moulmein, though many were built
for him in Great Britain. It is reported that as many as
eight ships flying his house flag were in one of the Thames-
side docks at once. His later vessels, built at Moulmein,
included the *Albuera*, 852 tons, *Hougomont*, 962 tons,
Cospatrick, 1,119 tons, and *Lincelles*, 904 tons; the
Ballarat, 713 tons, at Aberdeen; and at Sunderland the
Rodney, 877 tons, *Talavera*, 916 tons, *Pyrenees*, 830 tons,
Vimiera, 1,037 tons, *Dunbar*, 1,167 tons, *Duncan Dunbar*,
1,374 tons, *La Hogue*, 1,331 tons, and others. The first
English built vessel he put into the Australian trade as a
passenger ship was the *Duncan Dunbar*, launched by Laing
the year following the *Kent* at Blackwall.

John Willis, the elder, after starting as ship's boy and
working himself up to be master and then ship owner,

owned four vessels by 1853, the *John Willis, St. Abbs,
Borderer,* and *Janet Willis,* and shortly afterwards added
the *Merse,* then being built at Sunderland, to his fleet,
to be followed some time later by the famous clipper
Lammermuir which was his favourite. Captain Shewan,
senr., was her commander up to 1860. Upon Willis's
death, his son John took over the business and extended
it. He was famous for two things, his white hat, and his
ownership of the *Tweed* and *Cutty Sark.*

The *Norman Court,* owned by Baring Brothers, was
another fine ship which was reckoned as fast as the regular
clippers. Captain Shewan, junr., reports that when in
1871 his ship was running down her easting, after rounding
the Cape of Good Hope, he fell in with the *Thermopylae*
which had been running the easting down a couple of
degrees further south. "As a proof," he writes, "that
there was little difference in the speed of the two ships I
would say that on the day, March 2nd, the *Thermopylae*
entered Port Phillip Heads, we in the *Norman Court*
rounded Cape Pillar, the south-east point of Tasmania."

Wigram's first ship in the Australian trade was the *Kent;*
she was 927 tons, and 186 feet in length with a beam of
33 feet. Her masts and other spars were of unusual length
even for a Blackwaller. She was a great favourite with
passengers. After a few years an advertisement asserted
that she had made eight passages to and from Australia
"of an average duration which has not been equalled by
any vessel afloat." It is quite possible, when one remembers how she beat three or four of the China tea clippers.
In 1854 she and the *Marco Polo* sailed from Port Phillip
on the same day, and the *Kent* landed her mails at Hastings
in 84 days, the day before the *Marco Polo* reached the
Mersey. The *Kent* was then under Captain Coleman. In

1859 Captain Clayton had her, and the *Kent, Blue Jacket* and *Marco Polo* left England within two or three days of each other. Off the South American coast a storm interfered with them, but Captain Clayton managed to turn it to his advantage and gained a lead on his competitors and arrived in Port Phillip Bay 88 days out, and several days ahead of the others. The *Kent* generally averaged about 81 days to Melbourne, though her maiden voyage in 1853 was done in 83 days and her second voyage, in the same year in 74 days.

By the way, chanties were not allowed in the Blackwall frigates, a fiddler being carried to supply the music for the crew to work to. Chanties were deemed undignified. Captain Clayton, who was one of the most popular commanders that ever trod a deck, was up to all sorts of expedients to get his ship along in calm weather. Once he rigged platforms on each side of the ship and with volunteers from the passengers to assist the crew, set them to rowing their hardest from the platforms to get the ship along. There was a fiddler on each side to encourage the rowers to put their backs into it. This healthy and unusual exercise lasted two days, and it had the desired effect of keeping her on the move till she got a wind. A boat was towed astern in case anybody fell into the sea.

It is an eloquent testimony to the care with which the Blackwall ships were built, equipped and sailed that throughout what may be called the days of the Blackwall frigates only four catastrophies stand out with startling prominence : the *Northfleet, Cospatrick, Dunbar* and *Dalhousie*. The last named was built at Moulmein in 1848, and as one of the White Horse Line of passenger ships she sailed from the Thames to Sydney, with a few passengers, intending to embark the remainder of them at Plymouth.

On the way from the Downs, she capsized and sank. The only survivor was taken off the floating wreckage by a passing brig.

The *Northfleet*, when outward bound from London for Tasmania in the '70's, with a cargo of railway iron and a large number of passengers, most of whom were navvies, was run into and sunk by the steamship *Murillo*, a foreign owned vessel ; out of the 350 emigrants on board 293 were drowned; those lost included Captain Knowles who, revolver in hand, had tried to save the women and children.

One of the best performances by a Blackwall frigate is said to have been that of the *Anglesey* in 1871, when she ran from the Start Point to Port Phillip in 72 days, and on the homeward run covered 3,397 miles in thirteen days, an average of 261 miles a day, and the run from Port Phillip to Cape Horn in 23 days.

Green's passenger ships in the Australian trade in the '60's and early '70's were among the most popular afloat for the better class of traveller who appreciated comfort and not being overcrowded like the majority of the ships from Liverpool.

Thompson's Aberdeen White Star Line started in 1825 with the *Childe Harold*, a brig of 116 tons ; all this line's ships were built by Hood, and till iron was adopted, all were of wood except three, the *Thyatira*, 962 tons, the *Thermopylae*, 948 tons, and the *Centurion* 965 tons, which were composite. The line's subsequent vessels were of iron. The largest of them was the *Kosciusko*, 1,192 tons. All the hulls of the ships of this line were painted green. It was only in the gold rush that any of them carried passengers in the 'tween decks. The *Star of Peace*, 1,113 tons, was one of the fastest, and under Captain Sproat made four voyages to Sydney in 79 days or under.

The *Thermopylae* on her maiden voyage in 1868-9 was
commanded by Captain Robert Kemball, formerly of the
China clipper *Yangtse*, which was afterwards well known in
the Sydney trade, and later of the *Fairlight*, another
favourite in the Melbourne trade. She sailed on November
6th, 1868, crossed the equator 28 days out, rounded the
Cape of Good Hope on December 16th, 38 days out, and
arrived on January 7th, 1869, a voyage of 62 days. Her
fastest day's run was on January 4th, when she covered
336 knots. She arrived while the *Moravian*, the pioneer
vessel of the line, was loading and about to sail for London.
This passage by the *Thermopylae* was the fastest ever made,
and certain other alleged record voyages, such as 56 days
from London to Melbourne or Sydney, may be dismissed
as inventions.

What one might call the genealogy of the *Cutty Sark* is
interesting and romantic.   A French frigate was sent to
India a century or so ago, and was much admired.   Her
measurements were taken and her lines or shape noted,
and a steamer called the *Punjaub* was built on them for
the Indian navy at Bombay. She was very strongly constructed of teak, and after some years' service as a steamer,
transporting troops and doing other work, she was sent to
England.   Here the second John Willis bought her, had
her engines taken out, and converted her into a sailing
ship in 1863. This became the famous *Tweed*, 1,745 tons,
one of the most talked-of ships of her time, an exceptionally fast vessel. Willis gave the command to Capt. W.
Stuart, at one time of the *Lammermuir*, and he retained
the post until 1877. Under Stuart she made many good
passages, such as London to Bombay in 77 days, and on her
first voyage to Melbourne she went in about 76 days and
did the return run in 83. She took a big ship load of

TWEED

From oilpainting, by permission of Mr. J. Rothon

FERREIRA (ex CUTTY SARK) AS A BARQUENTINE

Photo by R. A. Fletcher

emigrants to Otago, New Zealand, in 1874 in under 80 days, and the homeward voyage from Sydney to London was about 90 days. In the following year her outward and homeward runs to and from Sydney were made in even better time. A year later, under Captain Byce, she gave another proof of her speed, as she ran 230 miles one day and 300 the next, arriving in 81 days at Sydney, and thence to Hong Kong in 44 days. Her next commander was Captain John Whyte, formerly of the *Blackadder*, under whom she made a one day run of 362 miles, and reached Sydney in 75 days. Another change of masters followed, and the old ship did not again distinguish herself; she was getting old, and probably felt the effects of her strenuous career. Her end came when she was wrecked on the South African coast in 1888. Even then she had not exhausted her usefulness, for some of her timbers, as staunch as the day they were put into her, were bought for a church at Port Elizabeth, and have since done duty in supporting its roof.

So pleased was John Willis with the early performances of the *Tweed* that he is said to have decided to build on her lines a ship which should beat the flying *Thermopylae*. This was the *Cutty Sark*. She was built at Dumbarton by Scott and Linton, but they failed before they could complete her and Messrs. Denny Brothers were responsible for finishing her. Some of the work and material put into her was not of the best quality. However, she proved herself exceptionally fast in all weathers. Captain Moodie, her first commander, ascertained by log that the ship was doing over 17 knots through the water, and he stated that once she covered 363 knots in the 24 hours. If so, it is the fastest run ever made by a ship built to be a tea clipper. Another writer states that on the previous day she made 362 knots.

Other exploits really performed by this gallant little ship are a run of 3,737 miles when running down her easting between the Cape of Good Hope and Cape Leeuwin in 1890, 220 miles from Green Cape to Sydney in seventeen hours, in 1889, and in running the easting down in the South Pacific to round Cape Horn she covered 353 knots in a day, and 2,180 miles in a week; and at another time 7,678 miles in thirty days. These later runs, Lubbock says, were made after her sail plan was reduced. Coming home from Anjer in 1872 she made three runs in the south east trades of 340, 327, and 320 miles on consecutive days, as compared with the *Ariel's* 330, 315, and 314 on consecutive days in 1868, and the *Thermopylae's* consecutive runs of 267, 290, and 318. Captain Woodget, the last commander of the *Cutty Sark*, before she was sold to the Portuguese in 1895, has said more than once that the *Cutty Sark* while he had her was never passed by anything.

The Adelaide trade was in the hands of a few firms only, the principal ones being Devitt and Moore, the Orient Line, and the Elder Line. The captains in this trade were notorious sail carriers, and though the ships going to this port were not so large as those going to the other ports they were driven for all they were worth, and if Cape Borda, on the west end of Kangaroo Island, were not sighted in 70 days it was regarded as a bad passage. I have seen many of these ships come bowling up the Gulf of St. Vincent under a big spread of canvas before a strong south-west or south wind, and with " a bone in her teeth," heading towards Port Adelaide. It was an old saying among their captains, if they had a wet passage, as they almost invariably did, that they dived after passing South Africa and came up for breath off Cape Borda. Certainly they had plenty of water over them as they ran down their easting. The crews did not like this sort of driving and they often deserted on arrival, and made their way overland to Melbourne or Sydney to ship at double the wages or more for the homeward trip.

The Orient Line, known in its early days as Anderson, Anderson & Co., had some fine vessels. The *Orient*, 1,933 tons, their first ship, built in 1853, had a long and successful career. She was first engaged as a transport in the Crimean war. In 1856 she sailed from Plymouth for Adelaide with passengers and cargo. It was her custom to return by the Cape, not the Horn. From 1856 to 1877 her longest passage appears to have been 104 days, which was in 1877 when under Captain Haffner, and her shortest, 73 days, in 1866 when Captain Harris had her. When homeward bound in 1861 her cargo caught fire. Water was pumped into her through holes cut in the deck and pumped out again, and the deck was flooded. The boats were provisioned and lowered and towed astern, and the women passengers were transferred to a Dutch ship which came on the scene and stood by. The fire was subdued, and after the women had been taken on board she sailed for Ascension where some necessary repairs were effected, after which the ship continued her voyage to London. This ship must not be confused with another ship of the same name which was wrecked on the coast of Cape Colony.

The *Heather Belle*, 479 tons, was a splendid specimen of the type of small sailer. She left Port Phillip in October, 1856, and Captain Harmsworth, finding a strong easterly wind when he got outside the heads, and having no mind to try to beat against it in the rock-strewn waters of Bass Strait, sailed his ship down the western side of Tasmania— not the first shipmaster before or since to adopt that course—and ran down her easting to Cape Horn in 26

days, or only a week longer than the *Lightning's* record of
19 days in 1854.   Then she made the remarkable run of
21 days from the Horn to the equator, and she was signalled at Start Point 67 days after leaving port.   Truly a
fine performance for such a small vessel.

The *Murray*, 903 tons, which was in the Adelaide trade,
was the last wooden ship the line ordered.   Once, in coming
home by way of the Cape she had the company of the
Blackwaller *Hotspur* for several days and reached the
Channel only a day behind her.   With Captain Legoe in
charge she made passages out from Plymouth of from 73
to 83 days.

The Orient Line, in 1863, went in for composite vessels.
The smallest was the *Coonatto*, 633 tons, and the largest
the *Yatala*, 1,127 tons.   The *Coonatto* once ran to the
Semaphore, at the entrance to the Port Adelaide river, in
66 days.   Captain Legoe left the *Murray* to take the
Yatala, and ran to Port Adelaide in 66 days.   The Orient
Line in the '70's went in for steam, with a number of
vessels chartered from the Pacific Steam Navigation Company, and thereafter owned their own steamers.

Elder's *Beltana*, 734 tons, another of Laing's composites,
was chiefly famous for her race against the *Yatala*, which
ended in the latter being wrecked off the French coast, and
for the way Captain Richard Angel drove her.   After
running down his easting at a pace that scared his mate he
sighted a ship beating round Cape Horn to the westward.
For some reason he decided to " sail round her," and
actually did so in the stormy weather of that part of the
world.   It would be interesting to know what the people
on the other vessel said.   On another occasion, when his
mate suggested the advisability of taking in one of the
topgallant sails, he replied by ordering him to set the

royals. The story is told of this " flying Angel," to give
him one of his nicknames, and of other captains too, that
he added to the order to set the royals, instructions to
borrow the lady passengers' petticoats and set those if he
could not find anything else.

Others of Elder's ships were the *Glen Osmond*, the *Collingrove* and the *Torrens*. All three were composites. The
Torrens, built by Laing in 1875, was of 1,276 tons. She
was the last ship in the Australian trade to carry stunsails.
Glad the crews must have been when stunsails went out
of use, for they were a lot of trouble. She was a splendid
sea boat in any weather, and as for calms she could keep
steering way on herself merely by the flapping of the sails
as she rolled in the swell. In a letter in the " Nautical
Magazine " Commander Shrubsole, R.N.R., describes a
voyage he made in her. He says she passed a big American
ship, the *Jessie Harkness*, which was carrying every sail
she could spread and was travelling well, and the *Torrens'*
band played " Yankee Doodle " as she left her behind.
Another time " we passed a large ship running the easting
down. She was under her topgallant sails, while we were
under upper topsails with weather upper and lower stunsails set. The old ship was never driven ; she did not need
it, neither would she stand it. But she sailed rings round
anything sighted." She was then commanded by Captain
H. R. Angel, who previously had the *Glen Osmond* and the
Collingrove. Captain Angel was her chief owner, and
superintended every detail of her building, and then
commanded her for fifteen voyages. She has logged 14
knots, and her best day's run was 336 miles. Her passages
from Plymouth to Port Adelaide were generally made in
about 64 days. Her popular commander retired in 1890,
and was followed by Captain Cope and then by Captain

F. Angel, a son of the former master. Under both her new masters she had a series of accidents, and seemed to be as unfortunate as she had previously been fortunate. Captain Angel, senr., got weary of paying for repairs and sold her to Italians. They ran her ashore, repaired her, ran her ashore again, and broke her up at Genoa in 1910. The *Collingrove*, when under Captain Sanderson, ran from Port Adelaide to the Horn in 26 days, and on a later voyage took 48 days.

One of the most beautiful ships that ever floated was the composite *Sobraon*, of 2,131 tons register. She was ordered by Lawther, Maxton & Co. from Hall of Aberdeen, and was launched in 1866. She was commanded on her maiden voyage by Captain Kyle and then by Captain J. A. Elmslie. Her first five voyages were to Sydney, after which she sailed to Melbourne. She always returned to England via the Cape of Good Hope, the captain having a keen regard for the comfort of his passengers. Like the *Torrens* she was known as a hospital ship, not because of any special sickness on board, but because of the large number of wealthy invalids who sailed in her for the benefit of their health. " You ought to take a voyage to Australia and back in the *Torrens* or the *Sobraon* " used to be the advice fashionable doctors gave to rich patients, and they often took it. Some liked Australia so well they stayed there. The *Sobraon's* outward passages varied between 70 and 80 days, and were seldom longer. Devitt and Moore, after running her on charter for some years, bought her. Captain Elmslie retired from her in 1891. This was not the only famous ship he had. Much earlier in his career he had the *Cospatrick*, which he left in 1867, and was succeeded by his brother who was in charge of her when she was lost in 1873. Captain J. A. Elmslie also commanded the *Parramatta* and the *La Hogue*, both fine ships and great favourites with those who travelled in them. The *Sobraon* had the reputation of being the most comfortable passenger ship afloat, and she was certainly the most luxurious, as luxury was regarded in the days that preceded the ocean palaces of modern times.

On the death of Duncan Dunbar in 1862 Messrs. Devitt and Moore became financially interested in many of his ships, including *La Hogue*. In the Adelaide trade their *City of Adelaide* and *South Australian* were as popular as those of any other firm using the port. Captain David Bruce had the *City of Adelaide*, and all his three sons served their time under him, and rose to be captains.

This firm also managed the famous *Thessalus* and *Mermerus*, and also acted for a Mr. Walker who had a number of barques in the Tasmanian trade. One of them, the *Berean*, was sold to Norwegians and was a frequent visitor to the Regent's Canal Dock in London two or three years before the war; I have often seen her there. She was built by Pile of Sunderland in 1869, and had forty years of service to her credit when I last saw her. Captain Wyrill, who at one time had the *Berean* was 44 years in command of sailing ships, mostly in the Tasmanian trade, and sailed round the world 36 times.

A favourite ship in the Adelaide trade in the '60's was the *St. Vincent*, of about 800 tons, belonging to Messrs. Devitt and Moore. Partly because she was on the Adelaide service, and partly because the clippers which were then doing the round voyage by way of Melbourne or Sydney to China and then to England, were monopolising public attention, comparatively little notice was taken of her. She was, however, a fast ship, and would sail easily in any wind from a zephyr to half a gale; in a strong gale she was rather wet. It would have been interesting to note her performances had she been commanded by such a driver as Captain Woodget of the *Cutty Sark*, or Captain Kemball of the *Thermopylae*, or Captain Nichol Forbes of the *Marco Polo*, or any other master who could and would drive hard, and had her owners encouraged driving. Her second voyage out, in 1866, from Start Point to Cape Borda, was made in 69 days but was otherwise uneventful ; this was, I think, the record up to that time to Adelaide. Having discharged, she went to Newcastle, N.S.W., to load coal, and on the way encountered a " southerly buster," and being in ballast, was nearly capsized.

On returning to Adelaide she took in a cargo of wool and colonial produce and sailed in January, 1867, with a number of passengers. All went well as far as the Western Islands, when the cry of fire was raised. Captain Loutitt had all the hatches made as air-tight as possible to stifle the fire, and the boats were provisioned in case they should be needed. There was no panic and the weather was fine, but the smell that penetrated to the cabin from the smouldering cargo was so strong that the passengers had to sleep on deck that night. Next day the West India barque *Delta* was overtaken and took off the passengers, but like most of the ships in the West India trade she was very slow, so slow, indeed, that Captain Loutitt had to leave her behind. The slowness of the West Indiamen of those days was proverbial ; one of them is said to have carried away two of her masts when she was driven at the exciting speed of six knots, and another is said to have pushed a cocoanut in front of her for three weeks when crossing the Atlantic.

The fire gained for three days when, as an apprentice described it afterwards, " It was like living on the side of a volcano with an eruption brewing below." The captain decided to run for Plymouth and the way he pushed the little ship along showed that he might have made some record passages had he been encouraged to drive her throughout. Mr. W. G. Browning, in the " Nautical Magazine " writes :

" What a run that must have been. It warms one's old blood to think of it. The ship flying along with the wind on the quarter, doing every ounce she was worth. Decks asteam and so hot that they fairly blistered the feet that trod them. Smoke trailing from all three lower mast heads in a thin streak where the apertures could not be wholly blocked, and a crew of officers, men and boys, all ready to do their damnedest to save the good little ship which they, at any rate, considered to be the fastest afloat. And right well they did it. Early the following afternoon, with their ensign reversed, they ran into Plymouth Sound and without a stop shoved the little ' Saint ' ashore on the mud in the Cattewater."

Bluejackets from the fleet helped to extinguish the flames. After thirty-six hours the outbreak was suppressed sufficiently to enable the hatches to be opened. Both ship and cargo were rather badly damaged. Afterwards the *St. Vincent* was taken to London, and the captain, his officers, the boys, and crew received gifts from Lloyd's for saving the ship.

The tide of emigration from the United Kingdom set in early last century, and though it has fluctuated at times it has not died out yet. From 1815 to 1847 the number of voluntary emigrants from Great Britain to Australia and New Zealand totalled 613,615. In 1857, a few years after the gold rush started, there went to Australia from this country 61,248, and a good average was kept up for

some years later. Of course it meant a good time for the
shipowner, and he took full advantage of it. Whenever
there was a great shipping tragedy there was a falling off
in emigration, but thanks to government supervision of a
sort and a better class of ships being employed the year
1857 was marked by no great disaster to any ship cleared
out under the Passengers' Act. The mortality also was
very small, and this was attributed in part to the healthier
condition of the bulk of the emigrants. The mortality,
however, was greater on board the ships sent out by the
Emigration Commissioners, owing to the emigrants being
of an inferior class and having many children with them.
How great the emigration really was at that time may be
judged from the statement that in 1857 no fewer than
645 ships sailed from the United Kingdom with emigrants
for countries overseas, which at an average of 500 tons per
ship gives 322,500 tons of shipping thus employed.
Taking figures like these into consideration, it is not surprising to be told of vessels, which in these times we should
consider small, having on board anything from 200 to
600 or more passengers.

Liverpool became the chief port for emigration. The
leading Merseyside firms engaged in it were James Baines
and Co., who had the famous Black Ball line, which must
not be confused with the earlier American Black Ball
line of North Atlantic packets ; Messrs. Pilkington and
Wilson, owners of the Liverpool White Star line ; James
Beazley, whose firm was for many years a household
word in Liverpool shipping circles ; Henry Fox, owner of
the line named after him ; Miller and Thompson, owners
of the celebrated Golden line ; and Fernie Brothers, another respected name in Liverpool shipping annals, who
had the no less celebrated Red Cross line. There were

LIGHTNING

Picture supplied by F. G. Layton

Facing page 228

also several others, and as years passed, the firms connected with the sailing ship trade to and from Australia
numbered scores.

The rivalry among the Liverpool firms seems to have
been more intense than it was among the London firms,
though the latter showed plenty of enterprise on occasion.
The career of Mr. James Baines was extraordinary. He
started as a shipowner with one little vessel which had
seen her best days, and sent her on a return voyage to the
colonies and secured a good profit on his outlay. Then he
bought another ship, which was also profitable. Other
ships were acquired, but they were not fast or big enough
in his opinion for this trade in which he was determined to
take the lead. Accordingly he ordered four vessels from
Donald McKay, the great American shipbuilder. These
were the *Lightning*, 2,084 tons, the *Champion of the Seas*,
2,448 tons, the *James Baines*, 2,515 tons, and the *Donald
McKay*, 2,598 tons ; the first three were launched in 1854,
and the *Donald McKay* in 1855. They were very like the
later California clippers built by Mr. McKay. Baines also
bought from the same builder the *Japan* and the *Commodore Perry*, each of 1,964 tons, while they were under
construction. The *Lightning* was built for speed, but she
was very strongly put together, and McKay did his utmost
to make her a credit to his reputation both in hull and aloft,
for her rigging and spars were as strong and firm as he
knew how. She was 244 feet in length, 44 feet in beam,
and 23 feet in depth. She was given long concave water
lines, which the "wood butchers of Liverpool" as
McKay used to term them, filled in with slabs of oak
sheathing. The *Lightning* made short work of one of these
on her first voyage, and left it somewhere in the ocean ;
the other was removed after she came back to Liverpool.

The better class emigrant ships, whether built in Great Britain or on the western side of the Atlantic, were not the dull things they are often depicted. Amusements were plentiful and varied, such as bands for dancing, concerts, mock trials, plays, debates, deck quoits and other deck games, and of course the inevitable cards ; in regard to cards, whist seems to have been the customary game on the outward voyage, and euchre, the favourite game in Australia in those days and for long afterwards, on the homeward voyage. On nearly all the ships there was a weekly newspaper printed on board, and all the captains were generally very careful to see that it contained nothing likely to cause serious controversy, religious and political contributions being consigned to the waste paper basket.

One advantage the large American built ships had was that their size and their comparatively light loading made them high out of the water; and their beam, greater in proportion to their length than that of the British built ships, made them steadier, thus accounting for their greater popularity. They were therefore drier ships, taking little water on board, and the 500 or more passengers they each carried were able to be on deck much of the time. These big ships were not so deeply laden as cargo vessels, their 'tween decks being devoted to passengers and not goods, emigrants not being as heavy as general cargo.

The *Marco Polo* did so well that other ships were built at St. John for British owners, the ships including the *Hibernia, Ben Nevis*, and *Guiding Star*, the last named, of 2,012 tons, being the largest. Many were also launched in Great Britain, chiefly of iron. The *Ben Nevis* and *Guiding Star* were ordered by the White Star firm to beat the *Marco Polo* ; it was said the British built ships were neither so fast nor so comfortable in their passenger accom-

modation as the vessels built on the other side of the
Atlantic.

The *Sovereign of the Seas*, which distinguished herself
in the Californian gold rush, was sent over from America in
1853, and as she crossed from New York in less than fourteen days, the Black Ball line lost no time in chartering
her. She sailed from Liverpool in September of that year,
and though her master, Captain Warner, had not commanded an American clipper ship before, he proved his
ability and made the passage to Melbourne in 77 days,
beating all the vessels that sailed at the same time, and by
ten days the English clipper *Gauntlet*. In running down the
easting she covered 3,375 miles in twelve days, her best
day's run being 412. The homeward passage was made
in 68 days. It was marked by a mutiny by some of the
crew who thought to seize the large consignment of
gold dust she had on board. The mutiny was suppressed
without loss of life and the leaders were placed in irons.

The White Star firm chartered three vessels, one of
which, the *Chariot of Fame*, sailed in one passage from
Liverpool to Melbourne in 66 days. The same firm also
chartered the *Red Jacket*, 2,006 tons, and the *Blue Jacket*,
1,790 tons. The latter made some fine passages, her best
being 67 days Liverpool to Melbourne and 69 days for the
homeward. The most famous, or most successful, of the
three ships was the *Red Jacket*. On her first voyage she
left New York for Liverpool in February, 1854, under
Captain Asa Eldridge, a noted packet and clipper ship
master, and reached the Rock Light, Liverpool, from
Sandy Hook in one hour over 13 days. It was a typical
winter voyage, with strong south-east or south-west winds
the whole way, and snow, rain or hail all the time. For the
first seven days she is said to have averaged only 182

miles a day, but on the other six days she averaged 353 miles. Captain Eldridge did not take her out to Melbourne, the command having been given to Captain Samuel Reed, and her first voyage took 69 days, and she is stated to have been back in Liverpool in 5 months and 4 days, her stay at Melbourne lasting only twelve days.

When Baines acquired the *Lightning* he appointed to her Captain Forbes, formerly of the *Marco Polo* which was now under Captain McDonnell who had been first mate on her under Forbes. On the arrival of the *Marco Polo* in 1853 the passengers, numbering 666, subscribed for a silver service to be presented to McDonnell " as a testimonial of respect for his uniform kindness and attention during his first voyage when his ship ran from Liverpool to Port Phillip Head in 72 days 12 hours, and from land to land in 69 days." After McDonnell, her later captains did not seem able to get the best speed out of the ship of which she was capable.

The *Lightning*, on her maiden voyage, in 1854, went by way of the north of Ireland and arrived at Liverpool in half-an-hour under 14 days. She made several fast runs ; her record run is stated to have been begun at noon on February 28th, and an abstract log published in Liverpool at the time contained the statement that the distance run in 24 hours was 436 miles, " the greatest day's run ever made by a ship under canvas," says Captain Clark. The *Champion of the Seas* was almost a sister ship to the *James Baines*, and she crossed from New York to Liverpool in June, 1854, in 16 days. The *Donald McKay* was the largest of the four, and with the exception of the *Great Republic* the largest wooden ship yet built.

The *Lightning* left Liverpool for Melbourne on her first voyage on May 4th, 1854, and the winds were not heavy enough to oblige her captain to take in her topgallant sails once in the voyage, and her best day's run was only 348 miles. She arrived in 77 days, and came back in 63 days. It is on this homeward voyage that she sailed 3,722 miles in ten consecutive days, and covered 412 miles in one day.

The *James Baines* is claimed to have made her first voyage to Melbourne from Liverpool in 63 days, in which she made a day's run of 420 miles, and to have returned in 69 days. An entry in her log for June, 1856, states that when she was doing 17 knots with her main skysail set she sighted at 1 p.m. a ship in the distance ahead, and at 2 p.m. the ship was out of sight astern ; this vessel, the *Libertas*, was under double reefed topsails. The clipper's log for the following day says she was going 21 knots. If so, it is the fastest speed ever recorded of a sailer. The *Champion of the Seas* and the *Donald McKay* did not specially distinguish themselves, though they made some good passages. None of these ships beat the passages they made at this time.

When the Indian Mutiny broke out, the *James Baines*, *Lightning* and *Champion of the Seas* were among those engaged by the government as troop ships. The " Illustrated London New " reports that the "*James Baines* left Portsmouth on August 8th, 1857, with the 97th regiment on board. Previous to her departure she was visited by Queen Victoria who highly eulogised the vessel and is said to have declared that she was not aware that so splendid a merchant ship belonged to her dominions." The *Champion of the Seas* sailed the same day from Portsmouth for Calcutta with troops, and nine days out the two ships were met by the steamship *Oneida*. The *James Baines* " presented a magnificent appearance, having in addition to her ordinary canvas, studdingsails, skysails, and moonsail, set and drawing, in all 34 sails, a perfect cloud of canvas—the troops all well and cheering lustily as the vessels passed each other. The *Champion of the Seas* was not far astern, both making great headway." The *James Baines* was under Captain McDonnell. The two ships arrived off the Hoogly in 101 days, almost side by side, with skysails set in a good breeze, the military bands on board playing, and the soldiers cheering in their excitement.

The next year, 1858, the *James Baines* was destroyed by fire while she was lying in the Huskisson dock at Liverpool, she having but recently arrived from India with a large and valuable cargo. The fire broke out on the morning of April 22nd. Notwithstanding that every effort was made to cope with the flames they spread rapidly throughout the ship, and other vessels in the dock, including one or two Cunarders, had to be moved out of danger. The burning masts in their fall set light to two sheds. The value of the ship and cargo was estimated at £170,000, and very little of the cargo was recovered. The ship was too badly burned to be worth repairing for sea, but her purchaser thought she was sufficiently sound in the lower part of her hull to be of use, and for many years she did duty as the floating landing stage at Liverpool.

The *Lightning* was also taken as a transport; sailing at a more favourable season she went to Calcutta in 84 days.

An advertisement, issued in December, 1857, and reproduced on another page is of considerable interest.

Several passages of 75 days or less were made by American built ships from this country to Australia, of which the best were 64 days from London to Port Phillip by the

Belle of the Sea, and 67 days from London to Sydney Heads by the *North Wind*. One of the most prominent lines in the New York to Australia trade was that of R.W. Cameron. Ships on this route made some good passages, including the *Mandarin*, 71 days, and *Flying Scud* and *Nightingale* 75 days each.

British builders did not like to see British owners going to America for their best ships, so Baines ordered the *Schomberg* from Hall and Co., of Aberdeen, in 1855. She was a big wooden ship of 2,600 tons, 262 feet long, 45 feet beam, with a depth of 29 feet, and was intended to show that as good ships could be built in Britain as on the other side of the Atlantic. Great things were expected of her when she was brought from Aberdeen to load for Melbourne, particularly when it became known that Captain Forbes of *Marco Polo* and *Lightning* fame was to command her. "Sixty days to Melbourne" is the signal Forbes is reported to have flown as she was towed down the Mersey. She did not show any great speed, the winds till she was long past the equator being light. Running down the easting after passing South Africa her best performance was 368 miles in a day, which was quite good enough to lead to the belief that she could do much better.

When 81 days out she was wrecked on the night of December 26th, on an uncharted rock near Cape Otway, about the most dangerous part of the whole coast of Victoria. Fortunately there was no loss of life. Captain Forbes' conduct, both before and after the stranding, was not satisfactory, and at the inquiry into her loss it was stated that after he found she was fast ashore he went below, leaving Mr. Keen, the mate, in charge, and that it was chiefly due to Keen and a saloon passenger named John Millar, that all the passengers were ultimately taken on board a small steamer, the *Queen*, the following day. Serious allegations were made against Forbes, and he was dropped by the Black Ball line.

A memorial casket was sent from London by the Shipwrecked Mariners' Society to Mr. Millar, with the Society's gold and silver medals for a Mr. Dixon and two sailors who accompanied Millar in a boat in search of a place where the people could land. The disaster to the *Schomberg* is said to have inspired Lindsay Gordon to write his fine poem " To the Wreck."

The conditions under which several vessels carried their paying passengers of the emigrant type were a disgrace to all responsible. So many had been the complaints of the accommodation for those emigrants who could not afford to pay for such luxuries as were provided for saloon passengers, that the government appointed a committee of inquiry. In some ships the accommodation for all except the saloon passengers was execrable ; the 'tween decks, where the second class, third class and steerage were carried, was innocent of daylight and fresh air except when the weather was fine enough to allow the hatches to be open or the ventilators to be used, and the sanitation was crude and inadequate. The water supply was often insufficient. The condition of the 'tween decks was described as filthy ; the stench, when the hatches were opened was nauseating, and the foul air was likened to a rising cloud of steam. No wonder reform was demanded. The passengers had to be kept below and the hatches had to be kept closed in dirty weather, whether the passengers liked it or not. The worst conditions prevailed in the comparatively small wooden ships. When larger wood, iron and steel ships were built the accommodation was better, though for the cheaper classes of passengers it was never much to boast about. During the last thirty years or so, the sailers have been driven by the steamers out of the passenger-carrying trade altogether. Some ships were not fitted to carry more than two or three cabin passengers, besides third class, or emigrants; others, perhaps, might carry a score, and many carried no other class at all. The old cabins were not entirely unused. Some captains packed them with cages containing parrots, for the importation of parrots, in spite of the heavy mortality among the birds, often brought in a few pounds when the ship reached London or Liverpool.

The barque *Ann Wilson*, one of the Black Ball line of packets from Liverpool, arrived at Port Nicholson, New Zealand, 1857, and as the death of a passenger on the voyage was attributed to neglect an inquiry was held, and the jury returned the following verdict :—" That the deceased, Jonathan Deverell, after an attack of diarrhœa, died from exhaustion, accelerated by the following causes : a short supply of water during the whole voyage, the want of proper medicines and medical comforts, the inadequacy of the cooking accommodation, the bad ventilation of the vessel ; and the jury hold the captain and charterers culpable for the same. The jury further record their opinion that great neglect attaches to the emigration officer at the port of Liverpool for not seeing a sufficient supply of water, medicine, medical comforts, and sugar put on board. They also consider the captain much to blame for not putting in at the Cape of Good Hope or other port for supplies of aforementioned articles when he knew the vessel was so badly supplied with them."

Bad as the conditions were on some ships conveying emigrants from Great Britain, they were not equalled by the ships carrying coolies from India to Mauritius, South

Africa and the West Indies, and Chinese from China to any place to which they could be tempted to go by promise of work and what seemed to them to be good pay. It was not unknown for over ten per cent of those who embarked in a vessel from India to die before they reached their destination. One of the worst cases on record is that of the American ship *Competitor*, of Boston, which sailed from Swatow with 380 Chinese coolies for Havana; 127 died on the way.

Competition was drawing the reign of the big American built ships to a close. Being constructed of soft wood, their continual repairs were expensive, and they were not always able to obtain sufficient homeward cargo to enable them to make a quick turn round and leave again for England. The smaller oak and teak-built British ships were able to obtain enough cargo and carry passengers as well, and after the worst of the rush was over they were able to hold their own against their larger and more powerful rivals. The days of the wooden ships, however, were approaching their end. Iron became the material of construction, and wooden ships, at all events in Great Britain, ceased to be built.

The building of iron ships, big and little, was taken up with enthusiasm all round our coasts, and some splendid craft were launched. Builders seemed to regard the good times that iron brought as likely to last for ever. As the demand for larger ships grew, because they were more economical to run and earned more money, and freights were beginning to fall, and steamers were steadily ousting sailing ships from trade route after trade route, or taking the bulk of what trade was on them, fewer small ships were wanted, and some of the smaller yards had to close. Steel came in to supersede iron, because it was lighter and stronger, though it has since been found that it did not last so long.

After a time all the wool and wheat carriers in sail from Australia were large iron or steel vessels. Cargo steamers, of steadily increasing size, invaded this trade and secured it nearly all, and now any of the few sailing ships left under foreign flags in this trade may consider themselves lucky if they get a cargo at all.

Among the older school of sailormen, the prejudice against iron was great. One of the old brigade, whom I told I had made a voyage in an iron barque, was very indignant.

" Wood is the stuff ships ought to be built of. It floats, and that's enough for me. Iron doesn't. That thing you were in isn't a barque, it's an iron tank with masts and sails to look like a barque, that's all she is. You take my tip and ship in a ship that is a ship, and that's a wooden one." Perhaps as a compromise, I sailed in a composite ship.

One of the earliest ships of iron was the *Lord of the Isles*, built by John Scott and Co. of Greenock. She was the first iron tea clipper, and was of 770 tons. She was not the first iron ship, that being the *Ironsides*, by Jackson, Gordon and Co., of Liverpool. Others were built in different parts of the country as the superiority of iron over wood became recognised. At first there was a tendency to put in more material than was necessary. A year or two before the war a small old steamer was dry-docked for repair on the Thames side, and when some plates were removed her ribs were seen so close together that only a thin man could have squeezed between them and they were thick and heavy, with plating to match. Later, when the strains and stresses iron could stand were better understood less material was used, and consequently the hull weighed less and could carry more cargo. Lloyd's, having no rules to deal with iron ships at the time they were introduced, adopted the specifications of the *Martaban* built by Scott in 1853. For some time builders used to go one better than those specifications, to make sure.

Of all the lines which have sailed between Great Britain and Australia and New Zealand none have surpassed the splendid vessels of the Glasgow Shipping Company, otherwise the Loch Line, managed by Aitken Lilburn and Company of Glasgow. As a fleet they were among the finest iron vessels to be found anywhere, and they held their own against the steam cargo vessels longer than any other proprietary, but even they had to bow to the inevitable at last. At first they were all three-masted ships. They were never famed for phenomenally fast runs, but they were known as good reliable vessels, whose voyages were made with far greater regularity than those of the average sailing ship, and they have some fast runs to their credit. The first to arrive in Australia was the *Loch Katrine*, on December 20th, 1869. Her graceful lines and evident power and carrying capacity were recognised at once and she was greatly admired. Her five sisters, the *Loch Ness, Loch Tay, Loch Earn, Loch Lomond,* and *Loch Leven,* arrived in that order, the last appearing on August 19th, 1870. They were all built in Clyde yards. The *Loch Tay's* maiden trip took only 73 days ; the greatest distance she logged in one day was 365 miles, and for nine days in succession she averaged 285 miles.

The *Loch Leven* was wrecked on King's Island, a few hours after leaving Port Phillip on her second homeward voyage ; her captain was the only man drowned, and her cargo of wool, valued at £150,000 was nearly all salved ;

he went back to the ship for her papers, and his boat upset in the surf. The next to go was the *Loch Earn*. She ran into the French steamer *Ville du Havre* on a clear night in November, 1873 in mid-Atlantic, and cut into her so badly that she sank in a few minutes. Captain Robertson managed to save 61 of the steamer's crew and 26 of the passengers, and the remaining 226 persons on the steamer lost their lives. The rescued survivors were transferred next day to an American ship, the *Tremontain*. The *Loch Earn* continued her voyage, but was, however, so seriously damaged that she foundered two days later ; all hands were afterwards picked up from the boats.

The *Loch Lomond* saw 39 years good service, being most of the time in the Australian trade, carrying wool or wheat to England and British manufactured goods to Australia, like the thousands of other vessels in the trade, and was sold in May, 1908, to the Union Steam Ship Company of New Zealand, which intended to use her as a coal hulk at Lyttelton, though it had been suggested to equip her as a training ship. For many years she was commanded by Captain Cameron, at one time marine superintendent and afterwards a director, of the Union S.S. Co., but at the time of her last voyage she was commanded by Captain J. Thompson, of North Sydney, who was making his first voyage in her. She sailed from Newcastle, N.S.W., on July 16th, 1908, and was never seen again ; some wreckage, washed up on Chatham Islands, was found a few months later and was supposed to belong to her.

The *Loch Ness* and *Loch Tay* were sold in 1908 and are now coal hulks at Port Adelaide. The *Loch Katrine*, after arriving dismasted at Melbourne in May, 1910, was sold locally and is now a coal hulk.

The ships *Loch Ard*, 1,624 tons, *Loch Maree*, 1,581 tons,

Loch Laggan, 1,435 tons, *Loch Vennachar,* 1,485 tons, and *Loch Garry,* 1,498 tons were built for the Loch Line in the years 1873-5, and the owners also bought the *Clanranald,* which some years previously they had chartered, and renamed her the *Loch Rannoch.* The *Loch Vennachar* was often spoken of as the finest of this fine lot of ships. In another chapter reference is made to the number of new iron clipper ships dismasted on their first voyage; no fewer than eight thus suffered in 1874, of which two were the *Loch Maree* and *Loch Ard.* The latter was an unlucky ship from first to last. After being refitted and resuming her maiden voyage she was dismasted in the Southern Ocean, and had to travel the remaining 4,500 miles under a jury rig. This distance occupied her 49 days and she crawled into Port Phillip on May 24th, 118 days after she left Glasgow the second time. Her third voyage proved her last, as she was lost near Cape Otway in June, 1878, two of those on board being saved and 50 drowned.

By a strange coincidence, the builders of the *Loch Ard* also built three 1,400 tons ships, the *America* (afterwards the *Loch Laggan*) the *Asia,* and the *Africa.* The *Asia* went to Australia in 1873, discharged her cargo, loaded coal for Bombay at Newcastle, N.S.W., and was never heard of after she sailed. The *Africa* was posted missing on a voyage from the Clyde to India in 1872, and the *Loch Laggan* went missing when bound from Liverpool to Melbourne in 1875.

The *Loch Maree* was built under instructions from the owners to spare no expense in turning out a ship of which everyone concerned would be proud, and was an exceedingly comfortable and seaworthy vessel. Her maiden voyage to Melbourne in 1874 took 74 days; she had eleven saloon and 30 second cabin passengers. For some years

LOCH CARRON

Picture lent by Captain Stainton Clarke

she made her voyages back and forth, but after leaving Geelong in October, 1881, she was added to the list of missing ships.

The *Loch Vennachar* had her share of mishaps. She was dismasted when outward bound in 1891 and put in at Mauritius for repairs. Captain Bennett, her master, received Lloyd's medal for saving the ship and cargo. In 1901 a steamer sank her in the Thames in a collision ; she was refloated in 25 days and repaired. She was wrecked on Kangaroo Island, not far from Adelaide, in 1905, all hands being drowned. More ships were added to the line in the years 1876-7, some of which came to grief, one being lost on Kangaroo Island. The *Loch Ryan* was bought by the Victorian state government and renamed *Murray*. Her record includes some good passages. In 1891 she sailed from the Clyde to Melbourne in 70 days and home in 89 days.

In 1881 the Loch line owners decided to have four-masted barques. The first were the *Loch Moidart* and the *Loch Torridon*, launched in 1881, by Barclay Curle and Co. on the Clyde ; they were each of 2,081 tons, and proved so satisfactory that the company ordered two more, the *Loch Broom* and the famous *Loch Carron*, sister ships of 2,075 tons. The latter pair had this peculiarity of rig, that they carried single topgallant sails on the foremast, and double topgallant sails on the main and mizen. The *Loch Carron* was commanded by Captain Stainton Clarke from her first voyage until she was sold to Norwegians, a period of twenty-five years. Captain Clarke had a great affection for his floating home, and I think I am right in saying that in all that long time he never lost a mast or had a really serious accident with his beautiful ship. I visited her often when she came to London, and I can say the same of every

one of the other Loch liners that came to London since this
century began. Her new owners called her the *Seileren*.
She was sunk in collision a year or two before the war off
the north coast of Ireland.

The *Loch Carron's* passages home were as a rule about
80 days. Coming up the Channel in 1908 she made, Captain Clarke told me, a good twelve knots, passing several
big steamers. I went to see her captain that year and found
she was the only sailing ship in London Dock, where years
before I had found sailing ships so packed that it was hard
to find room for another till one had sailed. He said that
close behind the *Loch Carron* was the *Loch Garry*, which
arrived 78 days from Melbourne, and the *Loch Broom*, *Loch
Ryan*, and *Loch Torridon* were on the way.

Captain Clarke, who was at one time second mate in one
of the Castle line of ships belonging to Skinner's, in the
China trade, was fond of relating an experience he had at
that time. He was sent by his captain to take a message
to Captain Dunn, of the celebrated tea clipper *Titania*.
All captains are very fond of their ships, especially after
they have been two or three voyages in them, and Dunn
was strongly attached to the *Titania*, and pardonably
proud of her.

" Is this the first time you have been aboard the
Titania ? " he asked. Mr. Clarke assured him it was.
Captain Dunn called his first mate.

" Mr.——," he said with his customary impressive
dignity, " this is Mr. Clarke's first visit to the *Titania*.
Take a lamp and show Mr. Clarke over the ship." So
ordered, so done. Captain Dunn was known as Dandy
Dunn, because of his habit on special occasions of wearing
a well-cut frock coat and a pair of lavender-coloured kid
gloves.

The *Loch Torridon*, which was commanded by Captain Pattman for many years, until she was sold to Russians, was lost in a gale in the north Atlantic soon after the great war broke out. The report that two liners saw her and signalled that it was too rough to do anything for her caused a great deal of comment at the time. One vessel that sighted her did not consider it too rough, and rescued all on board, including the ship's dog ; the *Loch Torridon* foundered soon afterwards.

One of the old stagers, which up to a few months ago was still going strong, was the four-masted full rigged ship *Lancing*. She was built as far back as 1866 at Glasgow by R. Napier and Sons, as an iron steamer, the *Pereire*. In 1894 her engines were removed and she was converted into a sailer of 2,764 tons gross and was for many years owned by a Norwegian firm. Throughout her long career, for she was over sixty years of age, she sailed in every one of the Seven Seas. She has made some very good passages, and her voyages have not been marked by many accidents.

Other instances might be given of the conversion of a steamer into a sailing ship, besides those mentioned in other parts of this book. Perhaps the most notable is that of the *Persia*, one of the early Cunard paddle steamers in that company's Liverpool New York service. She was built in 1855, and after running successfully for many years was sold. Ultimately she had her engines taken away, and achieved some success as the American sailing ship *May Flint*. The most historic converted iron steamer is undoubtedly the *Great Britain*, which, after a series of adventures as steamer and sailer which would have ended any ordinary ship, is now peacefully ending her days as a hulk at the Falkland Islands.

A famous ship I ought to mention is the old *Antiope*, an

iron barque of 1,496 tons gross, built by J. Reid and Co., at Port Glasgow as far back as 1866, as a full rigged ship. She has had her share of adventures, but came up smiling, so to speak, and was always ready for more. She was reckoned a very big ship in her early days, and was certainly a handsome vessel with her graceful clipper bows, her considerable overhang, and fine lines, and her well proportioned masts and spars. Captain Mathieson, writing to me some years ago, said he had had her then some years. He called her "a good old boat," and said he had grown quite attached to her. During the years she had been on the Pacific coast she had traded from San Francisco to South America, Australia, and the Hawaiian Islands, and said Captain Mathieson, writing from San Francisco, "she will probably lay her faithful old bones here." Being damaged in a gale she was brought into Valparaiso under jury rig, and a few months later, when bound for the Golden Gate, she lost the masts she got at the Chilian port. A Japanese warship at Nikolaevsk captured the *Antiope* as a prize during the Russo-Japanese war, and the Japanese prize courts condemned her. When both sides had fought each other to a standstill and peace was arranged, the old ship was sold. Her owners bought her back again, not without some opposition by Japanese would-be purchasers who scented a bargain, and refitted her and sent her to sea to earn her living. She was then strong and sound and in spite of her age able to make her twelve knots.

The *Antiope* was originally one of Heap's ships, another being the *Marpesia*, the line being afterwards bought by the Beazley firm. When in the Melbourne trade she went out in 68 days, which showed she had a good turn of speed. She carried emigrants and general cargo to Australia, and wool, wheat and other colonial produce home. Next she

FIGUREHEAD OF THE " CUTTY SARK "

Photo by R. A. Fletcher

LUCKNOW

Photo by R. A. Fletcher

Facing page 246

became a coal hulk at New Zealand, but owing to the demand for tonnage during the war she was refitted. She
went ashore soon afterwards, and after being stranded
nearly four months was got off and refitted once more, and
this time she went to Newcastle, N.S.W., and loaded a
cargo of coal which she took to Valparaiso. Two or three
other voyages followed and after a cargo had caught fire she
was sold yet another time and is now a hulk somewhere.

The *Charlotte Croom* was another well-known emigrant
ship which brought back wool or wheat. She was sold and
did good service as the *Astracana* for some years, and was
ultimately disposed of to Norwegians who re-named her
the *Nor* and used her as a depot ship for whalers in the
South Atlantic. Her peculiarity was that she had a three-
cornered cross-jack.

The *Lucknow*, a handsome iron vessel, had the usual
varied career of sailing vessels and was burnt in the North
Atlantic shortly before the war.

The ships of the Sierra line of Liverpool were all more
or less famous and were among the finest vessels afloat
of their time. They were known in all the chief ports of
the world. One need only mention their names for old
sailing ship men to recall their exploits. One of them, the
Sierra Pedrosa, a three-masted full rigged steel ship of
1,670 tons, built in 1883, was driven ashore during a gale
near the mouth of the Salt River, Table Bay, in July, 1889.
The captain, his wife and child, and all the ship's company
were rescued by the local lifeboat, except one man, before
the ship struck. The man left behind was saved the next
day, but he refused to leave the ship until he had changed
into his best shore-going clothes. The wreck was bought
locally and refloated and refitted, and was re-named the
Brutus. She travelled about the world for thirteen years,

and in August, 1902, she was stranded within a few yards of the same place at the mouth of the Salt River. Again those on board were rescued by the Table Bay lifeboat. The ship was refloated once more, and remained at her moorings for several years, being used for a number of purposes, including the storage of coal and the training of naval cadets. When the war broke out she was at Walfish Bay, which the Germans raided. The Union-Castle liner, *Armadale Castle*, employed as an auxiliary cruiser, arrived and finding that all the men, except one who was too ill to ride, had been carried off as prisoners of war by the Germans, took on board the women and children who had been left behind. A vessel on war service, looking for enemy ships, is not a suitable place for women and children, so the captain of the cruiser sent some of his crew to clean the *Brutus* and transferred the women and children to her, with the one man the Germans had left as commander. It is said that the task he had, to keep order among them, was no easy one. After some weeks they were all taken from the *Brutus* to Cape Town, and for the rest of the war the *Brutus* was inhabited chiefly by seabirds.

The *Sierra Lucena* afterwards became the Norwegian ship *Sophie*.

The shipping of convicts to the penal settlements in Australia and Tasmania was in full swing early in the last century. Some of the vessels employed in this ghastly traffic were by no means suited for it. Certain of them were such that it would appear to have been thought that any-thing was good enough to carry convicts, and that it did not matter what became of them ; the story of the convict ships does not make pleasant reading. The involuntary passengers or live cargo certainly included a number of criminals, but the treatment meted out to them too often was calculated to brutalise them and make them worse than they were. The treatment varied according to the kind of convict. Some made the best of their hard lot and the discomforts of the voyage, gave as little trouble as possible, endured the ill-treatment of the warders, and comforted themselves with the reflection that it would be over sooner or later. It was an educated man of this kind who, after settling down at Sydney, wrote the immortal lines :

> True patriots all, for be it understood,
> We left our country for our country's good.

The conditions under which the unfortunate convicts were generally carried, and the heavy mortality which marked some of the voyages, and the stories of the ill-treatment on board, induced the government of the day to insist upon certain improvements, one of which was that a naval surgeon had to be carried, and another was that the food had to be at least eatable, and the water fit to drink. The ships were supposed to be surveyed before being put into this service, but the rules were lax and easily evaded, and the owner of a painfully inferior ship had little difficulty in getting her accepted for the service, and it was his own affair how much profit he made out of the venture. Turbulent convicts generally had a sorry time of it.

One of the convict ships, the *Amphitrite*, with women prisoners, was wrecked on the Boulogne sands in 1833, a few days after starting on her voyage, and of 131 persons on board only three were saved.

Some distinguished men went to Australia at the government's expense. The " Illustrated London News" for July 25th, 1857, records that " On Monday notice was

given at Lloyd's that Her Majesty's government required
a ship immediately to carry 400 male convicts from England
to Fremantle, Western Australia.   Perhaps a more
remarkable set of convicts never left the country at one
time than will go out in this ship.   Among the 400 will be
found Sir John Deal Paul, and Co., the fraudulent bankers ;
Robson, the Crystal Palace forger ; Redpath, who committed the forgeries on the Great Northern Railway Company ; and Agar, who was connected with the great gold
robbery on the South Eastern Railway.   The notorious
bank forger, Barrister Saward, alias Jem the Penman, the
putter-up of all the great robberies in the metropolis for
the last twenty years, also goes out in this ship."

Another convict ship bound to Fremantle, included
among her assortment on one voyage the notorious Rev.
W. Beresford, Robson, and Tester.

NOTE.—The last four ocean-going sailing ships owned in the United Kingdom were the *Garthpool, William Mitchell, Monkbarns* and *Kilmallie.*   Two or
three years ago the last three were sold to foreigners. The photographs I took
of the *Monkbarns* and *Kilmallie,* upon the conclusion of their final voyages
under the British flag, should be of special interest.—R.A.F.

MONKBARNS

KILMALLIE

Photo by R. A. Fletcher

CHAPTER VIII

" ROARING FORTIES," ICEBERGS, SLOW AND FAST PASSAGES, ETC.

ON an ordinary map, on Mercator's projection, it would appear that the nearest and possibly the quickest way from off South Africa to Bass's Straits would be in a straight line. But if a globe of the world be examined it will be found that the nearest way is to go a good deal further south. A ship doing this not only saves distance, but has the advantage of the great " brave westerlies," as Maury calls them, which blow unceasingly all the year round in the latitudes of the south '40's and '50's. The same holds good in running from Australia or New Zealand to Cape Horn.

Apart from storms, which may be met with in any part of the world, and could generally be ridden out if there were enough sea room and the ship were not too old and over-loaded, the greatest dangers were rocks and icebergs, coupled in many cases with fog. Ships bound for Europe by the Cape Horn route had to go a long way south, where they had the risks of rocks, ice, fog and storms to face. But those same latitudes gave them the westerlies. That was the time to be on board a ship, if she were well found and not laden too heavily, and not like a half-tide rock with every wave washing over her from both sides and keeping her full to the gunwale without giving the faithful and struggling ship a chance to throw the water off herself and relieve the weight on her deck; when the wind was blowing as only the westerlies can blow, and screaming its defiance at man's creation, and every rope and sheet and halliard and brace was humming like the overstretched strings of a 'cello, and such sails as were set were as hard as iron, and the masts were bending under the strain, and the steering was of the best : that was the time when the driving captains carried on ; that was the time to realise that the ship was a living sentient being, with a consciousness that she was doing her best, and was proud to do it. That was the time and the way record runs and passages were made. The ships did not run to time tables in the roaring forties and turbulent fifties but as the great winds of heaven dictated.

There is probably no sight in the world more inspiring than that of the " greybeards " of the southern ocean, and to see them properly and appreciate the awfulness and beauty of that wonderful spectacle, you need to go aloft on some sailing ship when running down the easting.

" Everyone who has sailed in that southern girdle of waters which belt the earth on the polar side of 40 degrees, has been struck with the force and trade-like regularity of the westerly winds which prevail there," Maury wrote. " The waves driven before these winds assume in their regularity of form, in the magnitude of their proportions, and in the stateliness of their march, an aspect of majestic grandeur that the billows of the sea never attain elsewhere. No such waves are to be found in the trade-winds ; for, though the south-east trades are quite as constant, yet they have not the force to pile the water in such heaps nor to arrange the waves so orderly, nor to drive them so

IN THE "ROARING FORTIES." HOLYWOOD SHIPPING A GREEN SEA

Photo by Capt. M. M'Aulay

Facing page 252

rapidly as those ' brave ' winds do. There the billows, chasing each other like skipping hills, look, with their rounded crests and deep hollows, more like mountains rolling over a plain than the waves which we are accustomed to see. Many days of constant blowing over a wide expanse of ocean are required to get up such waves. It is these winds and waves which, on the voyage to and from Australia, have enabled the modern clipper-ship to attain a speed, and, day after day, to accomplish runs which at first were considered, even by the nautical world, as fabulous, and are yet regarded by all with wonder and admiration."

During the years 1909-10, several remarkably fine sailers came to grief in the Cape Horn neighbourhood. This is one of the stormiest quarters in the world. Westerly gales prevail about twenty-nine days out of every thirty, and the great seas encountered are something to remember ; the Cape Horn " greybeards " are not loved by sailormen. Vessels have been weeks trying to beat round from the Atlantic to the Pacific. It is no wonder sailors gave the Cape the name of Cape Stiff, or the Cape of Storms. A bleaker and more inhospitable place on the face of the earth it would be difficult to find. The westerly gales, however, are appreciated by the ships bound to Britain or the Continent from Australia or New Zealand, for they help such vessels along, and a run of twenty-six days from Adelaide to the Horn was not by any means unknown. I do not know of any aspect of the sea grander or more awe-inspiring than that of these waves, " such as creation's dawn beheld."

They have been estimated to travel at speeds varying between 23 and 27 miles an hour, and their vertical height from trough to summit has been calculated at from twenty to forty-three feet. When travellers tell you of waves over 120 feet high, don't believe them. A wave may appear as high as the mast head, particularly if a vessel is heeling over towards it, but if the wave and the ship could be kept still long enough for measurements to be taken it would be found that the mast head was a long way out of reach of the solid part of the wave. Spray, and the tops of waves cut off and carried by the wind, are another matter altogether, and may be blown as high as a mast head.

The adoption of Maury's sailing directions for the Great Circle, instead of the older directions recommended by the Admiralty, also meant that a ship going out by the Cape and home by the Horn sailed round the world. The Great Circle theory attracted much criticism, and not a few owners and masters expressed disapproval, asserting that the ships were more likely to be lost in the stormy waters of the higher latitudes.

Captain Godfrey, when in the *Constance*, one of James Beazley's ships, was one of the first to determine to test the theory. The time usually occupied at that time on a voyage from England to Port Adelaide was about 120 days, seldom less and often more. The *Constance* left Plymouth in July, 1850, and arrived at Port Adelaide in 76 days, as a result of adopting the Great Circle method ; the Adelaide people could hardly believe their eyes. Another surprise was experienced by those good folks when the *Runnymede*, Captain Brown, sailed from Liverpool to Port Adelaide in 72 days, and only the following month the *Anna*, of Henry Fox's line, arrived from the Mersey in 76 days. The *Runnymede* had a large number of emigrants, having been taken over by the Emigration Commissioners. These three vessels were under 1,000 tons each, and as they were not built to be clippers with speed as the main object, these performances are all the more remarkable. They afford another proof, if one were needed, that fast passages were more often than not due to the commanders, aided perhaps by the luck of the weather.

In southern and northern latitudes one of the greatest dangers sailing ships had to face was ice. Many a well-found ship is believed to have met her end with all hands from this cause. A ship is known to be likely to reach a certain part of the ocean about a certain time. If icebergs are reported to have been sighted in that locality at about the same time, the natural inference, if the ship is not reported, is that she struck the ice and was so seriously damaged that she sank. In the absence of definite information as to the cause of her not being heard of again, her name was added to the terribly long list of missing ships. Then the bell of the *Lutine* would be rung in Lloyd's Room, the news announced, and after a minute or two business would go on as usual.

It would be easy to draw imaginary pictures of the overwhelming of some vessel by ice ; instead, let me narrate some of the experiences which have befallen ships encountering ice, but before doing so I ought to give a few details concerning ice which may make the narratives more vividly understood by those who have never seen ice in large masses at sea.

Let the weather conditions be what they may, ice, when present, is a danger, and its most dangerous condition is when it is hidden by fog. It must be remembered that ice floats because it is very slightly lighter than water. For every ton of ice which may be visible above the surface of the sea there are between eight and nine tons beneath the sea level. Ice, as met with at sea, is classified as bergs and growlers. The former word is too well known to need explanation, but a growler is a large, more or less flat piece not more than two or three feet or so above the sea level, and often of very considerable extent. The growler is the more difficult of the two to see, and often has not been noticed until it was too late to avoid it.

The icebergs of the North Atlantic ocean start on their wanderings from the Greenland coast in the early spring, and by the early summer may be sighted by steamships crossing between European and New England or Canadian ports. When they get into the warmer waters of the Gulf Stream they melt rapidly, and very few have travelled further east than the middle of the North Atlantic. The bergs of the North Atlantic are seldom more than 200 feet high, with a front of half a mile, and a thickness of about the same.

It is believed that the highest icebergs ever seen in the North Atlantic were those of 1906, when some were reported of 700 feet, and one had an estimated height of 1,000 feet. In spite of the apparent smoothness of the exposed part of the berg its submerged surface may be as jagged as any reef of rocks, and as destructive to any vessel striking it. The projecting spur of ice below the surface, which is a common feature of bergs, may be a hundred or two hundred feet in length, or much more ; it may be far longer than the berg is high ; this is a danger which shipmasters have always sought to avoid. The mere fact that the sides of a berg or growler appear to descend perpendicularly into the sea is no indication of the absence of a spur or shelf.

Captain Grant, of the American ship *Lady Arbella*, from Hamburg for New York, in May, 1854, reported having passed one morning 24 large bergs and several small ones. " I should judge the average height of them above the surface of the sea to be about 60 feet," he wrote ; " some five or six of them were at least twice that height, and with their frozen peaks jutting up in the most fantastic shapes presented a truly sublime spectacle." Many other incidents might be given of icebergs in the North Atlantic. Not a summer passes without ice being sighted there. Ship captains do not indulge in rhapsodies over the beauty of the scene. Their log books merely contain a brief entry of the fact that so many bergs were sighted in such and such a latitude and longitude.

It is to the southern ocean that one must go to see icebergs at their best—or worst—in regard to both size and number. In both respects they far exceed those of the North Atlantic, and on account of their great bulk they last much longer. One is reported to have drifted for something like two years before it finally wasted away. Others have been seen within a few degrees of the latitude of the Cape of Good Hope. One immense berg was described by the captain who sighted it as being as large as the city of Liverpool. A berg 400 feet high is by no means uncommon. Several have been seen which had fronts of over a mile and a height of over 700 feet. These dimensions were not given as guesswork, but as the result of careful calculations made on the ships as they passed by.

The clipper ship *Red Jacket* in 1854 found herself surrounded by icebergs in the neighbourhood of Cape Horn.

The *Indian Queen*, 1,041 tons, launched in 1853 and for some years in the Black Ball line, made some good passages. The remarkable story of her experiences told when she arrived home in 1859 created some sensation. During her homeward voyage she collided with an iceberg at night in a fog. The second mate reported to the

17

passengers who came on deck that Captain Brewer, the
mate and most of the crew had gone away in a lifeboat.
One of those left on the ship was the captain's own son.
Leyvret, the second mate, took charge, and under his
direction matters improved. When day came the boat was
seen in the distance, but was soon lost to sight in the fog
and no more was ever heard of it. Leyvret had only the
ship's carpenter, five seamen, two boys, and the cooks and
stewards to work the ship; there were also on board the
doctor, purser, and passengers, among whom were seven
children and three women. All three masts had been
greatly damaged by the collision with the berg, but the
foremast still stood though it afterwards fell. The wreckage was cut away in the course of a few days, and two or
three sails were somehow set, and after avoiding two more
icebergs and riding out some gales the ship arrived off
Valparaiso and was assisted into the Roads by a French
warship and the boats of a British man of war just forty
days after the collision.

In 1884 the German barque, *Emil Julius* reported a
berg of 1,700 feet, and in 1893 the *Loch Torridon* and other
vessels reported bergs of 1,500 feet by measurement with
the ship's instruments. One of them was fifty miles long.
One gigantic berg is reported to have had a bay in it forty
miles wide, into which a vessel, thinking it was clear water
right through, might easily steer, without much chance of
getting out again.

Coming to a much later date, the years 1907-10 were
remarkable for the great number of immense bergs which
left the icefields round the south pole and drifted into the
track of shipping.

In February, 1907, the French barque *Vendee*, since
arrived at San Francisco from Cherbourg, reported having

passed in the South Pacific near Cape Horn a steel mast
with some rigging attached, apparently supported by submerged wreckage. The *Vendee* was herself wrecked in
September, 1908, off Cape Horn while homeward bound
from Portland, Oregon. The large French barque, *Fran-
coise d'Amboise*, when bound from Noumea for Glasgow,
counted between September 18th and 29th, 1908, no fewer
than 141 icebergs and floes, some of them being twenty
miles long.

An experience, which almost takes one's breath away to
read of it, happened to the Greenock barque *East Indian*
in September, 1908, and it would seem that she ran into
the same fleet of bergs which the French vessel reported.
Captain M'Kinley, of the *East Indian*, on arriving at
Queenstown, in the following December, told an extraordinary story, which was borne out by the ship's crippled
condition, she having lost her mizen topmast, and some of
the yards from her foremast. The barque sailed into a
mass of icebergs during a fog. She struck an immense
berg, fully 300 feet high, which towered above her mast
heads. Fortunately the hull did not strike the berg, but
the foreyard and some other yards did and came down.
By a piece of luck the wreckage became entangled in the
rigging and did not reach the deck, but huge pieces of
broken ice which overhung the *East Indian* fell on the
main deck with tremendous crashes. Two boats were
smashed by the falling ice.

An uncanny feature of the collision with the berg was
that it was accompanied by a loud report, and the barque
trembled from stem to stern, and those on board thought
she was going to founder. It was a time of great anxiety,
as the vessel was surrounded by icebergs and the fog had
thickened. After getting away from the berg she just

managed to clear another huge berg, but in doing so her mizen mast struck it and was buckled in two places. Next morning the *East Indian* came into contact with another large berg, but escaped without further damage. She also was damaged by ice a week later, and as though she had not had enough mishaps on her homeward voyage she struck an unchartered rock.

The Glasgow barque *Dee*, in the same Antarctic summer, sailed into what her master, Captain Yore, described as a sea of ice. He reported that the *Dee* rounded Cape Horn on September 4th and some days later found herself amid the ice. One of the bergs was at least fifty miles long and had an average height of 250 feet. It took the ship sixteen hours to pass it.

While going through this sea of ice the *Dee* sighted a partially dismasted barque, and bore down on her and offered assistance. She proved to be the Norwegian barque *Trafalgar*, bound from Lobos de Afuera for Hamburg. She had lost several of her spars and her bulwarks were stove in as the result of a collision with a berg. Her captain informed Captain Yore that he would try to get to Buenos Ayres. It is satisfactory to note that she succeeded in reaching Buenos Ayres on September 28th. This incident is another proof, if one were needed, of the brotherhood of the sea, for seafaring men, irrespective of nationality, are always ready to imperil themselves if they may render aid to a vessel in distress.

Altogether the *Dee* passed 150 bergs, some of which were from a mile to five miles in length. The presence of such a mass of ice in September so far north as latitude 49 degrees south, and longitude 50 west, was most unusual. Some outward bound vessels were reported overdue or missing that year, and it is to be feared that the latter

ASTRACANA

(Picture lent by former Captain)

AUSTRASIA

(Picture lent by former Captain)

were lost in this icefield, as it would be impossible to detect its presence until ships were in the midst of it.

Another sailing vessel, the *Arracan*, seemingly encountered the same icefield, and had to put into Monte Video for repairs. The following extracts from her captain's log show what she went through :—

September 14th, 1908—Encountered large icebergs, and was surrounded by ice.

September 15th—Set all possible sail, and steered various courses to north and west ; surrounded by ice as far as the eye could reach, some bergs being of great size.

September 19th—Icebound, with no visible way out. Took eight days to get through the ice, bumping heavily ; the field must have extended a thousand miles from north to south.

The well-known four-masted barque *Austrasia*, of Liverpool, which put in at Falmouth early in December, 1908, after a voyage lasting four months from Pisagua, reported having met a very large number of bergs off Cape Horn. These and the gales experienced in that stormy part of the world accounted for the unusual length of her voyage.

The *Largo Bay*, which put in at Queenstown in June, 1908, from Portland, Oregon, reported having passed 41 large icebergs in one day off the Falkland Islands, and many others between 49 degrees and 54 degrees south latitude. She also experienced heavy snow squalls, which rendered it exceedingly difficult to see as much as the vessel's head at times. The combination of icebergs and snow blizzards constituted about as serious a danger to shipping as can well be imagined, for a vessel may meet with disaster without a possible chance of avoiding it.

The ship *Carnarvon Bay* collided with an iceberg about

250 feet high during a fog, in latitude 50 south and longitude 59 west, and badly smashed her bow; altogether for about 300 miles she sighted ice.

Twenty to thirty years ago there were at most times of the year between three and four hundred sailing vessels on voyages which would necessitate their rounding Cape Horn. It is no wonder, therefore, that every now and then some large vessel was reported missing. In 1906 three splendid ships, the *Hautot*, the *Daniel*, and the *Netherby*, were expected to be in the Cape Horn neighbourhood in the latter part of the year. The first two vessels were French and were each of over 2,200 tons. The *Netherby* was a British ship of 1,400 tons. They never reached port, but were reported lost with all hands. It was thought at the time that all three collided with ice. Three ships afterwards reported that they had passed abandoned ships in that neighbourhood. A capsized derelict, the identity of which could not be ascertained, was seen floating among the bergs in September of that year; there was no trace of her crew. Some little time afterwards a large three-masted sailing ship was seen fast among the ice by the French ship *Chateau d'If*. Subsequently another French sailing ship, the *Emilie Galline*, herself collided near the Falkland Islands with an iceberg upon which a large ship had stranded. Fortunately the *Emilie Galline* was able to get clear. What happened to the crew of the stranded ship is unknown. They may have taken to the boats in the hope of being picked up by some passing vessel, and have been overwhelmed by bad weather. These three ships are supposed to have been the *Daniel*, the *Hautot*, and the *Netherby*. The *Daniel* and the *Hautot* were two of the government bounty-fed vessels. They were not old, the *Daniel* having been built only five years before, and the

other about two years before her. The *Daniel* was bound
from Bellingham Bay to South Africa with redwood, and
the other vessel from New Caledonia to the Clyde with ore.

A few weeks after they had been added to the long list
of mysterious disappearances at sea, one of the finest British
four-masted barques, the *Ormsary*, was reported missing.
She sailed from a South American Pacific port in September for England, and that was the last ever seen of her.
The loss of life through the disappearance of these four
vessels was over a hundred.

Other vessels posted missing about that time were the
Toxteth, *Carnedd Llewellyn*, and *Dundonald*, all among
the finest belonging to Liverpool, and the Glasgow ship
Falklandbank. The only one of the four ever heard
of was the *Dundonald*. She struck, when homeward
bound from Australia, an uninhabited and almost
inaccessible island some miles from the New Zealand
coast, and her crew were able to get ashore. The New
Zealand government maintained a food depot on the
island for the benefit of shipwrecked people, and there they
stayed until the government steamer paid her periodical
visit some months later and rescued the survivors.

Several ships are known to have been lost on one
or other of these islands of the Southern Ocean, and
wreckage washed up on some distant coast has been all
that has been found. Many victims of wrecks in the
Pacific have taken refuge on islands in the South Seas,
whence some survivors have wanted to be rescued, and
others have not.

Some of the older ships did good work to the last. The
Zemindar, built about 1885, by Harland and Wolff for the
Brocklebanks, was dismasted about 1898, and abandoned
as a constructive total loss, and sold by the underwriters

to Americans who re-rigged her at San Francisco and named her the *Homeward Bound*. In 1908 she sailed from Portland, Oregon, to the Mersey in the splendid time of 106 days, her master, Captain Thompson, evidently not having forgotten how to push a ship along.

Another veteran ship was the *Haddon Hall*, owned by C. E. de Wolf and Co., Liverpool, which after 38 years of work was still thought good enough to load a full cargo at Liverpool for Vancouver, and still another was the *Rollo*, built in 1876, which left Glasgow in 1898 for Australia. The *Haddon Hall* sailed in April 1908 for Vancouver with a general cargo, and had an uneventful run till she was making for Cape Horn, when she collided with the steamer *Amsterdam*, and was so badly damaged that she took in a great deal of water and the boats were provisioned and got ready for lowering. However, Captain Fookes got the hole plugged with cement, and the vessel was taken to Monte Video for repairs. These took two months, and she sailed again at the beginning of August. All went well till she rounded Cape Horn, and for six weeks she fought a north-westerly gale and made little or no headway. Twenty-two gales followed in quick succession ; sometimes the cabins were drenched with water, the men were washed out of their bunks, and then snow and sleet would follow. The cargo, chiefly pig-iron, shifted and the vessel listed till the cabins were half under water and the deck rail was out of sight. The crew worked hard to get her right, and on September 1st she had a south-west gale which lasted two days and she progressed 300 miles. Another north-west gale took her back almost to the old place. At last favourable weather enabled her to get within 200 miles of Cape Flattery, where she was becalmed for five days. On the fifth day a gentle wind took her a little further, and a tug came from Seattle and did the rest. Nearly everyone of the 22 men on board was laid up injured at one time or another during the voyage. Captain Fookes said it was the worst voyage he had ever made. From the time she left Liverpool it was 249 days before she reached Vancouver.

The *Inverness-shire*, a fine four-masted barque, belonging to Messrs. Thomas Law, had her share of misfortunes. When in February 1900 she was about to leave Honolulu the wind rose and signals were shown that she was dragging her anchor and the crew had refused duty. Captain Peattie, who was ashore at the time, engaged a tug, and with another captain went off with a number of kanakas to the ship. A great deal of chain was paid out but the anchor did not hold, and she was blown off the land into deep water and the anchor and chain were lost as the kanakas would not or could not get them in. The ship was blown about seventy miles to sea and did not return for some days. The men who had refused duty were severely punished, and a new crew shipped.

In February 1906 the *Inverness-shire* was only saved from being driven ashore near the Isle of Wight by a passing steamer and four tugs, a bit of salvage work which her owners found expensive.

Her most remarkable adventure, however, was in 1910 after she left Hamburg for Santa Rosalia. She spent about seven weeks trying to beat round Cape Horn into the Pacific, without success, and at last her then captain turned her head and ran her towards the Falkland Islands. On June 11th the Sea Lion islands were sighted, and the crew went ashore leaving the vessel at anchor while they waited for a more favourable wind, as the ship had been knocked about a good deal and needed repair. Somehow the news reached Port Stanley that the ship was there with no one on her, and a tug went out and towed the ship to the harbour, and then went back and collected the master and crew. The Falkland Islands were never a cheap place for repairs, and the islanders always looked upon a ship which needed them as a dispensation of Providence and to be made the most of accordingly. The repairs having been finished the ship sailed again and reached her destination at the beginning of February, 1911, the voyage lasting just about a year.

The *Merioneth*, a fine full-rigged ship of a little over 1,500 tons, built at Liverpool about 1876-7 for Messrs. Hughes & Co., is stated to have run from one of the South Wales ports to San Francisco in 95 days, the return journey to Queenstown taking only 96 days. These have been claimed to be records. Another time she made the homeward run to Queenstown in 110 days, actually arriving five days before the *Lord Cairns* which had sailed a fortnight before her.

One question often raised in connection with fast passages is whether the *Sheila*, when commanded by Captain W. H. Angel, actually on her maiden voyage passed the *Cutty Sark*. Captain Angel in his book on the *Sheila* said she did, but some people assert she did not.

The White Star liner *Red Jacket*, which plied regularly between Liverpool and Melbourne, made the outward passage in 69 days and the homeward in 74 days, the time occupied on the round voyage being 5 months 10 days.

The *Oweenee*, built in 1891, on her maiden voyage sailed to Melbourne from England in 65 days.

The big German five-masted ship *Preussen* sailed from New York to Yokohama in 1908 in 116 days. Captain Petersen in a letter to the firm stated that the voyage was the quickest ever made by a sailing vessel from New York to Japan by the eastward passage, and that it would have been quicker but for being becalmed in the Indian Ocean a day or two and being unable to go by the Straits of Sunda. After passing the north-west coast of Australia she passed up to the Lombale Strait and the Strait of Macassar and passed the Philippines and Pelew Islands, and so to Japan.

The barque *Sam Mendel,* a well known and popular vessel in her prime, is stated to have sailed in 1876 from London to Port Chalmers, New Zealand, in 68 days. She was sold afterwards to Swedish owners and renamed *Charlonus,* and sold again and renamed *Hanna,* and she got into the hands of the ship-breakers at Genoa about the end of 1909, and thus ended her 49 years faithful service in all parts of the world.

The splendid iron sailing ship *Leyland Brothers,* 2,291 tons, built in 1886 at Southampton, belonging to R. W. Leyland & Co., of Liverpool, made one of the fastest and one of the slowest passages on record. She left San Francisco on February 2nd, and on March 20th, only 46 days later, she passed Sydney Head, the distance covered being 6,600 miles. A year or two later, in 1906, she sailed from Antwerp for San Francisco and did not arrive until November 4th, thus taking 213 days for a voyage of 13,838 miles. On the earlier voyage she had very favourable winds ; the delay on the later voyage was due entirely to adverse weather, particularly in beating round Cape Horn. Another time she anchored in the Mersey 101 days after leaving San Francisco.

The little British ship *Arctic Stream*—she was only 250 feet long and 35 feet beam, and was built of iron at Port Glasgow in 1885—made in 1907 the passage with grain from the Columbia River to Queenstown in the remarkably

good time, for such a small ship, of 110 days ; it was the
record for a vessel of her size. She left the river the same
day as the big French ship *Andre Theodore*, also with grain
for Queenstown for orders. A few days before they sailed
the two captains wagered a new suit of clothes and a plate
of pea soup on the run home. Captain Charles C. Dixon
won the bet. His father, Captain Dixon, commanded a
transport on the Union side during the American Civil
war. He was master of the British ship *Glenesslin*, belonging, like the *Arctic Stream*, to Messrs. de Wolf and Co.,
of Liverpool, which was in the grain fleet from the Sound
the previous year, but the son made a much faster passage
than the father.

The American ship *Homeward Bound*, Captain Thompson, made the fastest passage that season from the Columbia River to England, taking only 108 days ; she was a
much larger ship than her little rival, and had a bigger
crew and a far larger spread of canvas.

The British four-masted barque *Muskoka*, when under
Captain Albert Crowe, who afterwards settled at Victoria,
B.C., made three runs from Victoria to Queenstown in
98 days, 101 days, and 108 days, all exceedingly fast runs.
The record passage from the Columbia to Queenstown,
according to the "Victoria Colonist," was made about 1888
by the British ship *Caithlock* in 89 days ; the average
passage was 130 days.

The American schooner *Alex. T. Brown* sailed from
Tacoma with lumber for Callao and passed Cape Flattery
on January 28th, 1910, and took 118 days for the passage.
The British ship *Wray Castle* sailed from the same port a
month later, and arrived 59 days earlier than the schooner.
A slow passage in the other direction was made the same
year by the British barque *Almora*, which took 232 days

from Newcastle-on-Tyne to Port Townsend, and was not spoken once on the way. A still longer voyage was that made a few years earlier by the British barque *Hawthornden*, which was 240 days from Dungeness to Puget Sound. The *Astracana* did the run from Sydney to England in 85 days.

The little iron Liverpool barque, *John Lockett*, 779 tons, ended a remarkable voyage when she put into Falmouth in April, 1909. She left the Thames in March, 1907, for the colonies, and sailed from Newcastle, N.S.W., to the West Coast of South America.

She then sailed to San Juan del Sur, Nicaragua, and while loading there was driven by a gale on a reef, but got off not much the worse, though three other vessels were wrecked within sight of her. She left for Falmouth on August 17th, and had calms and contrary winds and a gale which caused damage, and provisions began to run short. Bahia was reached on Christmas Eve, and provisions were taken in. A re-start was made a week later, but the vessel's bottom was so foul that she went so slowly she could hardly be steered. Again provisions ran short. When Falmouth was reached only a few morsels of meat and mouldy crumbs of ship's biscuits remained.

The Norwegian barque *Ester* left Amsterdam for East Indian ports in December 1907, and was spoken a few days later at the entrance to the English Channel. Months passed, and nothing was heard of her, and she became uninsurable. On August 7th, 1908, a telegram was received by Lloyd's from Macassar saying the vessel had arrived at her destination. Another remarkable case of a ship regarded as hopelessly overdue turning up was the *Lalla Rookh*.

The Portuguese iron barque *Albatros*, sailed from Lisbon

for St. Paul de Loanda in Portuguese West Africa, a journey that even in a Portuguese vessel should not have lasted very long. On the way she ran short of provisions, and obtained some from a passing British steamer. Some weeks later she put into Rio de Janeiro for water, and there she rested for a month after her strenuous exertions. Having recovered her wind, so to speak, and filled her tanks, she sailed again, and this time crossed the Atlantic in an easterly direction and duly reached Loanda in April, 1908, only 223 days after leaving Lisbon.

A few vessels have found the task of rounding Cape Horn from the Atlantic into the Pacific too much for them, and have given up the job in disgust. The *Denbigh Castle* left Cardiff for Mollendo on October 9th, 1908, and was spoken on November 22nd in 8 degrees north latitude and 26 west longitude, and again on December 8th in 9 degrees south latitude and 33 west longitude. Just about the time that her arrival was daily expected at Mollendo the steamer *Nerehana* arrived in the Thames from New Zealand and reported having sighted the *Denbigh Castle* off Diego Ramirez, near Cape Horn, steering east. This was thought to be a mistake in the reading of the ship's flags, and that it was some other vessel, but it was afterwards found that the report was correct. The vessel had been put on the re-insurance list and in consequence of the speaking the premiums were reduced, but they advanced again when nothing further was heard of her for some time and the re-insurances rose. On June 19th, it was announced that she had put in at Fremantle, West Australia, for provisions. Here she stayed sixteen days, replenishing her stores and getting ready to resume her voyage. After leaving Fremantle she was expected to reach Mollendo in 70 days.

Again no tidings were received of her, but at last she reached that port, and ended all anxiety as to her safety, arriving 409 days after she had left Cardiff. This is one of the longest voyages on record.

The records for 1907, to take one year as an illustration, show how remarkably sailing ship passages varied in length. The *Marechal de Turenne* sailed from San Francisco to Prawle Point in 108 days, and the *Eliza*, from San Francisco to the Lizard took 183 days. The *Europe* sailed from Astoria to the Lizard in 107 days, and the *Leon XIII* from the same port to Falmouth in 159 days. The *Lucipara* did the voyage from Tatoosh to Queenstown in 110 days, and the *Eugenie Fautrel* took 176 days from the same port to Falmouth. The *Erskine M. Phelps* covered the journey from Honolulu to the Delaware Breakwater in 103 days, but it took 156 days for the *William P. Frye* to sail from Honolulu to Barbados, near which the other would have passed on her way to the Delaware.

Going from east to west the *Gertrud* sailed from off the Isle of Wight to San Francisco in 119 days, and the *Medea*, from Christiansand, to San Francisco, took 223 days. The *Herzogin Cecilie* sailed from Leith to Honolulu in 108 days, and between the same ports the *Inverneill*, by no means a slow ship as a rule, took 177 days. Crossing the Pacific, the *Battle Abbey* sailed from Sydney to San Francisco in 60 days, the *Eliza*, from Melbourne to the same port, in 90 days, and the *Gertrud* from San Francisco to Newcastle N.S.W., in 41 days.

A list of the longest and shortest passages from Newcastle N.S.W., to San Francisco in the years from 1890 to 1910 shows some remarkable contrasts. It was published in San Francisco and reproduced in New York "Shipping Illustrated" in 1910. In 1890 the longest voyage was that of the French barque *Iton*, 114 days, via San Diego, and the shortest by the British ship *Clan Buchanan*, 51 days. No fewer than 107 sailers arrived in 1891, from Newcastle, N.S.W., this being the greatest in any year ; the longest passage was 126 days by the British barque *Lord Canning*, and the shortest, 49 days by the British ship *Talus*. The American barque *Fresno* had the distinction of the longest voyage in 1892, being 107 days, and the *Hiawatha* and the *California* tied for the shortest with 53 days. In 1893 the British ship *Cedarbank* took 144 days, calling at San Diego, being the longest, and another British ship, the *Eulomene*, made the shortest in 50 days. The next year the British ship *Osborne* made the shortest passage in 47 days, compared with the 90 days of the American barque *Palmyra*, the 135 days of the British ship *Scottish Moors*, calling at San Diego, and the 163 days of the French barque *L'Avenir*, which called at Honolulu.

The British ship *Celtic Race* made the longest passage, 104 days, in 1895, and the German ship, the *Christine*, 40 days, the shortest on record up to then. The fastest trip in 1896 was made by a French vessel, the *Pierre Corneille*, in 50 days ; the British barque *Hollinwood*, via Lyttelton, took 74 days, and the French barque *Jules Verne*, 114 days, the longest. The celebrated Loch liner, the *Loch Torridon*, headed the list in 1897 with 46 days ; the British ship *Cressington* was 106 days. The British *Kate Thomas*, via Sydney, took 85 days in 1898, the American barque *General Fairchild* 116 days, and the British ship *Pericles* 53 days. In 1899 the extremes were the British ship *Crown of India*, via Sydney, 296 days, and the British ship *Metropolis* 51 days, with the British ship *Hyderabad*, 197 days, between. The British ship *Marion Frazer* made the shortest passage, 55 days, in 1901, and the French barque

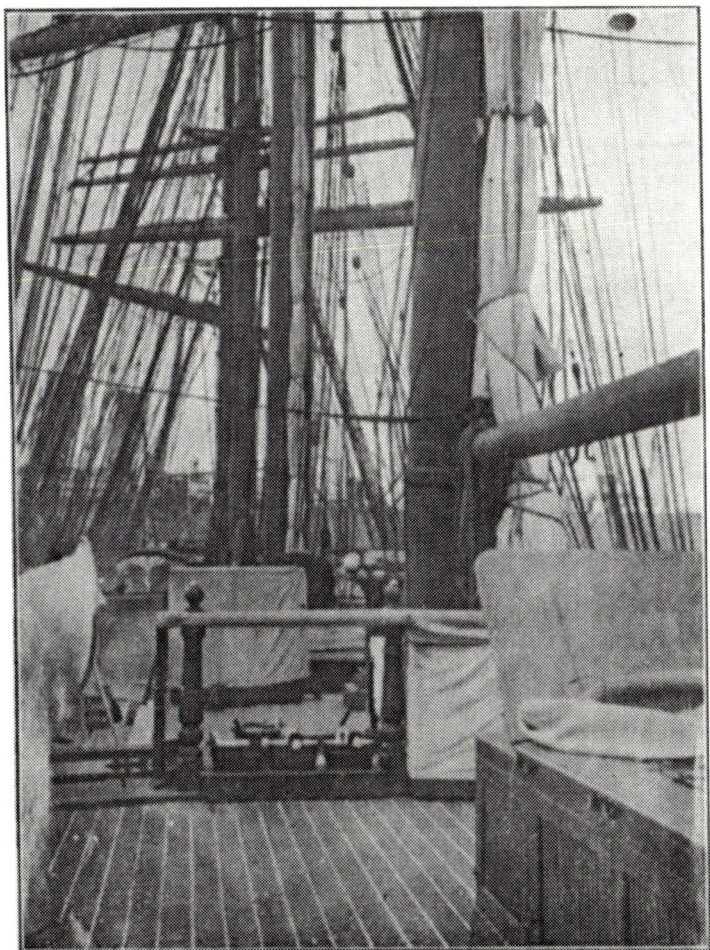

DECK OF LOCH TORRIDON

Photo by R. A. Fletcher

Dupleix and the British ship *Arracan* each took 103 days.

Though in 1902 the British ship *Osborne* again made the shortest passage, she took 61 days ; this year was remarkable for number of long voyages, these including the *Netherby* 111 days, *Windsor Park* 113 days, *Clydesdale* 125 days, these being British vessels ; the German ship *Peru* 136 days via Valparaiso, and the American schooner *Alice McDonald* 210 days via Pago Pago. The *Loch Torridon* again in 1903 made the fastest crossing in 45 days, as against the 116 days via Auckland of the American ship *Mary Cushing*, and the 108 days of the French barque *Marie Molinos*. Some American ships distinguished themselves by their slow passages in 1904, among them the barque *Holliswood*, 127 days, which included a stay of 62 hours at San Pedro, the barque *Carrollton* 114 days, and the *Sea King* 112 days ; the British ship *St. Mirren* took 115 days. On the other hand the British barque *Inverclyde* crossed the Pacific in 52 days. Two more of the " Invers," the *Invercoe* and the *Invermark* each took 87 days in 1905, these being the longest passages this year, and the British barque *Balmoral* made the shortest in 68 days.

The year 1906 showed a striking contrast, the longest being the 226 days of the French barque *Beaumanoir*, which included 97 days at Sydney, and the shortest the 61 days of the American barquentine *James Johnson*. Steamers were steadily invading this trade to the detriment of the sailer, and no fewer than 58 of the 76 arrivals were steamers in 1907. Among the sailers the British barque *Andromeda* took 101 days and the French barque *Armen* 60 days.

The record for 1908 states :—" Seventy-nine arrivals,
18

23 of which were steamers. American ship *Reuce* 229 days
via Sydney 83 days ; American barque *Big Bonanza*, 182
days via Sydney 77 days ; British barque *Willscott*, 124
days ; British barque *Andromeda* 120 days. The French
barque *Marthe Roux* and the American barque *Amazon*
were tied this year for shortest passage—54 days ; the
French barque *Emilie Galline* made the passage up from
Hobart in 50 days in this year. The *Willscott*, which
arrived dismasted, has since been purchased by the Alaska
Packers Association and has had her name changed to the
Star of Iceland."

In 1909 the forty arrivals included twelve steamers.
American vessels made the longest and shortest passages,
the *Henry Failing* taking 194 days including a stay of
90 days at Sydney, and the schooner *David Evans*, 56
days. The French barque *Thiers* occupied 113 days. The
details for 1910 are incomplete, but two American vessels,
the *John Palmer*, and *Henry K. Hall*, took 105 days.

Another good passage, which included a trip round the
world, was that of the *Kirkcudbrightshire*, under Captain
D. Roberts, in 1909. She sailed from Glasgow to Sydney
in 81 days, from Newcastle, N.S.W., to Junin in 39 days,
and from Caleta Buena to Queenstown in 93 days, the round
voyage occupying 10 months and four days. A long voyage
was that of the *Springbank* ; she left Hamburg in June
1908, and arrived at Santa Rosalia on December 29th,
210 days.

While the east coast of the United States has preferred
the fore-and-aft schooner, the west coast has had a number
of barquentines. The fore-and-aft schooner is more suitable
for coasting work, especially on the east coast, but the
westerners have found out the utility of the barquentine.
Vessels of this rig have made some remarkable voyages.

The *John L. Stanford*, 970 tons, in 1906, sailed from Port Ludlow, Wash., to Santa Rosalia in the good time of 22 days. In that year, also, the *Amaranth*, 1,109 tons, sailed from Shanghai to the Columbia river in 23 days, about 6,500 miles, and is credited with having run 340 miles from noon to noon, thanks to taking advantage of the steady strong westerly winds of the higher latitudes. So far back as 1896 the schooner *Aida* sailed from Shanghai to Tacoma in 27 days, and her track and the winds prevailing during her voyage were printed on the back of a pilot chart as a guide to other vessels.

The most remarkable barquentine that ever sailed was the *E. R. Sterling*, which only this year arrived in the Thames dismasted and was taken to an east coast port and broken up. She was formerly known as the *Everitt G. Griggs*, and was a six-masted vessel, and began her career as a four-masted ship the *Lord Wolseley*. After being knocked about in some dirty weather in the Pacific she was bought by some speculators on the west coast and re-rigged as a six-masted barquentine. Her foremast carried a foresail, double topsails, double topgallants, and a royal ; all the other masts were fore-and-aft rigged. She was a well-known trader in the Pacific, visiting Australian ports as well as those on her own side of the ocean, and proved herself a fast vessel and a good seaboat under her curious rig. A writer in a Dutch paper, thinking it necessary to give a name to such a vessel, called her a " schoonerbrig," but did not explain how much was brig and how much was schooner, or where one began and the other left off. She was certainly not a brig.

While on the subject of speed I should like to say that no one knows which was really the fastest sailing ship ever built. Many factors contributed to speed, and they did not all appear in all the vessels every time, or all in any one at any time. One was the design and shape of the ship, another was the personality of the commander, another was the nature of the cargo, another was the method of its loading, another was its trim—so sensitive was the *Ariel*, for instance, that Captain Keay at one time had a heavy box which could be dragged forward or aft along the deck as needed in order to suit her, and some tea clipper captains used to load tea into their cabin accommodation to improve the trim—another was the condition of the sails and rigging and copper plating of her bottom, another was the weather, the most fickle of them all, and another was the steering. When all these conditions or nearly all, and a few more might be added, synchronised, really good passages were made.

A good steersman was worth a mile an hour to some ships. One old sailor I knew had a habit when he took his trick at the wheel of throwing the vessel a point off her course, weather permitting, just to bring her on it again. Then he would pat the wheel gently with one hand while holding it with the other, and talk to the ship, as one might to a favourite and skittish mare. " Gently, old girl, I'm looking after you. Don't stick your nose into it that way, lift your head and show your forefoot. That's better, that's the way, my little beauty." And the little beauty did her part with him at the wheel as a spirited mare will respond to a kind word and the slightest pressure on the reins by a driver whom she loves and trusts. There was some mystery about that man, which none of the rest of us could fathom. Mystery or no, he was a splendid sailor. He had been in some of the racing tea clippers, and the stories he told in the dog watches were listened to by everyone in the ship, from the Old Man downwards. He

SHIP ILLAWARRA

was a believer in the counting of the waves, to know when a big one was coming, and taught me his system, and I never found it wrong.

Captain Shewan, in his book, boldly expresses his disbelief in some of the " wonderful runs " in a day or week, said to have been accomplished by some of the American built ships. His explanation is the same as that given me by another ship captain years ago. It is pointed out that many of these great runs were made when the vessel in question was running down her easting in high southern latitudes. Captain Shewan writes, "Running the easting down, below the 50th parallel of latitude—no infrequent course to be chosen in the days of Maury and Great Circle sailing—a degree of longitude would not be more than about forty miles of actual distance. A ship, therefore, making, let us say, 280 knots from noon to noon, would cover seven degrees of longitude. As there are sixty miles of longitude to a degree, the vessel would have ' covered ' 420 miles. Nautical miles were confounded with miles of longitude to the infinite enhancement of the particular clipper's reputation."

I may add it would also increase the clipper captain's reputation. Calculations of this sort pleased the passengers, who were gratified to think that they were bowling along at this phenomenal speed, and when they got ashore again they advertised the vessel and her captain, as the astute captain intended they should. Fast runs from port to port in so many days are a different matter, and can generally be checked by references to the shipping papers which recorded departures and arrivals, but even here newspaper records and ships logs do not always tally by a day or two. Not one of the American built vessels, claimed to have made such wonderful runs of 400 and more

miles a day, ever equalled the record established by the
Thermopylae on her famous first voyage. The later China
tea clippers were faster than the earlier ships built for that
trade, and they were also larger and more capable of being
driven. Such of them as were put into the Australian
trade, during the round voyage from London to Melbourne
or Sydney, and thence to China and home to London,
made good passages, but they were little better than the
iron and steel vessels built to be cargo carriers first and
speed merchants afterwards.

A very popular vessel in the London and Sydney trade,
with both shippers and passengers, was the *Illawarra*; she
made several fast voyages both out and home.

NOTE.—In regard to the height of waves mentioned at the beginning of this
chapter, it should be understood that abnormal waves of unusual size—often
miscalled tidal waves—are occasionally encountered in mid ocean; their cause
is unknown. They have been estimated at fully 8oft. from trough to summit.

CHAPTER IX

DISASTERS, RESCUES, ETC.

THE sea has always exacted a heavy toll from shipping. It is simply appalling to read the list of disasters, month by month, or year by year, which befell sailing ships. Hundreds were lost every year on the coasts of the British Isles alone, and to these must be added the ships which met their fate in other parts of the world. Many of these wrecks were of what would have been classed in the latter part of the nineteenth century as small vessels, but in the early part of the century these little ships and barques undertook ocean voyages that would be regarded nowadays as reckless adventure; it was all in the day's work, and what is more, many of them went their voyages year after year. They were commanded by men of the old sea-dog type, which is now as extinct as his ships.

Some of them were not much bigger than our larger coasting schooners. Vessels of 500 tons and under carried thousands of emigrants to America, and some of those that went to Australia and back were no bigger. The conditions under which they carried their passengers would not be tolerated now. The casualties which befell the ships in the emigrant trade were heavy enough in all conscience, but when one remembers that they were built entirely of wood, that steel wire rigging was almost unknown, and

that the seas they traversed were imperfectly or in-
correctly charted or not charted at all, the wonder is that
losses were not more numerous. The same may be said of
the ships in the trade to and from India and the Far East.
But there never was a shortage of British sailors for
British ships in those days, as there was in the closing
years of the last century, and as there is now.

Owing to the numerous disasters to shipping, several
localities have earned the unenviable reputation of being
ocean graveyards. The coasts of Australia have been the
scene of many lamentable disasters, not a few ships
meeting their doom when within a few hours of the end of
their journey. The west coasts of North and South
America have seen the end of many a fine ship. The
dreaded Cape Horn neighbourhood has claimed innumer-
able victims, how many can never be known. The Pesca-
dores are no mean contributors to the tale of lost ships.
In one year over 2,000 vessels were wrecked on the coasts
of Great Britain. The continental shores of the Channel
and Bay of Biscay have many wrecks to their discredit.
The African coasts are studded with ocean graveyards.

On the other side of the Atlantic the rocks of the Baha-
mas and of the West Indies generally have added in no
small measure to the melancholy record. The seas and
gales off Cape Hatteras, " America's Cape of Storms "
as it has been called, have caused the loss of many a splendid vessel.

Sable Island, off the coast of Nova Scotia, has always
been one of the most dreaded spots in the North Atlantic,
and steamers as well as sailers, which have to pass that
way, give it as wide a berth as possible. Sable Island is
one of the worst places in the world for a ship to get away
from, because it is surrounded by shallow water and is

exposed to the full fury of every storm wind there, no matter from what direction it blows. Wind, sea currents, shoals and fog seemed to have combined to make it one of the most to be dreaded places on the face of the globe. The island is about 85 miles east of Nova Scotia. It is narrow and crescent-shaped, nowhere more than a mile and a half in width, and a few years ago was estimated to be about twenty miles in length, though it has suffered considerably since from erosion. It is estimated that at the beginning of the nineteenth century it was fully forty miles in length. Some years ago it was reported that at the northeast end there was something like nine miles of roaring breakers before a depth of six fathoms was reached, and that for four miles more there were heavy cross seas over a depth of ten to fourteen fathoms. At the north-west end there were seventeen miles of shallows covered by breakers and cross seas before the water could be considered deep. As the process of erosion has been going on steadily, the dangerous shallows will have been increased by some miles. A hundred feet of the island have been known to disappear in a single gale.

The number of vessels wrecked on Sable Island may be counted in hundreds, but cannot ever be accurately known. Often only fragments of wreckage and a few bodies have been washed ashore to show that some vessel has been broken up on the shallows, miles from the island.

A French brigantine, the *A.S.H.*, from St. Pierre to Boston, with fish, struck on December 9th, 1884, on the West End bar and soon began to break up. It was learned afterwards she had seven persons on board. They took to the rigging and were drenched by the heavy seas which swept over them. The temperature was 12 degrees below zero, and their clothes froze till the wearers were encased in

ice. Three sailors were washed overboard. The steward
went mad and cut his throat, and a wave carried off the
body. The captain, mate and the remaining sailor managed
to cling to a spar and reach the shore. They tried to walk
to the lighthouse which they could see about three miles
away. The captain soon fell from exhaustion and was
frozen to death as he lay. The mate and sailor pushed on ;
the sailor fell, and he too was frozen to death. The mate,
now the sole survivor, who must have been a man of
unusual endurance, struggled on alone till he also fell, but
he managed to complete the journey on his hands and knees
in six hours from the time he landed, and was more dead
than alive when he was found. Every attention was given
him, and he soon recovered.

The records of the island contain one marvellous escape.
In 1856, a large schooner, the *Arno*, was seen running
before a storm dead on a lee shore. The sea was breaking
everywhere round her, but none broke over her. The
watchers saw her advance till she struck on the beach.
The life-saving corps men learned afterwards that two
large casks filled with fish oil had been lashed in the fore-
rigging, and securely lashed beside them were two of the
strongest sailors with long wooden ladles with which they
threw the oil into the air as high as they could. It was
caught by the wind and carried far in advance of the vessel
and spread over the seas sufficiently to stop them breaking.
The *Arno* thus reached the shore. No lives were lost.

It would be easy to fill a book of twice this size with a
record of nothing but disasters to sailing ships. I do not
intend to do more than mention a few of the better known
ships which met their end through fire, collision or wreck,
or being reported missing, with a few typical examples of
the heroism shown by those on board. I am intentionally

omitting descriptions of many such occurrences because they have been narrated so often.

The *Abergavenny* was wrecked off the Bill of Portland in February, 1805, with a loss of over 300 lives. There was nearly as heavy a loss of life when the packet *Prince of Wales* and the transport *Rochdale* were wrecked on the Irish coast a year or two later.

The loss of the *Kent*, East Indiaman, has been often described. She was a fine ship of 1,350 tons. She left the Downs at the beginning of February, 1825, and encountered a storm into the Bay of Biscay on the 28th, and the next day caught fire. Fortunately the sailing ship *Cambria*, a much smaller vessel, arrived, and thanks to the heroic efforts of her master, Captain Cook, and his crew, rescued nearly all on board the *Kent*. On March 2nd the burning ship blew up. This ship must not be confused with a later Blackwall ship of the same name.

In 1857, two fine ships were lost within a few hours of the termination of their voyage to Sydney. One, the *Catherine Adamson* struck the rocks 25 miles from Sydney Heads, and twenty of those on board were drowned. Two months later, in August of that year, the clipper ship *Dunbar* from London was wrecked at the Heads about six miles from Sydney. She had on board 140 passengers, besides her crew, and all were lost except one seaman named Johnson.

The *Dunbar* belonged to Duncan Dunbar. The ship stranded on the rocks in dirty weather just outside Sydney Harbour, a place called " The Gap " having been, it is supposed, mistaken for the Heads, and as she had been sighted approaching it and did not arrive, search parties went out. Johnson was rescued by a youth who was lowered down the cliff with a rope.

His rescue is thus described by a Sydney paper :—

" Johnson, who was thrown upon a shelf of the rock, was
enabled to obtain some shelter behind a projection, and
there he slept. When the morning broke he saw the wreck
and the bodies of his late companions. He endeavoured
to make signals, but was undiscovered. He uttered cries,
but the boiling ocean prevented them being heard. A
careful search was, however, making. Every spot where
there was a chance of seeing any object below was occupied
by spectators. At last a cry was heard, 'There is a man
upon the rocks.' A rope was lowered without delay.
After some failures it was brought within his reach. There
was danger from the projection of the rocks, but having
entwined the rope with seaman's skill around him, he
gave the signal and he was drawn up, some 200 feet, and
was received by the crowd with cries of congratulation and
joy. He passed about thirty hours on the rocks."

The emigrant ship *British Admiral* struck the rocks at
King's Island, between Tasmania and Australia, in 1874,
and eighty out of 89 on board were drowned. As sharks
abound in those waters it is to be feared that some of the
shipwrecked persons were devoured by them.

One of the most serious ocean tragedies on record was
the destruction of the emigrant ship *Cospatrick*, when on
her way to New Zealand. She was discovered to be on
fire about midnight on November 17th, 1872. Only five
or six persons out of the 476 on board were saved. They
were picked up in an open boat ten days later by another
vessel which conveyed them to St. Helena, where they
arrived on December 6th.

How dangerous a fog may prove at sea was illustrated
by the loss of the barque *Cromartyshire*, sunk in collision
off Sable Island by the French liner *La Bourgogne*, in
July, 1898. The steamer was on a voyage from New York

to Havre, and was about 150 miles to the north of her
proper course, and in spite of the fog prevailing she was
travelling at fast speed. The collision resulted in the
captain of the *Cromartyshire* and over 500 of her passengers
and crew being drowned ; the saved numbered 165.

As a contrast to this appalling disaster, it may be mentioned that when the Danish emigrant ship *Denmark*
was lost 800 miles east of Newfoundland in 1889, the
Atlantic Transport liner *Missouri* rescued 735 persons. For
this splendid piece of work Captain Murrell of the *Missouri*
and his officers and crew were very widely praised. A
public subscription was organised in London, and Captain
Murrell was presented by the Lord Mayor at the Mansion
House, in the presence of a crowded gathering, with a
suitably subscribed silver salver and about £500, and the
officers and crew also received due recognition of their
bravery.

A tragedy in the Australian trade, and one which ought
to have been avoided, was the sinking of the outward-
bound emigrant ship *Kapunda*. She was run into by the
barque *Ada Melmore* off the Brazilian coast, about three
o'clock one morning in January, 1886, and not far short
of 300 lives were lost. At the subsequent inquiry the
officers of the *Ada Melmore* were censured.

Another disaster, which attracted great attention, was
the sinking of the four-masted barque *Kate Thomas* while
being towed from Antwerp to Liverpool ; she was run into
and sunk by a steamer off the Land's End in April, 1910,
19 persons perishing.

Another disaster, which it would be hard to beat for the
horror of the picture which the mind may conjure up, was
that of the *St. Paul*. She left Hong Kong for Sydney in
1858 with 327 Chinese emigrants, and was lost on Rossel

Island in September of that year. Captain Pennard, her master, and eight of his crew sailed in one of the ship's boats in the hope of obtaining assistance for those left behind on the island. They were picked up by the Danish schooner *Prince of Denmark*, which in due course reported the disaster. The French vessel *Styx* was despatched to Rossel Island, where she arrived in the latter part of the following January. She was only able to bring away one survivor, the remainder having been massacred and eaten by the natives.

A tragedy, almost without parallel in sea annals, was reported in 1841. The ship *William Brown* struck ice and was so badly holed that she sank. Passengers and crew took to the boats, which were seriously overloaded, and no fewer than sixteen passengers in the long boat were thrown overboard by the crew in order to lighten her.

The years 1907-10 were disastrous to shipping from other causes than ice. The cargo itself may be a source of danger. More than one ship has been lost through her cargo shifting while the ship has been rolling heavily in bad weather; sometimes this has been due to insufficient care having been taken in stowing it. Coal cargoes have been known to ignite spontaneously, and it has not always been possible to subdue the outbreak either by smothering it by cutting off all possible supplies of air, or by pumping water into the hold and pumping it out again when the fire was extinguished, both being remedies only possible of application under favourable conditions. The first of four big coal-laden ships to go missing in those years was the Liverpool ship *Silberhorn*, in 1907. She sailed from Newcastle, New South Wales, for Iquique and presumably made a good passage across the South Pacific, for she was sighted by a German ship, the *Anny*, off the South American coast.

HOLYWOOD OFF CAPE HORN

From photo lent by Capt. M. M'Aulay

At that time, the *Anny* reported on arriving at Pena Blanca, she was on fire—if she was the *Silberhorn*—drifting some 90 miles off the island of Mas Afuera ; the masts were burnt, the foremast lying across the deck. Nothing was seen of the crew. The painting was scorched, and the only letters visible were " ool." Nothing has been heard of the *Silberhorn* or her crew from that day to this. Her boats were gone, so it is supposed her crew took to them in the vain hope of saving their lives. An exhaustive search was made, but nothing was learned.

The *Arthur Sewall*, of 3,209 tons, one of the finest steel ships ever launched from an American yard, built in 1899, by Messrs. Sewall, sailed from the Delaware Breakwater in April, 1907, for Seattle, with a cargo of coal. It was thought, as she never arrived, that she may have shared the fate of the *Silberhorn*. Two other fine ships, the British *Falklandbank* and the American *Bangalore*, also disappeared with all hands when coal-laden. The former sailed from Port Talbot on November 9th, 1907, for Valparaiso, and was spoken by the Italian barque *Checco* shortly before Christmas in latitude 31 south, and longitude 46 west ; the *Checco* arrived at Monte Video on December 27th. The *Bangalore*, which left Norfolk, Virginia, for Honolulu on October 23rd, was spoken on November 24th in 7 north latitude, 26 west longitude. Spontaneous firing of their cargo owing to rough weather off the Horn may have been the cause of their disappearance, or it may have been due to ice. Occasionally, it is to be feared, vessels have been lost through collisions with each other.

With the terrible weather conditions to contend against in that part of the world, it is no wonder that sailors were always glad when they had passed the Horn, whether they were going east or west. Probably more vessels have been reported missing, which have been on voyages taking them round the Horn, in that part of the world than in any other.

The experiences of some of the vessels in that neighbourhood may prove interesting. One of them was the full-rigged steel ship *Deccan*, 1,986 tons, built at Glasgow in 1895. She left Port Talbot in August 1909, for a port on the west coast of South America, and certainly experienced her share of bad luck. In less than two months after leaving port, one of the apprentices died and was buried at sea. Captain Parnell was taken so ill that he decided to make a call at the Falkland Islands in order that he might be sent home. The stay at Port Stanley lasted ten days, and just as the voyage was resumed, with Mr. Rowlands, the chief mate, acting as master, a fire was discovered to have broken out on board, which it took an hour to extinguish. The usual westerly gales were experienced as the vessel beat round Cape Horn, and continued after she got round. On December 6th land was sighted some miles to leeward, and the wind having dropped more sail was set and an attempt was made to beat off the lee shore. This failed and the ship found herself among the breakers, and struck the rocks. Lifeboats were launched and in spite of being badly damaged were occupied by the officers and crew, and a hasty departure from the ship followed. A few biscuits and some tins of meat were all they had time to place in the boats, and fifteen minutes after the ship struck she had totally disappeared. After they had been in the boats for some hours they saw a small sandy beach and succeeded in landing. No lives were lost. The shipwrecked men numbered 27. They found grim evidence of the fate which might befall them in the shape of skeletons of previous shipwrecked sailors who had died of starvation, having nothing to eat but the few mussels they were able to gather. A scouting party, after they had been cast away for thirteen days, sighted a small sealing vessel and managed to make their signals seen. The captain of the sealer took the shipwrecked men on board, and in order to make room for them left some of his own men behind with provisions while he took the rescued men to Punta Arenas in the Straits of Magellan, whence they were sent back to England. Having seen to the safety of the *Deccan's* men, he returned and rescued his own men.

One of the survivors was Mr. Harold Pickering, and after this voyage he was appointed, as third mate, to the *Swanhilda*, another splendid vessel belonging to the same firm.

The *Swanhilda* was lost in the following May, while on a voyage from Cardiff to Antofagasta, through striking a reef off Staten Island, a few miles to the south of Tierra del Fuego. After she struck, an accident occurred in lowering one of the lifeboats and twelve of its sixteen occupants fell into the sea, including the captain, his wife, and the second mate. Only four of the persons in that boat reached the shore, and one of these became demented and wandered away. The survivors of the wreck managed to reach the Staten Island lighthouse which wirelessed the news of the disaster to Punta Arenas and a rescue steamer was sent.

The *Palgrave*, an iron four-masted full-rigged ship of 3,187 tons, the largest in the world, when she was built in 1884, was wrecked near Coquimbo, Chili, in August, 1908. She was dismasted on her second voyage, and again a few years later. Her owners, Messrs. Hamilton and Co., bought her back from the underwriters and had her refitted, and for fourteen years she escaped serious accident until she

19

met the mishap which ended her career. One incident in her career is almost unique, when she saved her time by an hour and benefited her owners by £6,000. She was to load at Calcutta for New York, and her freights amounted to about £12,000. She was delayed by light winds in the Bay of Bengal, so Captain Higgins anchored off Madras and telegraphed to his owners in Scotland, and they immediately cabled to Calcutta for a tug to go and assist the ship. The tug brought her into Calcutta within an hour of the expiry of the cancelling date, a piece of good fortune for the owners as freights had fallen by about fifty per cent.

The *Palgrave* is said to have been built according to what her designer conceived to be the dimensions of Noah's Ark. She has been described as a difficult ship to handle.

Rescues at sea are regarded by seafarers as ordinary incidents of the day's work. A landsman reads in his newspaper that the crew of a vessel has been rescued in a gale by the crew of another vessel, but he has no idea of the risks that the rescuers run, voluntarily of course, but the risks are none the less great, and more than one man who has set out on his errand of life-saving has lost his own life as the reward of his heroism. The " County " line was a famous line many years ago, but it has gone like others. The British India steamer *Oolobaria* twenty years ago sighted in the Indian Ocean a sailing ship in distress, with her masts broken off short by the deck, her boats stove in, and drifting towards a lee shore. She was the *Fathal Rahman*, of Muscat, Arab owned and Arab manned. Captain Addenbrooke, of the *Oolobaria*, wanted to take the wreck in tow. Second officer Cocks and a volunteer crew of lascars went in a boat, and for five hours struggled to reach the ship, which, like their own boat, was at times completely hidden by the great seas from the steamer. At last the boat's crew succeeded in passing a line to the ship, but the line parted before a hawser could be made fast. The only alternative being the abandonment of the ship, it was decided to try to rescue the crew. Chief Officer McArthur relieved the second officer, and another boat's crew of volunteer lascars made two trips to the sinking vessel and brought off the men. Every man had to jump into the sea from the ship, and be hauled into the boat, and when they reached the steamer they had to jump into the sea and be hauled on board the *Oolobaria.* Not a life was lost, and 38 Arabs were saved, and so well was everything carried out that even the ship's boat was got on board. Describing the rescue Captain Addenbrooke says, " The rescuers were in the cutter for many hours in a high cross sea, with cyclonic squalls and blinding rain, and it was entirely owing to their coolness and judgment that the abandoned ship's crew were safely transferred." For this brave and dangerous rescue the committee of Lloyds awarded Lloyd's silver medal to Chief Officer F. D. McArthur and Second Officer A. T. Cocks, and its bronze medal to a number of lascars. Since 1837 Lloyd's have presented medals in recognition of conspicuous acts of bravery at sea, but many an heroic act and brave rescue has little or nothing said about it and the rescuers neither seek nor get reward. Perhaps in this case, if they had been men from some old steam tramp, instead of one of the liners of a well-known company, the rescue would have passed unheeded. The sailing ship was one of the old " County " line, the *County of Lancaster.*

The famous old tea clipper, *Sir Lancelot,* also owned and manned by natives, went down in a gale in the Indian Ocean, most of those on board being rescued.

One of the saddest wrecks connected with Liverpool sailing ships was that of the well-known *Dalgonar*, one of the largest and finest ships of the port. While in ballast she was capsized in an exceptionally severe gale in the South Pacific, her decks being almost perpendicular and her keel visible. During the launching of the lifeboat Captain Isbester and three men were drowned, but the remainder regained the ship after a terrible experience. A small French ship, the *Loire*, sighted the *Dalgonar*, and stood by her for four days and nights, burning flares at night to let those on the sinking ship see that she was still there. At last the gale moderated sufficiently for the *Loire* to launch her lifeboat, and eventually 26 men were rescued in an exhausted condition. The rescue has been described as " one of the most heroic deeds of bravery at sea on record." The *Dalgonar*, however, did not founder at once, but drifted about the South Pacific for some time, and went ashore on a reef near one of the mid-ocean islands.

The *Galgate* was a fine steel four-masted Liverpool barque of 2,356 tons which had more than her share of ill-luck. She was dismasted two or three times. Once she was towed into Rio de Janeiro having had the worst of an encounter with a gale, and a powerful tug was sent from Liverpool to bring her back. Another time when she required the help of a tug, she and the tug parted company in dirty weather, and the tug reported accordingly. Later the *Galgate* put into Queenstown, and inquired if anybody had seen her tug.

The Liverpool four-masted barque *Alice A. Leigh*, 3,000 tons, also had her share of bad fortune. On one voyage she sailed from Hamburg in 1909 for Santa Rosalia, and meeting with heavy weather she lost several sails and spars and put into Falmouth for repairs. She also arrived in the

Thames with considerable damage aloft. After a change of owners and the war, she was in the New Zealand trade, and as the *Rewa* made two or three voyages to London.

The ship *Wallace*, of Leith, commanded by Captain Cormea, which left Quebec in November, 1857, with timber, was capsized by a tremendous sea when 800 miles from Cape Clear. She righted, and another sea carried away the foremast and bowsprit, and drowned the chief officer and steward. All the provisions were spoilt by the sea, and a great wave stove in the water casks. No vessel came in sight, and to keep going and alive the sailors killed and ate the ship's dog. For ten days they were confined to the rigging, and then the barque *Clyne* rescued them when they were well-nigh exhausted. An apprentice, who was taken off the wreck insensible, died soon afterwards.

The iron ship *Waverley*, Captain Rose, was chartered at Shanghai in 1857 to take about 400 men of the Chinese contingent to Swatow. She had not been properly ballasted, and when she was thrown on her beam ends in a gale her mud ballast shifted and she stayed capsized. The English schooner *Nora*, under Captain Porter, sighted her some hours later and managed to get close enough to rescue the captain and his officers and crew and about 300 of the Chinese, and left the ship to her fate with about 100 Chinamen clinging to the rigging. The *Nora* made for Foo-chow whence the authorities sent a steamer to search for the wreck. In the meantime the *Intrepid*, Captain Gardner, had sighted the wreck and rescued the Chinamen.

The following statement by Captain Spencer, of the packet ship *Northumberland*, which went down in mid-Atlantic during a voyage from New York to London, tells its own story :

" Queenstown, December 16th, 1857. I, Captain S. L. Spencer, beg to report that I am indebted to Captain Percy, officers, and crew, of the brig *Jessie*, of St. John's, Newfoundland, for the lives of myself and passengers through their gallant conduct in rescuing us from my ship on Friday, December 4th, which was a perfect wreck, having been reduced to that condition two days previously by a fearful gale of wind. But for their timely assistance we must have perished, as everything had been done that was possible to keep her afloat, and all the hands worn out and exhausted ; the masts were gone to the deck, and the sea had swept away everything in the cabins, and some of the women had nothing but a blanket to protect them from the weather. There is the greatest praise due to the noble captain that as soon as he perceived the wreck he made to us, though he had but a small vessel of 140 tons, heavily laden, and had already suffered considerable damage from the gale, and expressed his willingness to take us off. This was not accomplished without imminent peril to themselves, a heavy sea running at the time, and the brig under close-reefed topsails, so that the whole day was occupied in passing four boats to her. Sixty-three souls, bringing but few provisions, were a serious addition to their cargo, but we were welcomed with every kindness ; and here I have to record an act of pure benevolence that must command the admiration of everyone : The brig was bound to St. John's, Newfoundland, the home of Captain Percy and his two sons, first and second mates (their absence had already been protracted by accident from six weeks to six months). With the knowledge that all was anxiety at home, they were calculating on the happiness their return would bring to their family ; yet as soon as we were all on board, they immediately, and unasked, turned the ship and sailed again for England. It is but a poor tribute to such kindheartedness to say that they did more for us than their own safety warranted, a heavy gale the following night obliging them to throw overboard part of their cargo. My passengers, I am sure, share with me in the feelings of gratitude that prompt me to make this testimony, and to them also I am indebted for their praiseworthy exertions before leaving the unfortunate ship."

A more touching tribute, or one more eloquent in its simplicity and genuineness, I do not think I have ever read. For a little brig to rescue sixty-three persons from a sinking ship in an Atlantic gale is a piece of seamanship as remarkable as it is heroic.

A thrilling story of the wonderful escape of the barque *Adelaide* from total destruction by fire in 1853 was afterwards told by one of the passengers. According to his version in the " Illustrated London News," the vessel, commanded by Captain A. R. N. Tremearne, left Port Adelaide for London on New Year's day with eighteen passengers and a valuable cargo which included 40,667 ounces of gold, a large quantity of copper, and other produce. When the ship was in longitude 67.23 east and latitude 25.13 south it was discovered at half past three on the morning of February 4th that the wool had ignited from spontaneous combustion. The smoke was first seen issuing from the after hatchway, and the deck was opened and immense quantities of water were poured down. The captain decided to make for the island of Rodriguez, 400 miles away, and a boat was provisioned and got ready for launching. The flames burst through the cover of the after hatch, but these were extinguished. The launch was lowered, and the quarter boats were provisioned and made ready for lowering at a moment's notice. At four o'clock in the afternoon flames broke out round the main-mast, but were suppressed. Mr. E. W. S. Driffield, the passenger who tells the story of the fire, continues :

" At 4 p.m. we expected the fire to overpower us and break out every minute ; so the ladies, married men, children and servants were put into the launch, which towed astern very easily : Mr. Ellis, the chief officer being in charge with three hands. The captain, however, encouraged all hands to continue the efforts that had been already made to save the ship, and the water was kept as abundantly supplied as previously. In the steward's cabin and pantry the smoke and heat were very great. At midnight the breeze was increasing, and the weather squally. Double-reefed the topsails, and furled the courses, as they created a draught on the deck ; also furled the light sails. Smoke to be observed issuing from every crevice. The water kept going all night.

" Saturday, February 5th, 4 a.m. Set maintopgallant sail. The fire to all appearance seemed to be between the main and mizen masts. The carpenter cut holes in the deck—one on each side of the main mast, one amidships, one in the steward's cabin, pantry, and in the cuddy, also just abaft the mizen mast—for the purpose of admitting water into the hold : all these holes being immediately covered with wet blankets, etc. to exclude the air. The bulwarks being perfectly tight, the deck and cuddy were flooded with water, and the hands stationed at the different holes to uncover them when, with the motion of the ship, the water rolled over them, and to cover them again the instant that the water receded so as to admit no air at all into the hold.

" 10 a.m. Had three good lines fast to the launch, which

towed astern very well. Smoke appeared somewhat less.
Set flying-jib, main-royal, and gaff-topsail. Threw all the
hay overboard, keeping only sufficient for the present use
of the stock ; and as all the grain was below, the poultry
were all killed. The greatest quantity of smoke now
issued from the steward's cabin.

" 12 p.m. Island of Rodriguez distant 330 miles.
Moderate trade wind, and fine. Water as plentifully supplied as ever. The heat in the cuddy was most intense in
the afternoon ; and it was considered advisable to knock
down all the cabins and throw them overboard, which was
effected with considerable difficulty, and great destruction
consequently took place of the passengers' baggage ; but
it was for the safety of the ship and therefore unavoidable.
Threw two hen coops overboard that were in the way.
The carpenter then cut several holes in the poop and cuddy
decks, and hose were led between the two decks into the
hold, every hole in the poop deck being covered with
blankets, etc., except at the time the water was being
poured down ; water was supplied to these holes in immense quantities.

" At 8 p.m. the fire to all appearances was very much
subdued, but the water was kept going as usual, and all
hands were divided into quarter watches for the night.
The weather being squally at times, all small sails were
furled.

" Midnight : Weather fine, everything quiet and all
apparently buried in deep sleep, except the water gang on
duty."

On the Sunday the captain read prayers twice. The
pumping in of water was maintained night and day. The
captain read prayers twice on Monday and again on
Tuesday morning. By half past three that afternoon, as

the fire appeared subdued, the captain considered he might venture to take the passengers in the launch on board again, and this was done, but the launch was towed astern all night in case of need. At six o'clock Rodriguez was sighted twelve or fourteen miles distant. As immediate danger from the fire appeared so much less, and as dangerous reefs surrounded the entrance to the port at the island, and for other reasons, Captain Tremearne decided to run for Mauritius, " as under existing circumstances there was every probability, if he attempted to put in at Rodriguez, that he would be obliged to run the ship ashore where she would inevitably become a total wreck, and most likely the extremely valuable cargo would have been lost with her—to say nothing of the great sufferings and inconvenience it would have occasioned to the passengers."

On the Wednesday and Thursday the heat in the interior of the vessel continued very great. On Thursday night very heavy rain fell, and passengers and all hands being on the poop got drenched. On the Friday, when passing Round Island, a signal was hoisted for a tug, and no notice whatever was taken of it. At 7 p.m. a pilot came on board, and at 10 p.m. the ship was anchored off Port Louis. On the Saturday Captain Tremearne lodged his passengers at a hotel, the *Adelaide* was towed into harbour, and the fire brigade turned out with two engines and after playing for some time into the cuddy to cool it, pumped fresh air down into the after scuttle to enable the men to get up the gold, which was done with much difficulty, the heat still being most intense ; and Captain Tremearne saw it safely lodged in the bank by 10 p.m.

During the time the launch was towing astern with passengers, provisions were cooked in the ship and lowered to those in the launch, in order not to touch those already in the boat lest the ship should have to be left in a hurry. A clergyman was among the passengers, and after they returned to the ship he relieved the captain of the daily reading of prayers. After the ship had been repaired, and sugar had been taken in to replace the burnt or damaged wool, which was removed at Port Louis, the *Adelaide*, with her original passengers, resumed her voyage on March 24th and reached London on June 13th.

The American ship *Harkaway*, 545 tons, of Charleston, left that port in August 1857 with a cargo of turpentine, cotton and resin for Liverpool. She had a captain, two mates, a crew of 14, and ten passengers. Something exploded in the hold on the evening of September 5th, and set the cargo on fire. By 5 a.m. on the 5th it was seen to be impossible to save the vessel, and the crew began to cut away two of the masts to fill the ship with water. The flames ascended the fore-hatches and came through the starboard side of the ship. A vessel attracted by the smoke and glare steered towards the *Harkaway* about 9 p.m. This vessel, the *Sarah and Dorothy*, of Newcastle, put out a boat and rescued the passengers and some of the crew with much difficulty. The ship was then in flames. The captain and the rest of the crew were rescued just in time, as the turpentine exploded and blew up the vessel a few minutes after they had left it. A small vessel, the *Advice*, of Liverpool, fell in with the crowded *Sarah and Dorothy* and took seven of the crew. The captain and mates and the ten passengers were transferred the next day to the R.M.S.P. *Atrato*. The other seven members of the crew stayed on the *Sarah and Dorothy* for St. John's.

The ship *Eden* which sailed from this country for Valparaiso included in her cargo 150 tons of gunpowder. Her captain went mad and set fire to the vessel, which ultimately blew up. The crew took to the boats and were picked up by the *Juanita*.

Emigrant ships furnish a long list of disasters. Among these may be mentioned the *Exmouth*, from Londonderry to Quebec, which was lost in the North Atlantic in April, 1847, when nearly all of the 247 persons on board were drowned.

The American emigrant ship *Ocean Monarch* left Liverpool for Boston in August, 1848, and caught fire a few hours later when only six miles off the Great Orme's Head. There were nearly 400 persons on board, and 178 lives were lost. The Brazilian frigate *Alphonso* and the yacht *Queen of the Ocean* between them saved 156.

Another vessel, the *Annie Jane*, with emigrants from Liverpool, stranded on Barra Island, on the west coast of Scotland in September, 1853, with a loss of 348 lives. The wreck of the *Tayleur*, a new ship, on the Irish coast a few hours after she had left Liverpool, when 380 persons were drowned at the very beginning of their voyage, seemed to cast a gloom over the country.

In May of the following year the *John* struck on those terrible rocks, the Manacles, near Land's End, and 200 persons were drowned. It used to be an article of faith with sailors that no ship that struck the Manacles was ever saved.

In 1848 the ship *Omega*, with 336 emigrants was reported to have sustained an injury of so serious a character that it was necessary to transfer all on board to another vessel. One, called the *Barbara*, came on the scene and took all on board from the *Omega*, which was stated to have foundered soon afterwards. The *Barbara* herself was wrecked on the American coast, and nearly 200 of the emigrants were drowned. The *Omega* did not sink, for she was passed by the barque *Franklin*, perfectly sound, some eighty miles west of the Scillies, with not a soul on board, and drifting with the currents. There is little doubt that had her passengers and crew remained on board all would have been saved.

The wreck of the convict ship *Neva*, with 240 persons on board, occurred at King's Island, to the north of Tasmania, at the western end of Bass Strait, on May 14th 1835. She had 150 female convicts, 55 children, and nine voluntary emigrants, the officers and crew comprising the remainder. About 2 a.m. land was sighted, and breakers were soon seen ahead, and the ship went on the rocks and began to go to pieces. The doors of the prison were burst open by the violence with which the ship had struck, and the convicts swarmed on deck. A boat had just been launched, and into this many of them jumped, and capsized her before she could get away from the side of the vessel. The captain, the surgeon, and the superintendent of the convicts and two of the crew were already in the boat. All but the captain and two sailors were drowned. These three managed to regain the ship, and the captain had another boat launched, and care was taken that it should not be overcrowded. Soon after it was pushed off from the wreck it was capsized in the surf. The master and chief mate, being good swimmers, got back to the ship, which was now rapidly falling to pieces. Many of the terror-stricken convicts still on board were clinging to planks and fragments of the ship and screaming for help. The wreck was lifted by the waves off the reef and dropped into deep water. Some of the crew and a few of the convicts drifted ashore on wreckage on King's Island, which was nine miles from the scene of the disaster, and of the

22 who reached the shore alive seven died from exposure and exhaustion. A few provisions were washed up, on which the survivors lived for fifteen days.

A small vessel, the *Tartar*, belonging to a man named Friend, of Hobart Town, was lost on another part of the island, and its crew saved. They erected a tent and waited for rescue. Seeing an unusual quantity of wreckage on the beach, they made a search of the island and found the survivors of the *Neva*, and the two parties joined forces. On June 15th, another small vessel belonging to Mr. Friend called at the island, being attracted by the distress signals flying, and ultimately all were rescued and taken to Tasmania. Before leaving King's Island they buried over a hundred bodies which had been washed ashore.

The *General Wood*, while carrying nearly a hundred convicts from Singapore to the Penang settlement, was lost in 1848 under circumstances which caused much comment. The convicts mutinied, murdered most of the crew, and afterwards caused the destruction of the vessel. She had sailed without the protection of a military convict guard, and the convicts took advantage of this.

But no tragedy can equal in its horror that which marked the end of the celebrated American clipper *Bald Eagle*. The ship, which was under Portuguese officers and a crew mostly of the same nationality, was carrying some hundreds of Chinese coolies to islands where guano is obtained. Trouble arose between the Portuguese and the coolies, so they fastened the coolies below, under gratings, and shot at them with their revolvers. Somehow the ship was set on fire, and the Portuguese took to the boats and left the unfortunate Chinamen to burn to death.

One vessel well known on the Pacific coast and in Australian ports in her day was the old wooden barque

Hesper. She was built at Port Blakeley on the Pacific coast in 1882. She spent most of her career in the lumber trade from the Puget Sound and Columbia river ports to Australia and China. In the early '90's, she was homeward bound from Australia with one of the hardest crews afloat on board, the "Pacific Monthly" reports. Captain Sodergren treated them well, but their leader, a big Irishman named St. Clair, talked them into mutiny.

"He told them the captain had some 20,000 dollars freight money aft in his cabin and that it would be an easy matter to kill the officers, secure the money, run the vessel ashore on one of the South Sea islands, and give out to the world that they had met shipwreck. He won over the majority of the crew, and hostilities were opened by killing FitzGerald, the second mate in cold blood.

"Their plan was to kill off the officers one at a time, and they would probably have carried out the plot to the full had not the captain's wife surmised that something was wrong, and put the cabin in a state of siege. Seeing their plot was known, the mutineers made no further attempt at secrecy, but began a determined attack upon the cabin, in which the officers and several of the sailors who had refused to join their comrades were barricaded. The siege went on for several days, when the mutineers found there was not one among them who could navigate the ship. Thereupon they began to weaken, and opened negotiations with the captain, who managed the affair with such skill that ere long he had the ringleaders in irons." Ultimately they were taken to San Francisco where the mutineers were tried, and St. Clair was hanged and several of the others were sent to prison for long terms.

The old barque *Gatherer,* a Pacific coast veteran, had an even more unenviable record. She was known as one of the hardest vessels afloat, a veritable hell-ship, and her decks were bloodstained more than once. In 1882, her master, John Sparks, who is described as a fiend aboard ship, had a big bully of a mate named Watts, who joined with him in hazing the crew. One man, who had been brutally ill-used by Watts, ran aloft off Cape Horn and after cursing the officers soundly jumped into the sea. No attempt was made to rescue him. Watts deliberately shot another man, and a third, after being ill-used by the mate climbed upon the rail and cut his throat with a knife and fell into the sea. Watts' worst exploit was to gouge out the eye of a young sailor ; the details of this atrocity are said to be too sickening to be related. When the *Gatherer* reached San Francisco the captain was dismissed his ship, and Watts was arrested and given a long term of imprisonment.

The *Harvester* was another Pacific ship with a bad record. Her captain had one man put in a barrel, the head of which was then fastened up, and nails were driven into the sides of the barrel. When the captain thought it had enough spikes, he rolled the barrel up and down the deck. The unfortunate victim was nearly dead when released. Another time the captain put some of the crew into a pig pen and kept them there for days.

Another American captain once put one of his mates into a fowl house on deck and compelled him to come to the bars and take grains of corn from his hand and try to eat them.

Probably one of the most unfortunate fleets that ever existed was that associated with a well-known American ship-owning family named Palmer. The line was founded by William E. Palmer, of Roxbury, about 1903, the first vessel being the *Dorothy Palmer*. All fourteen vessels of the line were named after members of the family, and very handsome fore-and-aft schooners they were. After owning them for six years William Palmer died, and then began an extraordinary series of catastrophes. The first to go, within a month of her owner's death, was the *Minnie Palmer*, a vessel of 1,900 tons gross register, and valued at £12,000 besides her cargo, which was worth almost as much. She sprang a leak in bad weather off Cape Hatteras, and though she had two tugs in attendance, she stranded on the dreaded Frying Pan Shoals, and was wrecked. This was in November 1909. At Christmas the same year, the *Davis Palmer* sank with all hands off Boston Harbour. Disasters happened to the other vessels of the fleet. One, the *Harwood Palmer* was torpedoed by a German submarine in 1917. Fire, collision and storm accounted for the others. The last to be lost was the *Dorothy Palmer*, which was abandoned by her crew off the New England coast early in 1923.

If the adventures of the crew of the Norwegian barque *Alexandra* were not known to have occurred, the account of them would be dismissed as fiction. She was caught in one of those terrible long spells of calm weather which are to be met with sometimes in the Pacific and were as much to be dreaded by sailing ship men as any storm. They were said to be worse than any calm in the Atlantic, owing to the almost entire absence of swell in the sea. In the Atlantic there is always a slight amount of swell, even on the calmest day, which causes a ship to rock sufficiently to slat her sails against the masts and thus get along at about three or four miles a day, but in the Pacific the ocean seems asleep too, and as calm as the wind. Get out of the calm area the *Alexandra* could not. At last provisions began to run short, and the crew were in danger of star-

20

vation. It was decided to leave the ship to her fate and abandon her, and to take to the boats. The calm must have come to an end some time, or she drifted out of it on ocean currents, for she was found to have stranded on one of the islands of the Galapagos group. The boats, after leaving the ship, kept together for a little time, and parted in the darkness. One of them reached the South American mainland; the other went in a westerly direction and finally brought up on one of the many islets in the middle Pacific. There its occupants remained for close upon six months before they were discovered and rescued. It was then that they learned that their ship had been posted as missing and they themselves were mourned as dead. The *Alexandra*, it may be mentioned, was built at Aberdeen in 1874, and for many years sailed under the British flag.

The Norwegian ship *Theodor*, a ship with a history, was posted missing in 1907. She was known to thousands on both sides of the Atlantic as the Cunard steamer *China*, having been built on the Clyde in 1862, and being sold out of that Company's service, had her engines removed and was converted into a four-masted sailing ship of 2,437 tons. Her Norwegian owners were evidently proud of her, for she was kept up well, and retained her 100 A1 classification to the last. Altogether this famous vessel saw 45 years service; she disappeared with all hands while on a voyage from Tampa, Florida, to Yokohama. It is conjectured that she was overcome by a cyclone in the South Indian Ocean.

The Meritorious Service medal, established by Lloyd's in 1893, was first awarded to William Shotton, third mate of the British sailing ship *Trafalgar*. She was going from the East Indies to Australia, and soon after leaving port fever broke out on board, and the captain and first and second mates were among those laid up. Some of the crew became mutinous. Shotton, almost a boy still, took command, and assisted by John Lee, the steward, who stood by him loyally, brought the ship into an Australian port.

A particularly ghastly tragedy of the sea was reported when the big Norwegian ship *Alonso* put into Falmouth in January, 1914. Her captain had died of beri-beri, and the first mate and six of the crew were suffering from the disease. The vessel had 8,500 barrels of whale oil which she had brought from the whaling station at Elephant Bay, and the disease broke out soon after she left there. Captain Hansen had to take to his bed on Christmas Day and died as the vessel was entering the Channel. The chief officer took command, but was himself stricken by the disease, and then several of the crew were taken ill. The ship was short of fresh provisions. Three days before she was towed into Falmouth a telegram was received stating that a large vessel was seen dangerously near the Lizard rocks ; tugs went out, and one of them found the *Alonso*.

Another recipient of the Meritorious Service medal was a Norwegian, Captain Mattson, of the Norwegian barque *Flora*. The resourcefulness of sailors has long been proverbial. The *Flora* sprang a leak below the water line. For the safety of the ship it had to be stopped. The captain had a long watertight canvas bag made, with a glass window in the side. He crawled into the bag feet first, put his arms through two sleeves let into it, and when these had been securely tied at the wrists to keep the water out he was lowered over the side of the ship till the window was level with the leak, and he then hammered pieces of old tarred rope into the open seams and stopped the inflow of water sufficiently to save his vessel.

CHAPTER X

THE very nature of the seafarer's life has always caused him to view things from a standpoint peculiarly his own. This was more especially the case in the days of the Tall Ships with their long voyages and protracted isolation at sea than it is in these days of floating hotels and travelling warehouses crossing the seas according to schedule and in a minimum space of time. The round voyage of a sailing ship might last a couple of years or even more. The conditions of life afloat strongly influenced the temperaments and moulded the characters of the men of the sailing ships, and made them almost a race apart from the land dwellers. One important factor was loneliness, and another was the always present sense of danger. They were simply small companies of men living on floating specks on a vast ocean. They were sailing in little ships that sometimes were remarkable only for the hardships they inflicted on those aboard them ; they, or some of them, felt the intensely close communion with nature, as represented by the wind and sea, which was inseparable from their waking moments and sometimes was with them in their dreams ; they felt, too, the companionship of the stars by night ; there was the never ending study of the ever varying clouds by day and the

weather indications they give ; they saw the fickle and
wanton beauty of the always changing sea, and the cold
brilliance of the moon and Southern Cross in southern
latitudes ; they felt the consciousness of the possibility
of hidden and sudden peril, even in the finest weather : all
these conditions, and many others, helped to make the
sailor of the wind-driven ships the self-reliant cheerful
man he always was, risking his life more often in a single
voyage than most landsmen do from a sense of duty in ten
years, and laughing death in the face.

Probably the loneliest man on a sailing ship which did
not carry passengers was the captain. Apart from their
officers they had no one to speak to, and except in comparatively rare instances the necessities of maintaining
their official position made intimacy with their mates
very difficult. On the other hand there were many close
friendships between masters and their mates, but it is to
be feared that these were the exceptions that proved the
rule. Some ship owners allowed their masters to choose
their mates themselves, and where this was done the results
were almost always satisfactory ; other owners chose the
mates for them, irrespective of suitability to one another,
and in spite of the spirit of give and take and of mutual
toleration which prevails at sea the results were not always
satisfactory.

Many owners permitted the captains of their ships to
take their wives with them, and a few extended this
privilege to the first mate—if the husbands and their
wives happened to be personal friends. The presence of
the captain's wife usually added to the comfort of all
on board, particularly on British vessels. On such, there
was little or no brutality by officers towards the men, and
little inclination on the part of crews to be turbulent and

cut up rough. The mere presence of a good woman on board had an influence which was all for the good.

Captain T. Y. Powles, one of the best known and respected of modern sailing ship masters, whose home was at Liverpool, was accompanied on many of his voyages by his wife, and very comfortable ships his were. Without interfering in any way with the management of the ship, and always with the utmost tact, Mrs. Powles sought to do something for those under her husband's command. The boys and sailors used to speak of her as " mother " among themselves, a testimony to their regard for her, and her slightest wish was law to them. In fine weather she would, if possible, get up a concert in the saloon, and every member of the crew not on duty was always invited to be present ; there were seldom any absentees. Mrs. Powles died on her husband's ship, the *James Kerr*, and was buried at San Francisco. Her husband died some years ago at his home at Liverpool.

Captain Powles was fond of a joke. Some of the others on board one of his ships were fond of a joke too. On a voyage from Calcutta to San Francisco, in 1881, when he commanded the *John O'Gaunt*, he had a well known American scientist, Dr. Foord Clark, among his passengers, who took great interest in electrical manifestations and St. Elmo's Fire in particular. Captain Powles, who knew something of the subject, and was not without imagination, gave him what information he could, of all of which the professor made voluminous notes. A mysterious light appeared on a yard arm one night. The doctor was summoned ; he was delighted at the sight. A boy was sent aloft to try and capture the strange fire ; one story is that he had a box with him for the purpose, and took it along the yard, and that when he reached the light it disappeared ; he shut the box lid with a snap and returned with it to the deck and handed it to the doctor. Dr. Clark spent much of the rest of the voyage in writing a learned treatise in which he described what he saw and stated his theories, and on reaching San Francisco he gave a newspaper an account of the affair. Captain Powles now thought the joke had gone a little too far, and sent a letter to the "San Francisco Bulletin" in which he said :

"Dr. Foord Clark, during his voyage from Calcutta to San Francisco, often expressed a wish in his scientific researches to see St. Elmo's Fire . . . One day a midshipman borrowed the chief officer's bull's eye lantern and lashed it to the mizen royal masthead. The succeeding night was intensely dark, and on this night the lantern was lighted. After everything had been purposely fixed Dr. Clark was called, and I myself witnessed the phenomenon. Certainly the night was one on which St. Elmo's Fire might be expected to be seen, and, not being in the joke at first I considered the light to be the true St. Elmo's Fire. But on going to the fore part of the mast I could see no light, and consequently made inquiries, and was let into the secret. Meanwhile the doctor was in a sort of ecstasy, and was very busily engaged in making notes of the phenomenon. As the hoax was so perfectly conducted and so well carried out in every way I thought it would be a pity to destroy so admirable and so successful a delusion. But after reading Dr. Clark's description of the incident in the 'Bulletin' I considered it necessary for the benefit and in the interest of science to reveal the joke at the expense of my friend the enthusiastic doctor."

It only remains to be added that the boy who went aloft to the St. Elmo's Fire reported on returning to the deck that he had sustained an electric shock in his arm and described his sensations. The doctor took no end of trouble with him during the next twenty four hours, gave him some rum, and allowed him to smoke, and put his arm in a sling.

Captain Powles, when 23 years of age, was appointed to the command of the *Prince Oscar*, of the Graves Line, in 1870, and remained with the firm for nine years. Then for eleven years he commanded various ships for J. H. Beazley and Co., and from 1892 to 1904 he commanded the *James Kerr*, first for Geo. M'Allister and Sons and later for Wm. Thomas and Co.

Captain Ditchburn, who had the Liverpool barque *Sarah Bell* at one time, was often accompanied by his daughter, who was an accomplished pianist, and generally chose the dog watches as the time for practice ; it was not every ship on which the trick at the wheel was accompanied by a well played piano, and the sailors appreciated it accordingly.

Captain H. R. Angel, who had the *Sheila* and afterwards the *Collingrove* and finally the *Torrens*, was another master who was thoughtful for the comfort of all on board, passengers as well as sailors. Under him, there never was such a ship, those who had sailed in the *Torrens* used to say, for soft tack (bread) and good food. He was a great hand at getting up concerts in the saloon, and generally took part himself, sometimes giving a song and sometimes a recitation—he was no mean performer, either. Weather and duty permitting, the sailors were not only invited but expected to be present. He was often accompanied on his voyages by his wife or one of his daughters.

Captain Sanderson, who succeeded Captain Angel in the *Collingrove*, often had Mrs. Sanderson with him, and occasionally a daughter. The Captain was a great admirer of Burns's writings, and would quote them by the hour in his strong Northumbrian accent. He received a great shock when certain of his passengers told him that Burns was no good as a poet, and that when he was short of a rhyme he invented a word and said it was dialect.

One American captain, Patten by name, who had the *Neptune's Car*, had reason to bless the presence of his wife on board. On a voyage from New York to San Francisco, in 1856, he had to put his first mate under arrest for incompetence and neglect of duty. Captain Patten afterwards developed brain fever and became blind. The second mate was a good seaman, but knew nothing of navigation. The first mate asked if he might return to duty. Mrs. Patten did not trust him and decided to keep him where her husband had put him, and herself navigated the ship for fifty two days till she brought it into San Francisco. Mrs. Patten was twenty-four years of age at that time, and had learned how to navigate the ship when on a previous voyage with her husband.

About twenty years ago the ship *T. F. Oakes*, under Captain Reed, took 259 days to go from Hong Kong to New York, or more than three times as long as she should have done. She was navigated for many days by the captain's wife, as her husband and several of the crew were laid up with scurvy and other ailments. Besides acting as navigator, she had to be nurse also, and, an American newspaper reported, " carried her onerous duties to a successful issue despite an attempted mutiny." A series of storms drove the ship so far out of her course that the captain decided to try to get home by way of Cape Horn instead of the Cape of Good Hope. Before the ship had reached the Horn scurvy broke out among the crew ; the cook was the first to die. One by one the crew developed the disease. Somehow the *T. F. Oakes* rounded Cape Horn, with nearly half her crew dead or disabled. By the time she had crawled into the North Atlantic more than half the crew had died, and the survivors had to put the bodies overboard. The sight of sharks following the vessel did not improve matters. Mrs. Reed took her turn at the wheel like any of the sailors, day or night, besides navigating the ship, and did not hesitate to undertake or help in any work necessary when there were not enough men left to do it. In the North Atlantic the ship was picked up by an oil-tank steamer, and towed into port. The underwriters at Lloyd's showed their appreciation of Mrs. Reed's conduct by awarding her Lloyd's Meritorious Service medal, in 1897.

The barquentine *Kohala*, of San Francisco, 891 tons, was held up at Grey's Harbour, with a full cargo of lumber for her home port, owing to her master's inability to muster a crew under ten dollars a day per man. Sooner than pay this exorbitant rate of wages the master proceeded to sea with the assistance of his wife, the two mates and a Japanese cook, and reached San Francisco without mishap. The *Kohala* should have had eleven hands.

A few months previously the wife of Captain Reade, of the British barque *Mary Isabel*, of 300 tons, on a voyage from Mauritius to Sydney, took her trick at the wheel and her watch on deck in order " to cope with difficulties which had cropped up on the passage."

Theoretically, there is no reason why a woman cannot manage to navigate a ship by book and sextant, but circumstances may easily and often arise which would require an amount of nerve not often found in a woman. There have been other woman navigators, but I don't know of any who have distinguished themselves by their seamanship, though a few adventurous women have tried to go as stowaways.

The list of captains whose wives sailed with them would be a long one if it could be given. Most of the American clipper captains in the China tea trade were accompanied by their ladies, who certainly had a good time socially at the Chinese ports, and were quite as good as their husbands at boasting of the superiority of American ships over those of Britain.

The loneliness of the captain's position occasionally got on his nerves ; a few have become morbid and taken their own lives. Some captains went in for a hobby to occupy their spare time. Captain Sanderson, whom I have just mentioned, whom I knew personally, had taught himself wood carving, and he told me that some of the pictures in his home were in frames he had carved himself on his voyages. Many others have taken up photography. Some have been industrious readers. One shipmaster kept a list of all the novels he read, and in his spare time ashore he used to skirmish around the second hand book shops, and generally took thirty or forty novels with him every voyage. As a book was read, it was passed to the mate, then it was the second mate's turn, then the third mate had it, followed by the apprentices and the crew.

The old sailorman's attitude to literature, as to everything else, is tempered by his surroundings. Once I read Coleridge's " Ancient Mariner " to the crew of a vessel I was on, during the dog watches. Nearly every verse was keenly debated in detail. When the reading was finished my hearers were unanimously of opinion that the " Ancient Mariner " and his ship got no more than they deserved for the killing of the albatross. " The Tempest " was another book I read to them ; they liked the shipping parts, but

did not think much of the rest. Once they discussed the
story of Jonah and the whale. One of them had been a
whaler, and he frankly avowed disbelief in the "whole
yarn," saying that no whale ever found in the Mediterranean had a throat big enough to let even a little Jew
through it, and the story was as tough for him to digest
as the whale found Jonah.

Another captain used to take a few sets of boxing gloves
with him ; he was passionately fond of boxing himself,
and even after he had turned fifty he would don a pair of
gloves and "take on" anyone on board. He was a good
man at the game. But didn't the crew enjoy seeing the
boatswain set about him in one of the tournaments he
fixed up ! The Old Man had been lecturing the boatswain
that day, and the man tried his best to get his own back.

Captain Powles, when serving his apprenticeship, was
turned into the forecastle to fight his way, an experience
which he afterwards found useful. He became second
mate of the *Lancashire* in 1865, the captain of which though
nearly 70 years old was devoted to boxing. Learning
that Powles could take care of himself, he insisted upon
him taking on the crew in turn, and if any of the crew
objected the Old Man would roust the unwilling pugilist
out with a belaying pin and much strong language.

Other captains have made a practice of studying the
winds and ocean currents, and much valuable information
has been thereby obtained. The late Captain Simpson, for
many years an honoured commander in the Aberdeen
White Star line, made it a custom to throw overboard a
number of bottles every voyage. Every bottle contained
a piece of paper bearing the name of the ship, the date, the
latitude and longitude where it was consigned to the sea,
and a request that the finder should communicate with him

giving the date and place where the bottle was picked up. The bottles were well corked, and made as watertight as possible. Many of them, Captain Simpson told me, were never heard of again, but others were picked up years afterwards at places which showed that they had drifted half round the world.

For something like a quarter of a century Captain Simpson maintained his custom of sending bottle messages afloat ; he was responsible for fully ten thousand, and up to the close of 1911 he received a thousand of them back again.

Maury, in his " Physical Geography of the Sea," reports that Captain Beacher, R.N., prepared a chart showing the tracks of over a hundred bottles which had been thrown over to test the currents. This was before Captain Simpson made his experiments. From Captain Beacher's chart it appeared, Captain Maury wrote, " that the waters from every quarter of the Atlantic tend towards the Gulf of Mexico and its stream. Bottles cast into the sea midway between the Old and New Worlds, near the coasts of Europe, Africa and America, at the extreme north or farthest south, have been found either in the West Indies, or the British Isles, or within the well-known range of Gulf Stream waters." Two were thrown into the sea in south latitude off the African coast ; one drifted to Trinidad, the other to Guernsey, the latter having evidently performed the tour of the gulf. Another bottle, said to have been thrown over near Cape Horn by an American shipmaster in 1837, was picked up on the coast of Ireland.

It is astonishing how far a bottle may drift if securely fastened to keep the water out. One bottle, sent from the sailing ship *St. Enoch*, in July, 1893, in mid-Atlantic, a few degrees north of the equator, drifted 7,800 miles via the Gulf of Mexico to the Shetland Islands. Another ocean messenger, despatched from a steamer off the coast of Spain, was found after five years on the Cuban coast, having journeyed about 3,000 miles, but it probably lay on the shore for some time.

Probably the longest bottle drifts are those in the Southern Ocean. The ship *Allerton* sent one when she was south of the Falkland Islands in 1893 ; three years later it was found on the shore of the Great Australian Bight, having travelled 8,500 miles. The *Lord Ripon*, when near the Crozet Islands in 1896, dropped a bottle which arrived nearly three years later at a spot on the Australian coast, after a drift of 9,560 miles. From the barque *Eureka*, a bottle was dropped off Cape Horn, as the ship was beating her way into the Pacific. It contained a letter addressed to a person in England. It drifted about 9,000 miles east and was picked up on the Tasmanian coast. It is stated that three years after it had been " posted," the letter was delivered to the addressee.

More than once, bottle messages, when they have arrived, have conveyed the only information of a vessel's loss. The following was found on a slip of paper in a bottle in March, 1909, near St. Abb's Head : " Captain or anyone who receives this message shall receive the remains of the Dundee whaler *Snowdrop*. Collided with an iceberg. No hope. 14th November 1908." This was the only news ever heard of the vessel since six months previously.

Not many of the hundreds of messages consigned in bottles to the care of the ocean are ever recovered. No doubt some are broken against rocks ; others are perhaps not as securely corked as they might be, and the water gets in and down they go ; possibly a few when found receive no attention from the finder ; not a few become encrusted with barnacles and sink. Captain Bennett, of the well-known sailing ship *Thessalus*, dropped a bottle a day over as soon as he got into deep water during a voyage from London to Australia, and never heard of any of them.

Much valuable information as to ocean currents has been obtained from these drifting bottles. The Ministry of Agriculture and Fisheries is paying special attention to them. The United States Hydrographic Office has made a study of the question and has probably the largest amount of information in the world on this subject available.

It has often been said that sailors are, as a class, exceedingly irreligious. From the conventional standpoints of creeds and sects this was probably true in a great many cases. The habitual bad language of the old time sailor could no more be taken literally than the bad language used by the troops during the war. Still, it was regarded by landsmen as a proof of the spiritual degradation of the sailor, and the sprees he indulged in when ashore were looked upon as confirmatory evidence. They were not saints, and did not pretend to be ; indeed, if there were one form of professing piety which the old time sailor held in strong contempt, it was that which has been known ashore as " pi."

At one time Sunday services were the rule on passenger sailing ships. If a clergyman were on board he was expected to conduct it, otherwise it fell to the lot of the captain. On ships which carried no passengers services might or might not be held ; some captains would not hold them, some would. One master held his service in his saloon every Sunday evening in the second dog watch, and every member of the crew was invited to be present.

Some attended more to break the monotony of the voyage than from any other reason, but it was seldom that most of them were not there. The master never preached at them, but gave them simple Bible stories, and extracts from Bunyan's " Pilgrim's Progress," and himself presided at his little harmonium and led the singing of the hymns. The men by their presence showed their interest in religious matters, when given the chance, and, what was equally important, they were allowed to attend in their ordinary clothes instead of dressing in their best for the occasion.

When the old time sailors could be induced to attend a service afloat, their attitude was as devotional as one could wish, and afterwards they would discuss the whole proceedings with a respect which would surprise anyone who did not understand something of the seafarers' character. No men could live, as the old sailing ship men did, week after week and month after month, in close companionship with the sea and forces of nature, without recognising in some degree the great Omnipresence behind, and in, everything. Notwithstanding this, their language might be painful, and their outbreaks ashore the reverse of edifying.

One instance I may recall will serve as an illustration of the sailor's attitude towards the spiritual side of things. The ship on which I was, bound from Adelaide to London, sighted one evening near the equator a large sailing vessel bound south. The approaching vessel sailed so close to us that we could see the faces of those on deck, and read her name on her bow. She was the *Antiope*. The sunset was one of the most beautiful I have ever seen, even in the tropics. We were between her and the setting sun. As she neared us with every stitch of canvas set, the beautiful snowy cloths were illumined by the almost golden rays of the sun, and the spray at her bow flashed and glittered like showers of sparkling gems. Evening service was being held on her main deck. Just as she was passing from us her company began to sing that grand sea hymn " Eternal Father, strong to save." Instantly every head on our ship was bared, and remained uncovered as long as a note could be heard. The music, growing fainter in the rapidly increasing distance, seemed a message of hope sent over the water to us who were homeward bound from those sailing to the land we had left.

I have heard of Welsh captains who held forth extempore at great length, so that their congregations dwindled sadly ; and of a Scottish captain who read theological discourses to his crew, who were far from interested ; and of another who was holding a service in the saloon, the crew, or some of them, being present, when the second mate reported a sudden change of wind with a falling barometer. Instantly the Old Man bundled his congregation on deck with unscriptural language to hasten their movements, and when the necessary work was done to his satisfaction he announced " The service will now be resumed."

A man who was working his passage from Australia to England on a sailer, set himself the task of trying to convert the crew to the particular Baptist theories he favoured. His view was that any person who had not been completely immersed as an adult three times would be irrevocably damned. Any sailing ship man knows that the steering of a ship has a great deal to do with the amount of water she may take over her weather bow even in moderate weather. One day the Baptist was going along the main deck for'ard when a sea came over the gunwale and

21

drenched him. The Old Man had seen the steersman move the wheel slightly but enough to bring that about, and asked " What did you do that for ? "

" He says he is a Baptist, and that we're all going to be damned unless we're ducked three times," the man replied.

" Well, give him two more and make sure of his salvation anyway," was the captain's comment. So said, so done, as far as the duckings were concerned ; he had further similar duckings on later occasions, but made no converts.

" Give us some time to blow the man down." Probably the most picturesque feature of life in a sailer was to be found in the chanties, or sailors' songs and choruses—always pronounced, and sometimes written shanties. Everyone of these chanties consisted of a solo and chorus. The soloist was known as the chantyman, and many of the chanties were sung only when special duties were being performed. For instance " Haul on the bowline, the bowline haul " would only be sung when that order had to be executed.

" We'll pay Paddy Doyle for his boots," was reserved for the taking in of the courses. Paddy Doyle, thus immortalised in chanty, was the keeper of a sailors' boarding house. He used to cash his clients' advance notes, nominally for them but actually for himself, and when to keep the sailor any longer would make too much of an inroad into Mr. Doyle's profits, Paddy would ship him, half drunk, with a bag containing a few ragged clothes that even a tramp would despise, and a pair of sea boots always second hand and generally much the worse for wear. The sailorman certainly paid Paddy Doyle pretty dearly for his boots.

The chantyman was an important personage in his

watch, for upon his efforts often depended whether the men gave a long pull, a strong pull, and a pull all together. It may be questioned whether there ever was a known original or correct version of any chanty, and if one should be found it may certainly be questioned whether it would be fit to print.

Chanty singing began to decline when steamers became more common and sailing ships fewer, and its decline was hastened by the invasion of the British merchant service by foreign seamen, and it has declined so completely now that it has disappeared with the sailing ship. The captain of one of the few British sailing ships left a few years ago told me that on her last voyage there were no real chanties on board throughout the voyage because no one knew them except his mate and himself. In the old days it was different and a chantyman prided himself on his ability to improvise the words of a solo if the task in hand exhausted the usual verses of the chanty. The chanties as sung on British and American ships differed considerably. As sailors went from British to American ships, or vice versa, naturally they took their chanties with them, and altered them to suit their changed surroundings. Many chanties originated on shore and were adopted by sailors because they liked the tunes, and they adapted both words and music to suit their fancy. The negroes of the southern states and the West Indies were the best chantymen.

One chanty seldom sung except when heaving up the anchor to start a voyage was " Sally Brown." It began like this :

> Solo—Seven long year I've courted Sally.
> Chorus—Way-ay, roll and go.
> Solo—She said, my boy why do you dally.
> Chorus—Bet my money on Sally Brown.

One of the American versions of " Sally Brown " has this verse :

> Solo—Oh, Sally Brown is very pretty.
> Chorus—Aye, aye, roll and go.
> Solo—Prettiest girl in all the city.
> Chorus—I'll spend my money on Sally Brown.

Possibly this harpy was not unknown to a notorious crimp, or kidnapper of sailors, for a New York version of " Blow my bully boys, blow " has this verse :

> Solo—Oh, Shanghai Brown he loves us sailors.
> Chorus—Blow, boys, blow.
> Solo—Oh yes, he does, like hell and blazes.
> Chorus—Blow, my bully boys, blow.

Another anchor song was " Good-bye, fare you well," and it was mostly used when a vessel was getting up its anchor for the homeward voyage. Both American and British versions mention the captain. One American version begins :

> Solo—Bars to the capstan and run quick round.
> Chorus—Hurrah, my boys, we're homeward bound.

The English version was not only a farewell to the girls they were leaving at some foreign port, but anticipated the welcome the girls at home would give them.

> Solo—Oh, don't you hear the Old Man say—
> Chorus—Good-bye, fare you well.
> Solo—We're homeward bound this very day.
> Chorus—Good-bye, fare you well.
> Solo—She's a fine clipper, and we know she can go.
> Chorus—Good-bye, fare you well.
> Solo—The girls have the tow rope and they look for us you
> know ;
> Chorus—Hurrah, my boys, we're homeward bound.

It was an old saying in the fo'castle, when a ship was making a good homeward passage, that the girls at the destination had hold of the tow rope.

Another song was "Leave her, boys, leave her," and was sometimes the last chanty sung at the end of the voyage. " It's time for us to leave her," the chorus ran.

Another, equally suitable to such an occasion, was " One more day," which sufficiently explains itself. Probably the best known sea-song is the popular " A-roving." The sea version usually began " In Amsterdam there dwelt a maid," but the more modern English concert version opens with " At number five Old England Square."

One very well-known chanty was " Stormalong." Who the original of the song was is not known, but Captain Andrew Shewan, in his book " The Great Days of Sail," says, " Old John Willis," the famous London shipowner, " was the hero, it has always been my conviction, of the fine old chanty. There are points about it which indicate that Stormalong was none other than old John Willis ; ' old Stormy's son ' being John Willis the younger, and ' the ship he built ' the famous *Cutty Sark*. Old John was a seaman of the old school, and of the daring go-ahead disposition that gave ' Old Stormalong ' his cognomen." The best known version of the chanty runs :—

> Solo—O Stormy, he is dead and gone.
> Chorus—To my way, you storm along.
> Solo—Stormy was a good old man.
> Chorus—Ay, ay, ay, Mister Stormalong.
>
> Solo—I wish I was old Stormy's son ;
> Chorus—To my way you storm along.
> Solo—I'd build a ship of a thousand ton.
> Chorus—Ay, ay, ay, Mister Stormalong.

Solo—Now Stormy's dead and gone to rest,
Chorus—To my way you storm along.
Solo—Of sailormen he was the best,
Chorus—Ay, ay, ay, Mister Stormalong.

The chanty " Reuben Ranzo " is unlike most chanties as it tells something of a definite story, besides consisting of several verses. For some unknown reason, chantymen seldom attempted to alter its words much. It was sung a great deal when the topsails had to be hoisted, and its length was justified in ships that carried the old-fashioned single topsails. It began indifferently with the lines, sung as a solo, " O pity old Reuben Ranzo," or " Poor old Reuben Ranzo," or " Do you know old Reuben Ranzo." Every line was repeated twice, and the chorus was sung after every line and repetition. As far as I remember the second verse was :

Solo—Poor Ranzo was a tailor.
Chorus—Ranzo, boys, Ranzo.
Solo—Oh, Ranzo was a tailor.
Chorus—Ranzo, boys, Ranzo.

Sometimes the second time of the chorus was " Poor old Reuben Ranzo."

Subsequent solos were, each line being a verse :—

His father was a jailer.
He shipped on board of a whaler.
O Ranzo was no sailor.
He could not do his duty.
The mate, he being a hard man,
Took him to the gangway,
And gave him five and twenty.
O Lord, how he did holler.
The captain, being a kind man,
Took him to his cabin,
And gave him wine and brandy.
And taught him navigation
To fit him for his station.

About this time the mate's gruff " Bela-ay " ended the
story of Ranzo for the time being, and the topsail halliards
were made fast. The story does not end there, however.
One version is that he kissed the captain's daughter, another is that he married the owner's widow, and both agree
that " Now he's Captain Ranzo."   Who or what Reuben
Ranzo was I have never been able to learn.

Every chantyman was privileged to alter the words to
suit the needs of the moment. He had scope for doing so in
" Ranzo." He might make out that the captain was a
hard man and not the mate, or vice versa according to
their popularity on board, or that they were both hard
cases, or that being stung by remorse they vied with each
other in offering hospitality to Ranzo, but the last was
rare. It was an unwritten rule that the officers should not
interfere too much with the words of the chanties, and the
chantymen sometimes took advantage of this to express
the crew's opinions of the officers very freely. Cases have
been known where a chantyman has touched an officer
on a very tender spot, and a fistic lesson in poesy has
followed.

Another well-known chanty was " O Shenadore I love
your daughter," which tells what befell the Indian girl
whose father, the Indian chief Shenandoah, had a fondness
for the white man's fire water.

The version often sung of " Blow, boys, blow" on
English ships began about the middle of it with the
words :

> Solo—A Yankee ship came down the river,
> Chorus—Blow, boys, blow.
> Solo—Her masts and spars they shone like silver,
> Chorus—Blow, my bully boys, blow.

British sailors kept away from these miracles of neatness aloft. They knew, by experience or report, the back-breaking and heart-breaking time the unlucky crew had in getting the masts and spars to shine like silver or the decks to be so white that snow would make a dark stain on them, to use a sailor's saying.

With the British deep water sailing ships there have passed away the old customs which were dear to the heart of the fo'castle. When British ships had British crews these customs were rigidly observed. The first of them on a Cape Horner, or a ship bound for Australia, New Zealand or the Far East was that known as the Dead Horse. Sailors received an advance of a month's wages when they signed on. Sometimes they got them cashed by the keeper of the boarding house where they were staying, and went on a final spree before sailing ; and sometimes they handed the notes over to their wives, for not all the men before the mast passed their time ashore in drunken profligacy. But whatever they did with the money they always regarded their first month at sea as working for nothing, or for the "dead horse." So on the expiration of the month at sea the sailors made a procession from the forecastle, in one of the dog watches, usually the second, with a rough imitation of a horse. It was generally of canvas or sacking— sometimes an old mattress has done duty—and was ridden by a sailor in his oldest clothes and a battered hat, and he waved an improvised whip. This was dragged along the decks by the men :

> Solo—They say, old man, your horse will die.
> Chorus—They say so, and they hope so.
> Solo—They say, old man, your horse will die.
> Chorus—Oh, poor old horse.

Captain Whall gives the following versions of the next verse and the rider's final address to his mount :

Solo—Then if he dies, I'll tan his hide.
Chorus—They say so, and they hope so.
Solo—And if he lives, I'll ride him again,
Chorus—O poor—old—horse.

On reaching the quarter deck the rider dismounted and addressed the horse :

Old horse, old horse, what brought you here
After carrying sand for many a year
From Bantry Bay to Ballywhack,
When you fell down and broke your back ?
Now, after years of such abuse,
They salt you down for sailor's use ;
They tan your hide and burn your bones,
And send you off to Davy Jones.

After this, the horse was hoisted to the lee main yard arm, where a man was ready with a blue light. This he lit, and with a knife cut the rope holding the effigy and let it fall into the sea, the crew cheering lustily.

The next custom which was rigidly observed, as it afforded unlimited scope for rough play, was the visit of Father Neptune and his myrmidons. It has been described so often that it is unnecessary to give an account of the ceremony here. Anyone who had not crossed the equator before had to undergo the ordeal. Many a time the sailors have invaded the passengers' quarters, and dragged out their unwilling victims, and the more the latter struggled and fought the more the sailors enjoyed the fun, and the more thoroughly were the victims lathered and shaved and ducked in a sail full of sea water by Neptune's bears and other assistants. On some ships exemption could be purchased by a passenger buying a bottle of grog for the crew, on the principle of one bottle per passenger seeking to avoid the fun, but the great majority of captains forbade this because they preferred to have their crews sober. Even when tribute had been paid to Neptune, if there were not many victims, another group of sailors with a bear at their head might capture some unfortunate and put him through it again in order to keep the fun going. When there were only a few sufferers the ceremony was prolonged as much as possible, but when, as on the emigrant ships, there might be as many as a couple of hundred, they were put through the ordeal more quickly, but the fun was fast and furious for the best part of the day.

Practical jokes played by passengers on one another, or, by the ship's officers on the passengers, were common. One, near the commencement of a voyage, usually played by a sailor, was to tell a passenger that if he went on the fo'castle head he could see the dolphins playing about the vessel's stem. The passenger had no sooner mounted the ladder to the fo'castle head, than he was pounced upon by a sailor who made a white chalk cross on his boots, to indicate that the sin of trespassing where he should not have gone could only be expiated by sending to the watch a bottle of grog.

Passengers often got up a written weekly journal or newspaper, in those ships in which one was not provided and printed, and some of the paragraphs and personalities would have gladdened the heart of a lawyer on the look-out for libel actions ; the libelled person usually got his own back in the next issue.

A ship's apprentices were always ready for any mischief. They were generally underfed, and their exploits on board were mostly in the direction of adding to their scanty larder. More than once the galley has been robbed while the cook's back was turned ; that the stolen food was not properly cooked did not matter. A surreptitious visit to the store room could not often be paid, perhaps not once in a voyage, but the boys have been known to have jam when it had not been served out to them. One captain had a whole ham taken, and the boys had to share it with the crew who threatened to " split." Many a lad on first joining a ship has been told to go and ask the first mate for the key of the keelson ; the mate would disillusion him. The keelson was a great beam, or inner keel, next the keel at the bottom of the ship. Sometimes the mate would tell him to go down the forepeak and search till he found it, and then bring it up.

Those who have been privileged to make voyages in sailing ships and afterwards in steamers, and have compared the conditions in the two classes of vessels, must admit that the change brought about by the steamer is for the better. Even hard old shellbacks, when they have no longer been able to find a British ship to join and have been obliged to become one of the crew of a steamer, have been compelled to admit this, much as it may have gone against the grain to do so. Ships had a personality of their own. Over and over again, a captain could make a ship do wonders, and his successor could do nothing with her. A man may have been a splendid master of one ship, and almost a failure in another. Some ships seemed as obstinate as mules.

A certain ship had a reputation for misbehaving when " in stays." A new captain, an American, was appointed to her. The mate, by way of making conversation and being friendly, remarked " This ship's a bit awkward in stays ; we often have trouble with her then." " You don't say. I wouldn't have thought it," the new captain drawled. No ship could have behaved better afterwards, " in stays " or out of them.

Some ships seem to have been unlucky from the beginning. There is the well-known instance of a ship on which a man was accidentally killed a short while before she was launched. His mother, a Highland woman, went to see the launch, and cursed the ship thoroughly, and prophesied that she would never have a voyage without disaster. She seldom did. Sailormen believed in the curse, and it was sometimes difficult to get a crew for her. An officer seldom made two voyages in her. At last her owners got tired of her and sold her for a hulk, and years afterwards she foundered at her moorings and drowned one or two men. A run of misfortunes, such as that ship experienced, would be more than sufficient to justify any old sailorman in his belief that the ship was " hoodoo'd." A landsman would regard the misfortunes merely as a series of coincidences, and the sailor's belief as a superstition. Her sister ship, on the other hand, was uniformly successful, and was a favourite alike with her officers and crews, and praised by her passengers.

Sailing ship crews had many strange beliefs which in their opinion were founded upon their experiences, and many strange superstitions which they believed but could not justify. Even as late as the middle of the last century there were still old sailors who believed the story of Van der Decken, the " Flying Dutchman," and his phantom ship.

The belief in phantom ships was widespread and had a certain amount of justification. A mirage at sea is not uncommon, and many times it has taken the form of a ship under full sail. Sometimes it has been seen upside down ;

at other times, right way up and apparently floating, but above the water. Every phantom vessel thus seen in a mirage must be the replica of an actual vessel beyond the horizon, and reproduced with startling fidelity to detail. Sailors would see the phantom ship gradually assume shape, sail along for a half hour or more, and as gradually vanish again into thin air. It was enough for them that the whole ship's company saw the phantom ; the scientific explanation did not interest them. Occasionally it has been possible to identify the mirage ship by some peculiarity of rig. If anything happened to her the sailors who saw the mirage always declared afterwards that they accepted the phantom at the time as a premonition of disaster which must overtake the vessel sooner or later. Sometimes they said the phantom was the ghost of a ship that had gone down.

Another form of the belief in phantom ships has a strange pathetic beauty of its own. It was a firm belief among the sailors of the old school that the wraith of every lost ship returned to her home port. They believed in the individuality of their vessels, and that when a ship went down her spirit wandered back over the face of the ocean, slowly making its way to the port whence it had first sailed. Superstitious sailors have asserted that they have seen these phantom wrecks groping their way through the mists which are to be found on certain seas. These mists, as they are disturbed by the waves and torn by the wind, take strange shapes, and imagination does the rest. Anyone who has watched at one of our larger estuaries the sea mists crawling in above the flowing tide, and has noticed the strange shapes the mist takes as it advances and thickens, will realise why it was believed that these ghostly wrecks drifted to their home ports and vanished when they reached their old familiar moorings. Old shellbacks went further and averred that these ghost ships were manned by the ghosts of their lost crews.

A belief which probably originated in the days of the privateers and pirates, was that cruising somewhere about the Atlantic was a phantom ship known as the *Black privateer*, or *Black pirate*. Several stories used to be circulated about this mysterious vessel. They all agreed on one point, viz., that to sight it was an infallible sign of coming disaster. One legend was that this vessel, having turned pirate, captured a merchantman, and made many of those aboard her walk the plank. Then they looted the vessel and tried to sink her, but she would not go down. Then they tried to burn her, and when she was well alight the wind changed and carried her down upon the pirate which also caught fire and both were destroyed.

Other strange legends of phantom vessels used to be current in the West Indies and the Spanish Main generally. Possibly some owed their birth to the slight flickerings of the none-too-tender conscience of a retired pirate or buccaneer. Ignorance, superstition, drink and the approach of senility, coupled with the remnants of a conscience, may have caused the hallucination that he could see again the victims, whether ships or human beings, of his crimes.

There was a legend that a Spanish galleon which sailed from a Central American port for Spain, put into Santiago de Cuba, seeking safety from her piratical pursuers. The galleon stayed some days, and all being reported clear she sailed again for Spain. She was pounced upon by the pirates, and, unable to escape, drifted upon the rocks at the extreme eastern end of the island and went to pieces. The wreck is said to have been accompanied by shocking atrocities by the pirates. A priest on the galleon excommunicated the assailants for good. Now at intervals a phantom galleon founders at the same spot, and a pirate phantom ship founders in deep water with all on board and their ill-gotten gains.

Another phantom of the West Indies is the ship's boat which is reported to have been seen great distances from land, rowed by two men. Its appearance was always regarded as the forerunner of one of those terrible storms for which the West Indies and the Gulf of Mexico are famous. After the worst of the storm had passed the men were seen rowing their boat back in the direction whence they had come. The late Admiral Field, in his book of sea yarns, used this legend as the basis for one of his stories, to the effect that the boat was not only sighted but hailed as it passed close by one of the ships of the British navy.

If there were anything the average sailing ship man held in superstitious affection it was the seabird. It was an article of faith among the old shellbacks, whose belief nothing could shake, that the souls of drowned sailormen entered the bodies of the birds. To them, therefore, all seabirds, whether they were the giant albatrosses or the tiny Mother Carey's Chickens, were sacred. They knew that the birds followed the ships for the sake of the scraps of food thrown to them, and many an underfed and overworked sailor has given bits of his scanty meals to the birds because he loved them, and looked upon them as seafarers like himself. It was probably true that his generosity was due in part to the fact that the salt junk served out to him by a niggardly shipowner was too rancid to be eaten or too tough to be masticated, so it went overboard, the best place for it ; but the men sometimes gave more edible bits, and had their reward in the strange weird cries of the birds as they flew round the ship and clamoured for more. Captains and mates, too, often fed the birds.

Should one of the birds alight on the vessel for a few seconds, as has occasionally happened, or attempted to do so, it was looked upon as a sign that one of those on board would be lost before the voyage was ended. This belief is still held among the fishermen around our coasts. Seabirds resting on fishing boats riding at anchor with no one on board may be seen almost any day at our ports and seaside resorts and excite no comment among the fishermen, but should a bird come alone day after day and hover over one boat in particular, the fishermen will regard it as an omen that someone will go out to sea on her, and not return. If after the boat comes back it is reported that she has lost a man, and the gull should alight on the vessel, the fisherfolk will aver that the bird called him and that his soul is now in it. There is a Cornish story which says that a gull flew to a little fishing village, and, uttering its plaintive cries, brushed softly against the cheek of a young widow whose husband had been lost at sea, who had promised her that if he did not come back alive he would come in that way.

On some sailing ships the passengers were allowed to trap or even shoot the gulls by way of recreation and amusement, the excuse being that the skins were wanted. On other vessels the practice was strictly forbidden, not necessarily because the captain believed that ill-luck would follow injury to a gull, but on the grounds of humanity and because he objected to cruelty.

> "Lost ships beside them steering,
> Lost men at the weather earring."

These two lines indicate another strange belief held by the men of the old school. If two men were close personal

friends, and one were lost overboard, the survivor fre-
quently took it for granted that his mate had returned to
him, and worked beside him, accompanying him aloft
and sharing in his duties, whatever they were. Under this
belief a man would do the work of two, and show the
strength of two, and when his task was over he would say
he had been helped by the spirit of the dead man ; the
spirit always went to the weather earring if the living
man were sent to a yard arm, or to the most dangerous
place anywhere else, as a spirit could not fall into the sea
and drown.

It was also believed that if the wraith of a ship were
seen sailing beside one afloat, those on the latter must
regard it as a warning that the course must be changed lest
in following the present course she should go with the ghost
ship to the place of her destruction. Sailors have been
known to tell their captains of such warnings, and the
captains have been known to alter their course in order to
gratify the superstitious old salts and please the men, who
always worked better if they were humoured a little in
such matters. If after the change was made the ship
escaped accident, they always attributed it to the warning.

Sharks were another favourite object for the sailors'
imagination. They knew that the shark would eat anyone
who fell overboard if given the chance, and they knew too,
that the very young sharks may be made up into a tasty
dish. One big female shark is said to have had forty four
little sharks inside when caught and cut open ; this happened on a barquentine in the New Zealand coasting trade.
A still larger family was found in a ten foot shark caught
near Mauritius by Captain Kerr, of the sailing ship *Ard-
gowan*, she having 83 young ones ; one caught near
Amsterdam Island by Captain Johnson, of the *St.*

22

Lawrence, contained 65. The young sharks were only a few inches long. It has long been stated that female sharks swallow their young when danger nears. Sailors used to keep the little sharks in buckets of sea water where they swam about in blissful ignorance of the fact that they were to be eaten by the sailors instead of growing up and eating any sailors who might be unlucky enough to fall overboard. Sharks will snap at anything, even at the patent log trailing behind a ship. As for the old story that pilot fish would inspect a bait and warn the shark if they thought it dangerous, don't believe it any more than you would the other old yarn about sharks following a ship on which a death is about to occur. Sharks often followed sailing ships for days together, for the sake of the scraps of food thrown overboard, and if there happened to be a death in the ship that was merely coincidence ; the more persons on board, the more the waste food, and that is why sharks followed emigrant ships. What sailors thought of sharks is shown by their habit of calling those who preyed upon them ashore " landsharks."

Can the sailing ship be revived ? Can conditions be devised which will give it a new lease of usefulness ? The passing of the sailing ship has given rise to these questions. On the face of it, the answer would appear to be in the negative. The great advantage of the sailer was that its power was free. The great disadvantages were the impossibility of guaranteeing regularity of voyages, and the absence of any substitute for wind power. When internal combustion engines were first installed in ships a few years ago, the hope was freely expressed that they would provide the needed substitute. So they might have done, had there been no improvements in the engines as then known. Internal combustion engines have been so much improved that they are capable of being placed in almost the largest hulls, and compared with steam engines they take up little space, and the same comparison holds good as regards their oil fuel as against coal. The improvement of the internal combustion engine rendered it unnecessary to combine its use with sails ; the engines were powerful enough to do without sails above them altogether ; fewer men would be carried than if the vessel had sails. There is moreover, as already explained, a limit to the size to which a sailing vessel can be economically and safely built. So far as the mere building is concerned one could be launched as big as the biggest steamship, but it could not be handled at sea. In anything short of half a gale it might not have good steering way, and in an ordinary breeze it might only be able to answer its rudder and no more ; while as for going about, or wearing, or trying to beat off a lee shore the difficulties would be very great. Conditions may be brought about which will enable ships to take advantage of wind propulsion once more. As matters stand, however, history is repeating itself. Auxiliary steam engines to sails were displaced by more powerful engines, till steamers appeared which had no sails. The auxiliary internal combustion engine is disappearing, and the powerful internal combustion engine is taking its place.

The advantages claimed for the auxiliary motors were that they would assist the sailer in calms or very light weather, that they would cost nothing for fuel when not in use, that they could help the vessel in or out of port and possibly enable it to dispense with a tug, that the weight of the engines and the space they occupied would be more than counterbalanced financially by the saving of time, and that they would help a vessel to get away from a lee shore in time of peril. It cannot be said that these advantages have materialised to any great extent in actual experience. British sailing ship owners were interested, but not convinced. French and German owners were more optimistic, and decided to experiment. This was a few years before the war, when first costs and running costs were much lower than they are now or are ever likely to be again. The German firm of Rickmers have a very handsome five-masted barque fitted with engines ; she has been fairly successful.

Two remarkable French vessels were constructed and given auxiliary motors. One was the four-masted barque *Quevilly*—built originally as a sailing vessel for the Rouen— New York oil trade, and after a few voyages she was equipped with motors which enabled her to do another round voyage in the year. So satisfied were her owners with her performance that they decided to build a much larger five-masted barque and fit her with two Diesel engines, each of 900 horse power, and together driving twin screws. This was the famous *France*, referred to in a previous chapter. Her engines were expected to give her a sea speed of ten knots, and demonstrate the other advantages already mentioned. When the test came under sea conditions the engines did not give the anticipated results, and were ultimately removed. Several small motor vessels, some with and some without sails, have been built for the short voyages between British ports and the Continent, particularly the Baltic, and have proved successful. But they have not demonstrated that the internal combustion engine is going to bring about the revival of the large ocean-going sailing ship. It is to be feared, therefore, that the Tall Ships, as a commercial proposition, will disappear for good.

END.

INDEX

22*

Printed in Great Britain by Ebenezer Baylis & Son, Ltd., The Trinity Press, Worcester.

Printed in the United Kingdom
by Lightning Source UK Ltd.
124952UK00001B/70/A